THE TROPICAL AGRICULTURALIST

Series Editor
René Coste

Formerly President of the IRCC

General Editor, Livestock Volumes
Anthony J. Smith

Centre fᵒ ʳᵉⁱᵃˡ ʳᵉᵗerinary Medicine
Univeʳ ˥bᵘrgh

Animal Breeding

Gerald Wiener

Centre for Tropical Veterinary Medicine
University of Edinburgh
(formerly at AFRC Animal Breeding Research Organisation, now merged
into AFRC Roslin Research Institute, Edinburgh)

MACMILLAN

First published 1994 by
MACMILLAN EDUCATION LTD
London and Oxford
Companies and representatives throughout the world

www.macmillan-africa.com

Published in co-operation with the CTA (Technical
Centre for Agriculture and Rural Co-operation), P.O.B. 380,
6700 AJ Wageningen, The Netherlands.

ISBN 0-333-57298-X

11	10	9	8	7	6	5	4
08	07	06	05	04	03	02	01

This book is printed on paper suitable for recycling and
made from fully managed and sustained forest sources.

Printed in Malaysia

A catalogue record for this book is available from the
British Library

Cover photograph courtesy of Tony Smith

The opinions expressed in this document and the
spellings of proper names and territorial boundaries
contained therein are solely the responsibility of the
author and in no way involve the official position
or the liability of the Technical Centre for
Agriculture and Rural Co-operation

Technical Centre for Agricultural and Rural Co-operation (ACP-EU)

The Technical Centre for Agricultural and Rural Co-operation (CTA) was established in 1983 under Lomé Convention between the ACP (African, Caribbean and Pacific) Group of States and the European Union Member States.

CTA's tasks are to develop and provide services that improve access to information for agricultural and rural development, and to strengthen the capacity of ACP countries to produce, acquire, exchange and utilise information in these areas. CTA's programmes are organised around four principal themes: developing information management and partnership strategies needed for policy formulation and implementation; promoting contact and exchange of experience; providing ACP partners with information on demand; and strengthening their information and communication capacities.

CTA, Postbus 380, 6700 AJ Wageningen, The Netherlands.

Agency for Cultural and Technical Co-operation (ACCT)

The Agency for Cultural and Technical Co-operation, an intergovernmental organisation set up by the Treaty of Niamey in March 1970, is an association of countries linked by their common usage of the French language, for the purposes of co-operation in the fields of education, culture, science and technology and, more generally, in all matters which contribute to the development of its Member States and to bringing people closer together.

The Agency's activities in the fields of scientific and technical co-operation for development are directed primarily towards the preparation, dissemination and exchange of scientific and technical information, drawing up an inventory of and exploiting natural resources, and the socioeconomic advancement of young people and rural communities.

Member countries: Belgium, Benin, Burkina Faso, Burundi, Canada, Central African Republic, Chad, Comoros, Congo, Congo (Dem. Rep.), Côte d'Ivoire, Djibouti, Dominica, France, Gabon, Guinea, Haiti, Lebanon, Luxembourg, Mali, Mauritius, Monaco, Niger, Rwanda, Senegal, Seychelles, Togo, Tunisia, Vanuatu, Vietnam.

Associated States: Cameroon, Egypt, Guinea-Bissau, Laos, Mauritania, Morocco, St Lucia.

Participating governments: New Brunswick, Quebec.

Titles in *The Tropical Agriculturalist* series

Sheep	ISBN 0–333–52310–5	Animal Health Vol. 1	0–333–61202–7
Pigs	0–333–52308–3	Animal Health Vol. 2	0–333–57360–9
Goats	0–333–52309–1	Warm-water	
Dairying	0–333–52313–X	Crustaceans	0–333–57462–1
Poultry	0–333–52306–7	Livestock Production	
Rabbits	0–333–52311–3	System	0–333–60012–6
Draught Animals	0–333–52307–5	Donkeys	0–333–62750–4
Ruminant Nutrition	0–333–57073–1	Camels	0–333–60083–5
Animal Breeding	0–333–57298–X	Tilapia	0–333–57472–9
Upland Rice	0–333–44889–8	Plantain Bananas	0–333–44813–8
Tea	0–333–54450–1	Coffee Growing	0–333–54451–X
Cotton	0–333–47280–2	Food Legumes	0–333–53850–1
Weed Control	0–333–54449–8	Cassava	0–333–47395–7
Spice Plants	0–333–57460–5	Sorghum	0–333–54452–8
Cocoa	0–333–57076–6	Cut Flowers	0–333–62528–5
The Storage of Food		Coconut	0–333–57466–4
Grains and Seeds	0–333–44827–8	Market Gardening	0–333–65449–8
Avocado	0–333–57468–0	Forage Husbandry	0–333–66856–1
Sugar Cane	0–333–57075–8	Oil Palm	0–333–57465–6
Maize	0–333–44404–3	Alley Farming	0–333–60080–0
Food Crops and		Chickpeas	0–333–63137–4
Drought	0–333–59831–8		

Other titles published by Macmillan with CTA *(co-published in French by Maisonneuve et Larose)*

Animal Production in the Tropics and Subtropics	ISBN 0–333–53818–8
Coffee: The Plant and the Product	0–333–57296–3
The Tropical Vegetable Garden	0–333–57077–4
Controlling Crop Pests and Diseases	0–333–57216–5
Dryland Farming in Africa	0–333–47654–9
The Yam	0–333–57456–7

Land and Life series *(co-published with Terres et Vie)*

African Gardens and Orchards	ISBN 0–333–49076–2
Vanishing Land and Water	0–333–44597–X
Ways of Water	0–333–57078–2
Agriculture in African Rural Communities	0–333–44595–3

Contents

Acknowledgements   vi
Preface   vii
Foreword   viii

1 Livestock improvement   1
2 Performance recording and using records   9
3 Inheritance in general   18
4 Quantitative genetics   37
5 Selection I: Background   52
6 Selection II: Methods, schemes and rates achieved   77
7 Crossbreeding I: Background theory   103
8 Crossbreeding II: Systems and examples   117
9 Inbreeding   134
10 Special considerations for species and traits   148
11 Breed conservation   173
12 Postscript: The advance of biotechnology   180

Glossary   191
Bibliography   201
Index   204

Acknowledgements

I wish to thank most especially Dr Chris S. Haley (*AFRC Roslin Research Institute, Edinburgh*) for reading most of the chapters of this book and Mr John A. Woolliams (*also from the AFRC Roslin Research Institute*) and Dr Brian J. McGuirk (*Genus*) each for reading some of the chapters. I would like to acknowledge the contribution made by their helpful comments. Similarly, I wish to thank Dr D. Planchenault (of the Department d'Elevage et de Médecine Vétérinaire des Pays Tropicaux of Maisons-Alfort, France) for useful suggestions and additions. I am also indebted to Mr John D. Turton for help with references to provide background to the selection of livestock in the tropics. I am grateful to Dr Brian J. McGuirk for the data for Figures 4.2 and 4.3, and to the Scottish Agricultural College for the data for Figure 6.2.

The author and publishers wish to acknowledge, with thanks, the following for the supply of photographs, or permission to reproduce: Holt Studios International, (Nigel Cattlin) 3.5, 4.4, 7.2, 8.3 and 10.2; Roslin Research Institute (on behalf of the AFRC) Figures 4.1, 6.5, 9.5 and 12.1; Dr Anneke A. Bosma Figure 3.1; Dr A. J. Smith Figure 10.1; and David H. Holness Figure 10.3. (Figure 7.1 by the author).

GW

Preface

This volume has been written by Gerald Wiener, who has considerable experience of animal breeding both in temperate and tropical countries. Livestock kept in tropical countries are normally much less productive than farm animals of similar species kept on farms in temperate countries. The improvement of livestock in the tropics by the importation of breeding animals from temperate zones has, for a long time, been regarded as a relatively simple way of increasing the productivity of livestock in the tropics. However, many such programmes have been unsuccessful.

In this book Dr Wiener illustrates what can and cannot be achieved by animal breeding techniques. He starts by dealing with basic genetics and then deals with the various techniques used in animal breeding – selection, crossbreeding and inbreeding and the effects that each of these can have on animal populations. He gives examples of each and points out their limitations when applied in the tropics. At the same time he identifies systems of potential value, such as the use of multiple ovulation and embryo transfer which can be used to improve the efficacy of the selection process. He also deals with the specific considerations such as the effect of climate on animals, the problems faced when dealing with tropical species such as the buffalo and factors to take into consideration when dealing with individual traits, such as draught power.

This book provides a valuable guide for anyone concerned with animal breeding in tropical countries. The reader will find that topics as diverse as the need to conserve the genetic material from tropical breeds and the applications of recent advances in biotechnology are dealt with. This book, which should be read in conjunction with others in the series dealing with individual animal species, will provide invaluable basic and applied knowledge for all those interested in obtaining information about livestock improvement in the tropics.

Anthony J. Smith

Foreword

This book is aimed, mainly, at situations such as found in most of the tropics, where material resources for livestock improvement are limited and where the environmental circumstances for livestock production create special problems. The tropics are not, however, the only areas where limitations and obstacles to increased animal productivity exist. There are many countries, even with relatively benign climates, which have a shortage of material and feed resources for livestock production. This book will concentrate, therefore, on the principles of animal breeding which apply to all situations, rather than attempt to suggest particular solutions which depend on particular circumstances. One chapter is, however, devoted to the special considerations needed to adapt the breeding principles to the various livestock species and to their performance characteristics – in the context of their environment.

The rules of heredity as they apply to groups or populations of animals have been enlarged and developed, over the past 60 years, through mathematics and statistics into the science of quantitative genetics. This science underlies modern animal breeding schemes and their application. Advances in other disciplines such as physiology and in technological developments, such as artificial insemination and the manipulation of embryos have, however, increased the opportunities for progress in animal breeding – even if there are still constraints on their application. Some sophisticated and costly aids to animal breeding are often inappropriate in the materially less-favoured parts of the world.

Although quantitative genetics is the basis for this book, it has been thought necessary to avoid the use of mathematical derivations and reliance on statistical solutions. For those with more specialised or advanced needs, such matters can be found in other books, some of which are listed. However, in order to provide a cross-reference to such other books and to the specialised terms used by animal breeders, some of these terms and symbols are introduced.

It is hoped that this book will be of use to students, agriculturists, veterinarians, breeders and others concerned with livestock improvement, who want or need to understand the basis of animal breeding without the specialised detail, and in particular to those involved with the less-favoured countries in terms of climate and resources.

1 Livestock improvement

1.1 *Background*

Aims

Efficiency of production should be the objective of improvement. In economic terms this means that any increase in output, whatever the product, should be related to the costs of the inputs. **Improvement** will only have taken place if the **value of the output** then **exceeds the costs of the inputs**.

This can be consistent with increasing the production of milk, meat, wool, or whatever, but it is not exactly the same. There are other criteria by which the benefits of livestock production and of improvement schemes can be judged. A national goal might be to optimise production from the available resources of land, feed, or labour. Emphasis may have to be placed on sustainability of production. Whatever the aim, outputs should not be divorced from consideration of the inputs.

The inputs include the land, feed, labour, capital, veterinary services and other items required for animal production. It is not always easy to estimate the cost of these inputs accurately, but is important to recognise that they exist. This may appear self-evident where the inputs have to be directly paid for, but it is equally true when, for example, just natural grazing is used. Even in that situation economic improvement can only be said to have occurred if a given area of land produces more animals or animal products than it did before – and in a sustainable way. The returns obtained from animals (milk, meat, work, wool, hides, dung and other products) should be easier to quantify.

All too often in the past, livestock improvement – and genetic improvement in particular – has aimed simply at producing high-yielding animals. Often, high-yielding animals are the more efficient in economic terms, but not always. Especially in situations where feed and other resources are scarce and the climate is potentially stressful for animals, the costs of achieving high individual yield may be too high in relation to the returns. An intermediate yield, better than the old, but not as high as possible, is likely to be a better option. Where flocks and herds are large, or when considering a large area, perhaps a whole country or region, it is an improvement in the production from the whole system – in relation to the inputs required – which is more important than the size of the increase in the yield of the best individuals.

The overall objective of increasing the efficiency of the animal production system will often have to be attained by attention to some of the components. However, the first step is to decide what is meant by 'improvement' in any particular situation.

Methods

There are many ways of changing the productivity of livestock, whether judged on efficiency or yield. These include: feeding; management (including the physical environment); health care; physiological or pharmacological intervention; and animal breeding (genetic improvement).

This book is mostly about the opportunities for and methods of genetic change. In general, genetic improvement should not be considered in isolation from the aspects of the environment.

As a first step it will nearly always be better to consider the resources available for animal production and the limits to these resources, and to match the animal breeding objectives to these. Later on, improvements in any or all the resources (for example feed or management capability) can be matched by further improvements in the genetic capabilities of the animals.

To set about the process the other way around – to attempt to match the resources to the assumed genetic potential of the animals (for example an imported exotic breed or crosses with it) is risky and more prone to failure. The extra resources required to sustain the improved genetic type, for example the new breed or cross, may not be consistently available and the costs of providing them may be too high.

Extra feed, improved management, more health care, all cost money and have to be maintained continuously to increase animal productivity. It is important, therefore, to ensure that such extra inputs provide an adequate return in terms of animal production.

Genetic improvement does not come free of cost either, but once attained it is generally there without the need for further effort. Also, each step of genetic improvement can be added to the one which went before. The benefits from, for example, genetic selection accumulate over time – they are cumulative. Most other forms of improvement require the whole of the input to be made each time the improvement is wanted, for example through the supply of extra feed or veterinary medicines.

Sometimes a genetically improved stock immediately makes better use of the existing resources than the stock indigenous to the area. More often, an improved stock will also need some extra feed or other inputs. If these become available, the improved stock may well exploit the extra resources to better advantage. The extent to which these things happen can usually only be answered by making controlled changes in both the genotype of the animals and the environment in which they perform – and then assessing the consequences. Nature and nurture must be considered together.

Genetic options

Genetic change can be produced by:
- Substituting one breed for another
- Crossbreeding
- Inbreeding
- Selection (within a breed or a population, e.g. a herd)
- Gene transfer (not yet at the stage of regular application to animal breeding in unfavourable environments)
- and any combination of these.

The principles underlying each of these and how to proceed is dealt with in later chapters. From among the main options listed, genetic selection (within breed) is the only currently practical way of creating something new as distinct from something already in existence somewhere.

Genetic selection, because it moves forward in small, cumulative steps, allows any necessary changes in feeding and management to be assimilated slowly and steadily. In the long term, selection may provide the most secure option for sustainable improvement. Unfortunately, selection, particularly in the tropics, is not often enough given serious consideration. This is because its immediate effect is rarely as dramatic, as, for example, changes from crossbreeding.

Traits
The genetic options and the degree of complexity of a breeding programme will depend on the kind of trait which it is intended to improve. Trait (as used in this book) describes a product or attribute of an animal. Sometimes the word trait will be preceded by some other descriptive term:
- **production trait** related to some aspect of productivity, perhaps meat output
- **wool trait** related to the production of wool, perhaps fibre quality.

Some traits can be considered as made up of many components (**compound traits**). Meat output from sheep would be a compound trait

3

because many component traits contribute to meat output. Rather than select on meat output as a whole, the genetic selection in an improvement programme may need to be directed to one or more of the components or to a combination of them.

By contrast, the occurrence of horns in cattle should be regarded as a relatively simple attribute (a **simple trait**). Genetic selection aimed at ridding cattle of horns would concern itself only with the presence or absence of horns in the animals and in their parents and offspring. (These matters will be dealt with in more detail in later chapters.)

Interactions

Heredity and environment may interact. For example, two or more breeds compared in one set of conditions may not differ much in their productivity, but in another set of conditions they may differ a great deal.

EXAMPLE 1A HEREDITY AND ENVIRONMENT (FEEDING) INTERACT

Figure 1.1 shows, from tropical conditions in Australia, a comparison of the

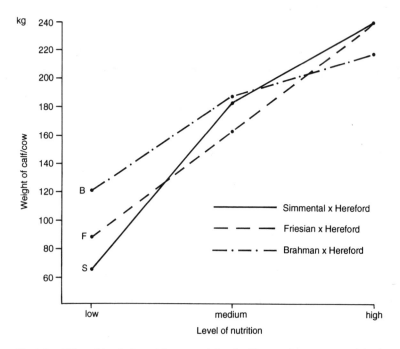

Fig 1.1 *Effect of level of nutrition on weight of calf weaned per cow mated in three breed crosses* (adapted from Barlow, Hearnshaw and Hennessy, 1985)

weight of calf weaned by crossbred cows of three types – crosses of Hereford with Friesian, Brahman and Simmental. All cows were mated to Hereford bulls. (The calves are therefore 3/4 Hereford.) The experiment was conducted on three levels of feeding: low; medium; and high.

*It can be seen that the Simmental crosses equalled the production of the Friesian crosses on the high plane of nutrition, they exceeded the Friesian crosses on the medium plane and were poorer on the low plane. The Brahman (*Bos indicus*) crosses were at a disadvantage to the other crosses on the high plane of nutrition but were the best on both the other feeding levels – and by a large margin on the low plane.*

The example 1A illustrates:
- The importance of the genetic and environmental (e.g. feeding) conditions and the opportunities for their improvement.
- The need to consider genotype and environment together.
- There can be an optimum genetic type for any particular set of conditions.
- Some genetic types increase their productivity more than others for any given improvement in the feed supply – or indeed other external factors which can affect production.
- The importance of comparing breeds (or other genetically different groups) under the same conditions of feeding and management if the comparison is to have any real value.
  The last of these points, comparing breeds under the same conditions, is an important matter which is often ignored.

For example, people often point to the very high yield of milk which Holstein cows give under the best conditions in North America and contrast it with the low yield of a zebu breed in Africa. Such a difference in yield is due only in part to the difference in breed and is greatly affected by the large differences in the environment (climate, feeding, management practices, disease incidence).

The relative importance of breed *and* environment in affecting yield cannot be assessed if each breed is kept only in its own, traditional set of conditions. When that happens, the genotypes (breeds) and the environments in which the cows are kept are said to be **confounded**.

The yield in North America gives little clue to the difference which would occur between the Holstein (or crosses) and the zebu under the conditions normal for the zebu.

Likewise, if one breed is kept in one herd and the other breed in another, differently managed herd – any breed difference is then mixed up (confounded) with other differences between the herds.

5

1.2 *Constraints on improvement*

In the tropics and in many developing countries of the world, the application of modern animal breeding techniques has to overcome a number of special problems which make progress more difficult than it might otherwise be. The special difficulties arise mainly from natural and economic constraints. It is important to bear these in mind so as to avoid false expectations from breeding programmes.

Environmental

Feed
Typically in the tropics, the feed base, particularly that available for ruminant production, is poor or very variable. Some of this arises from seasonal variations in feed supply, for example during dry and wet times of the year. Periods of prolonged drought or other disasters can severely reduce the supply of feed, whether from natural grazing or other crops. The costs of fertilisers and pesticides may preclude their use and further reduce the provision of feed, for example the availability of crop by-products.

Climate
Climatic extremes, heat or cold, have stressful effects on animals and, hence, on their performance. Many indigenous breeds are relatively well adapted to such conditions but breeds native to other environments are not.

Disease
A high incidence of animal disease and high mortality rates are common constraints on animal production. Disease and mortality often occur, or are increased, because of inadequate veterinary support. Both the incidence of disease and mortality rates are made worse through poor nutrition.

Apart from the direct effects on productivity, poor animal health has adverse effects on the rate of any genetic progress to be made in a breeding programme through:
- delaying the onset of breeding,
- lowering the reproductive rate and
- increasing mortality.

Animal disease also restricts other opportunities for genetic improvement, because most countries impose legal restrictions on the importation of breeding stock from outside their own territory – unless free from particular diseases. These regulations are intended to stop the spread of some important animal diseases, but they also have the effect of restricting the use of imported superior stock in breed improvement and in crossbreeding. The regulations apply to the importation of stock from all countries, but they make it particularly difficult for animals to be imported from tropical countries, where many of these diseases are endemic. The use of frozen material, in particular frozen embryos, may ease the restrictions on importation of stock in the future.

Structural constraints on genetic improvement

Infrastructure

Animal breeding programmes, at least on a national or regional scale, depend for their success on the ability to multiply and transmit the genetic improvement across the largest possible number of flocks or herds. Factors creating obstacles to the implementation of improvement schemes and their cost effectiveness include:

- Difficulties in transport for animals or semen
- Barriers to successful implementation of artificial insemination programmes (involving the production, collection, storage, distribution and effective use of semen)
- Absence of adequate marketing arrangements.

Investment in infrastructure may be necessary before genetic improvement is effective – but genetic improvement takes time to achieve. The first steps in a breeding programme should, therefore, perhaps be taken before the other improvements have been completed.

Herd/flock size

In many countries, including tropical countries, there are large numbers of individually very small herds or flocks. Small-holder farmers with only one or two cows, or with a very small number of sheep, goats or pigs are common. When the number of animals involved is large, progress in animal breeding is easier to achieve than when numbers are small. Also, the improvements which are wanted are likely to occur in a reliable way only if the numbers involved in the breeding programme are adequate. It is more difficult to extend the full advantages of genetic improvement to small units. For breeding purposes it may, therefore, be useful to associate small herds or flocks into larger groupings.

Animal resources

Absolute yields from many of the indigenous breeds of livestock, in for example the tropics, are often low – though an exotic breed may be no better or perhaps even worse under those exacting conditions. Just as it is wrong to expect too much from exotic breeds when they are transposed to unfavourable conditions, so it is wrong to dismiss the genetic

7

potential of indigenous breeds simply as 'low' and regard it as an absolute constraint on improvement.

The concept of genetic potential should always be related to the conditions under which the animals are expected to perform. Wrong expectations interfere with the proper planning of improvement schemes and lead to disappointment in the results.

Human resources

A shortage of adequately trained specialists creates problems for the design and implementation of breeding improvement schemes. It is important to match any scheme to the availability of competent people to carry it out.

Record keeping

Recording the performance of livestock is one of the pre-requisites for livestock improvement (chapter 2). Absence of records is a barrier to implementing and evaluating breeding schemes.

2 Performance recording and using records

2.1 *Why have records?*

Performance records are essential for the successful design and execution of breeding programmes. Records can be few and simple or more extensive depending on circumstances. Even a simple crossbreeding scheme requires some records on the performance of the indigenous breed(s) relative to the crosses and the relative performance of different types of crosses. This is necessary for devising the right crossbreeding system and to judge its cost-effectiveness.

For breeding schemes which involve the selection of individual animals – the superior ones from among a group – performance records are even more important. The skills of the farmer's eye are not good enough for picking out genetically superior animals in respect of most of the important characteristics of livestock. Subjective impressions of performance and reliance on memory are almost useless. The difficulties are well illustrated by reference to reproductive rate.

EXAMPLE 2A THE ANIMAL'S LOOKS ARE NOT A SUBSTITUTE FOR RECORDS

The reproductive rate of farm animals has usually a large bearing on profitability and on the opportunities for genetic progress. Looking at a cow or a ewe will not tell how good or bad she is in this respect. Nothing can be deduced about the potential for transmitting 'good' genes for reproduction by looking at a ram or a buck. Records of performance are essential.

Often it is necessary to keep simple pedigrees so that the performance of parents can be related to that of their offspring. This is essential for selection schemes. For many crossbreeding schemes pedigree recording might be restricted to identifying the breeds involved at each stage, and probably the identity of the sire (the reason for this is to avoid accidental

9

mating of close relatives, i.e. inbreeding, chapter 9).

The cost of undertaking performance recording should be accepted as part of the necessary cost of achieving improvement.

2.2   Which animals to record

The choice of animals for which records are made depends on the circumstances of any particular breeding programme and its current and future objectives.

Sufficient records may often be available from institutional herds or flocks for purposes of designing breeding schemes and for decisions about breeding policy. Such records are often a useful starting point. They are, also, often the only records which it is practical to use without incurring the costs and delays in gathering the information afresh for each particular scheme. It is, however, important that the conditions under which the animals are kept in these institutional units are reasonably similar to the conditions under which the commercial animals – the target of improvement – are kept (or will be kept in the future).

Once a breeding programme has started, more recording will be needed in order to execute the plan and assess progress. For the herds (or flocks) from which actual breeding animals are chosen, or in which breeding animals are tested, all the animals should have the appropriate aspects of their performance recorded. In addition, at least a sample of the herds and flocks associated with the improvement scheme should have some recording done from time to time, in order to monitor any changes that take place and to assess the value of the breeding programme. This sample might be from the commercial herds in which some of the newly improved animals (perhaps bulls or rams, or their semen) are used.

Mason and Buvanendran (1982) have discussed these matters in some detail. They point out that no standard system of recording is suitable for all farming conditions. The level of recording which it is possible to maintain depends on the management system for the animals and the stage of development of the livestock industry of the country or of the particular animal enterprise.

2.3   What to record

The best advice is:
• To restrict records to those essential for the conduct of the improvement scheme and its cost-effectiveness.

- Only to undertake recording that can be maintained.
- Only to collect records that can be analysed.

Taking records without using them for the purposes for which they are needed – decisions about breeding, feeding and management – is a waste of time and money.

For details pertaining to different species, see Mason and Buvanendran (1982) and see Faugere and Faugere (1986) for an example of recording procedures for small ruminants in Africa. As a general rule, the records most needed are those directly related to the aspect of performance which it has been decided to improve, for example milk yield, body size or litter size. In addition, some characteristics require observation which are related to the principal trait even though they are not the direct object of improvement. Such additional traits may have a bearing on production efficiency or costs and they may themselves change in consequence of changing the primary trait. Given below are some specific examples of recording for inter-related aspects of performances but the same principles apply to all traits and to all species.

EXAMPLE 2B MILK YIELD AND MILK COMPOSITION

Assume that it is the intention to increase milk production in cattle. If so, some estimate of milk yield has to be made, perhaps from monthly records. This may not be difficult in large institutional herds, even in the tropics. It may present greater difficulties in small-holder herds where problems can arise because of poor educational level of farmers and poor access of the farms to field workers, acting as recorders. (Less accurate but still factual ways of recording yield may have to do.) However, cows which produce more milk often produce milk with a lower proportion of fat and protein.

If cheese- or butter-making is the objective it may be that milk yield alone is the wrong criterion for improvement. But even when extra milk quantity is the aim, some measure of milk composition will be useful in addition to total yield if the maximum economic gain is to be made or quality (in terms of milk composition) is not to be lost.

EXAMPLE 2C MILK YIELD AND BODY SIZE

As a generalisation (not true in every case), cows which yield more milk are often larger than those which produce less. Big cows, however, eat more than small ones and that may not be desirable, or may not be cost-effective. Some records should therefore be taken to note the milk yield/body size relationship and any changes that occur – and perhaps to take account of the relationship in the improvement programme. The relationship of milk yield to body size is also highly relevant when part of the farmer's income from cattle is derived from their use for meat or work, in addition to milk.

11

EXAMPLE 2D MILK PRODUCTION AND REPRODUCTION

*Milk production is related to the regularity of calving. The level of milk pro-
duction can affect the timing and ability to conceive. Thus, minimum records on
calving performance are needed to relate to the changes in milk production. In the
same way, records of health, or at least of overt illness, are necessary in order to
interpret milk records. A cow with mastitis or other disease will have reduced milk
production.*

Minor traits

It is important to avoid spending time and effort on recording minor
points which make little or no contribution to the main trait, or to the
efficiency of production. Such minor points overload the capacity to
gather the essential information and if considered in the selection of the
breeding animals will actually retard the improvement progress.

Efficiency

In relation to the paramount importance of *efficiency* of production, it is
useful to record those items which contribute significantly to the costs of
production. The financial returns from the production process can be
gauged by the output – more easily quantified for items which are sold
than for items which are used by the farmer.

The costs of production may also change as genetic improvement
proceeds and productivity increases, for example, feed inputs may change.

Feed intake, one of the major components of the costs of animal
production, is difficult or expensive to measure. If considered important, as it would be in a large-scale enterprise, the recording may need to
be restricted to the costs of purchased feeds or feeds which are given to
the animals instead of being sold. For grazing situations, an indication of
stocking rate may be all that is feasible. For common grazings even that
exercise may be impossible – or pointless.

In the present discussion it is necessary only to stress that some indication of inputs is useful especially for large improvement schemes, such as
those on a national scale. The information may be obtained from perhaps just a small sample of herds – for example the larger, institutional
ones – on a periodic basis rather than as a frequent routine.

Culling poor animals

Performance records can be used as a basis for culling unproductive
animals. Such culling improves herd performance and profitability, quite
apart from any possible genetic benefits.

Correcting (adjusting) performance records

It is always necessary to relate performance levels to the conditions under which the performance is achieved.

A number of external factors influence the performance of animals, such as the year, the season of the year, stage of lactation, sex of animal, age and many others. The average effects of such external influences should be taken into account when comparing the performance of different animals.

This process is called correcting the performance records. It is based on the use of **correction factors** which are calculated from the average effects of these outside influences. Once this has been done, it becomes easier to separate animals on genetic merit.

If it is not done, the effects of heredity can be greatly, even completely, masked by the effects of other factors. The degree to which this occurs will be greater for some traits than for others, but the principle applies to all traits and especially to those, such as milk or meat production or reproductive efficiency, which are most often the target of improvement.

EXAMPLE 2E CORRECTING PERFORMANCE RECORDS: THE PRINCIPLES IN RELATION TO SHEEP

A twin-born lamb will generally be smaller than a single. Males are generally heavier than females. A lamb born to a mature ewe will generally be bigger and grow faster than one born to a young female lambing for the first time. The season when the lamb is born may well affect its growth and survival, because the season will affect climate, feed supply and animal health. One year may well differ from another for similar reasons.

To compare the weights and growth rate of lambs of a mixed group:
- *First correct the raw data on weights and growth of each lamb for these external influences.*
- *Only then compare the relative merits of different lambs – merits which will be partly due to the genes they carry.*

Similarly, only after taking account of these various factors can the more productive ewes – in terms of lamb production – be distinguished from the less productive.

EXAMPLE 2F CORRECTING PERFORMANCE RECORDS: NUMERICAL EXAMPLE FOR SHEEP

Assume there are two male lambs weighing 18 kg (lamb A) and 21 kg (lamb B) at 6 months of age.

If increased body size is the criterion for improvement, which of these two should be kept for future breeding?

The following information is available on each lamb:

Lamb A: born as twin in September (during the long dry season), dam 5 years-old.

Lamb B: born as single in December (during the short dry season), dam 2 years-old.

The flock records over several years show that, on average, by the age of 6 months:
- *twin-born lambs still weigh 3 kg less than singles;*
- *those born in September are 3 kg lighter in weight than those born in December;*
- *lambs from 2 years-old ewes are 1 kg lighter than those from 5 years-old dams.*

Using these average values as correction factors to bring both lambs to the same basis (i.e. single-born in December to 5 years-old ewe) the following occurs:

	Lamb A	Lamb B
Observed 6-month weight	18	21
Correction for twin effect	+ 3	
Correction for month effect	+ 3	
Correction for age of dam		+ 1
Corrected weight	24	22

Because lamb A had suffered more disadvantages to its growth than lamb B, it is seen that, after correction, lamb A is really the better of the two.

2.4 Using the records

Records which are not used may as well not be taken. For decisions about feeding and management the unadjusted data on performance will often provide sufficient guidance. For this purpose, and for individual herds, written records will often suffice. But for decisions about choice of breeding animals – either to keep or to cull – more information is needed. Many factors influence performance – it is important to sort them out and estimate their effect on the recorded performance level.

If a breeding scheme is very simple and decisions relate to perhaps only one trait (for example a weight at a particular age or a milk yield), written records will again provide substantial help in correcting records and choosing animals for breeding, or for adjusting their feeding in relation to yield.

Often, however, situations are more complicated. It might then be difficult to make accurate decisions about breeding and feeding in the time available on the basis of written records alone. Here are a few examples of such situations.

- *The individual herds or flocks may themselves be large involving a very large volume of records over several years.*
- *Some breeding schemes include many herds or flocks.*
- *A genetic selection programme may be based on a combination of several traits.*
- *Decisions about present and future breeding stock may have to be taken over a short period of time, such as a first decision about lambs needed as breeding replacements in the future to be taken either at the time lambs are weaned or at the start of a long dry season when surplus stock may have to be sold because feed will be in short supply.*

Written records alone seldom suffice when animal numbers are large and extend over many years and perhaps involve several farms, when the breeding scheme is concerned with more than one trait, if many external factors influence animal performance which require corrections to be made, and when decisions need to be arrived at quickly. Under such circumstances a computer becomes not only a valuable aid but probably a necessity.

Computers

A computer, with suitable program, will allow the rapid sorting out of the inter-related factors affecting choice of breeding animals and those surplus to requirements. Many personal computers (desk top or lap top) are adequate for most of the likely requirements.

First step is to put the data (information) on each animal into a **database program**. This is a program which allows all information on an individual to be stored in an ordered way and to be interlinked with the information on all other individuals – including parents and other relatives. The program allows the data to be sorted and accessed by different classifications, for example by herd, by sire, by season, by age of animal or by breed.

Second step is to feed the data into a program capable of correcting the data on each individual animal for the external, environmental factors which have affected production – as illustrated by the earlier examples.

Final step, at least where genetic choices are involved, is to rank the animals in order of merit for the trait being improved, or for an appropriate combination of traits.

Breed comparisons

Where a comparison of the performance of different breeds and crosses is involved, the need to correct the performance data of individual animals may not be necessary – especially if the breed groups being compared are large enough for the factors other than breed to be averaged out. That will, however, not always be the case. Herds, for example, may differ in management and feeding practices and may even be in different parts of the country with differences in climate. If the breeds or crosses to be compared are unequally distributed over several herds differing in these ways, it could invalidate any breed comparison. To overcome this problem, one way is to make breed comparisons within herds and average the breed differences over all herds. In other situations it may be more appropriate to calculate the average effects which different herds have on animal performance and correct the records accordingly. This again is more easily done if the records are stored in an appropriate way on a computer.

2.5 *Statistical confidence*

When devising and trying out new feeding, management or breeding practices, it is important to find out how much confidence to place on the effectiveness of these new practices before recommending their use more widely. Any new treatment, or new breed type, can at first appear beneficial but can later be found to be useless – and it is important to avoid making such mistakes – or at least to reduce the possibility. This is done by *estimating the probability that the effect* (for example, the difference between two levels of feeding) *might have arisen by chance.* Differences between groups of animals can arise simply by chance because the animals involved are only ever a sample of all the possible animals – and especially if the numbers in the groups are small.

EXAMPLE 2G DIFFERENCES DUE TO CHANCE

If groups of 10 sheep were drawn at random from a mixed flock of 500 and the sheep are weighed, it is highly likely that the average weights of different groups (samples) of 10 would vary simply because of the random way they were drawn – a chance effect.

There are statistical tests to examine these points (see books on statistics for details). In general, the statistical tests end by giving a probability (likelihood) that a difference as large as that found could have occurred by chance once in some larger number (in gambling terms it gives the 'odds'). (For instance, it might be asked: What is the probability that a difference of 2 kg in the weaning weight of lambs between a local breed and a crossbred group arose just by chance? The answer, after the appropriate calculations, might be: less than 1 time in every 20.)

By convention, less than 1 chance in 20 (5%) is usually taken as reasonably good evidence that chance alone is unlikely to have produced the effect. The effect itself (in the above example, the difference between the local lambs and the crosses) is then said to be **significant** at the 5% level of probability. Less than 1 chance in 100 (1%) would give even greater confidence in the effectiveness of a change of breed, or of the usefulness of a treatment (significant at the 1% level of probability).

The way this probability is calculated always depends on relating an average value, based on a series of observations, to some measure of the scatter or spread around that average (chapter 5). The most commonly used measures of such scatter are:

- **standard deviation** (SD) – for the scatter of individual observations
- **standard error** (SE) – for the spread of the averages of a number of groups.

Standard errors, themselves derived from standard deviations, reflect the fact that more reliance can be placed on averages based on a large number of observations than on those based on just a few. For instance, if deciding on the potential merits of a new breed, a milk yield for that breed based on the average of 500 cows should give much more confidence than an average based on the yield of only 5 cows. The standard error based on the 500 would be much *smaller* than that based on the 5 – given the same underlying variability.

Often, the statistical analysis of observations on animals is complex and standard deviations or standard errors cannot be readily applied. Such situations arise when many factors act simultaneously to affect the performance of animals and the effects of these various factors have to be disentangled and estimated. The principle of testing the significance of the effects, however, remains the same.

Computers make all these calculations easier to perform; the more complicated of the calculations are not practical without them.

2.6 Conclusion

In order to make the right decisions about the choice of animals in an improvement scheme, the importance of recording animal performance and of using the records cannot be over-stressed. Even without a formal improvement scheme, performance recording can be very educational and an aid to better management.

3 Inheritance in general

If sheep are mated to sheep we expect offspring which are sheep and not goats. Similarly, if Zebu cattle are mated together we expect Zebu calves and not Herefords. This, in essence, shows something about the workings of heredity. The fact that animals of one species or of one breed resemble each other is because they share a common inheritance. On the other hand, there is also variety. Even within a breed of livestock, all individuals are not alike. Offspring resemble their parents but are not identical copies of them.

These observed facts arise from the way the hereditary units of animals, the genes, are maintained in the population and from the way they are passed from one generation to the next.

3.1 Cells, chromosomes and formation of gametes

The hereditary material of an animal is contained in the nuclei of the cells of the animal body and is situated on chromosomes – seen through a microscope as rod-like structures at certain stages of cell division. Within each chromosome is a long double strand of deoxyribonucleic acid (DNA) and it is this which contains (encodes) the genetic information passed from parent to offspring.

The chromosomes occur in pairs (the members of such a pair are called **homologous** chromosomes). The number of chromosomes in each of the cells of the body (except the gametes) is referred to as the **diploid** number. This diploid number is, for example, 30 pairs (60 chromosomes) in cattle, 27 pairs (54) in sheep, 30 pairs (60) in goats, 19 pairs (38) in pigs (Figure 3.1) and 39 pairs (78) in chickens.

Cell division

Life begins with a single cell, the fertilised egg, called a **zygote**. It has the diploid number of chromosomes. When the zygote divides, each daughter cell receives an exact copy of the full complement of chromosomes. This form of cell division is called **mitosis** (Figure 3.2). The same thing

18

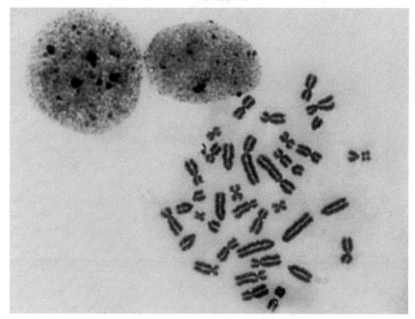

Fig 3.1 *Chromosomes of the pig* (photograph by Dr Anneke A. Bosma, Faculty of Veterinary Medicine, University of Utrecht)
Metaphase chromosomes from a blood lymphocyte of a male domestic pig. The chromosomes are stained with aceto-orcein. The 'balls' at the top of the picture are nuclei of cells which were not in mitosis when the preparation was made.

then happens repeatedly as cells continue to divide to form the different parts and tissues of the animal's body. Immediately prior to each cell division, the chromosomes double up in number. The duplicate pairs then separate – one pair to each of the daughter cells.

Thus, each cell contains the identical diploid complement of chromosomes – irrespective of the fact that the cells may be in different parts of the body. (The process of differentiation into different body parts and tissues starts very early in embryonic life.)

Gamete formation

The zygote, the starting point of a new individual, is formed by the fusion of two special cells (the **gametes**). One gamete comes from each of the parents: a sperm from the father; and an unfertilised egg from the mother. Something special happens in the formation of these gametes, the sperms and the eggs:

- Only half the number of chromosomes appear in each gamete that are present in all the other cells of the body.

19

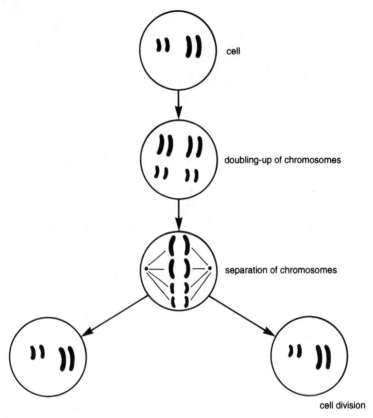

Fig 3.2 *Mitotis*
Cell division, for simplicity, of an imaginary cell with a total of only 4
chromosomes – in 2 homologous pairs. After doubling, the chromosomes
separate to the daughter cells which, therefore, retain the diploid number of
chromosomes.

- Only one of each member of the homologous chromosome pairs goes
  into each gamete (but see also crossing-over, section 3.4).

   If this halving of chromosome number did not occur during gamete
formation, the fusion of two cells each with the full (diploid) complement of chromosomes would double the total number of chromosomes
in each generation – and that would quickly become an impossible
situation. The process of cell division leading to gamete formation is
called **meiosis** (Figure 3.3).

   The number of chromosomes which appear in the gametes is called
the **haploid** number. The choice of which member of any one chromosome pair goes into any one gamete cell (individual sperm or individual
egg) is purely a matter of chance (Mendel's first rule, section 3.3). Thus

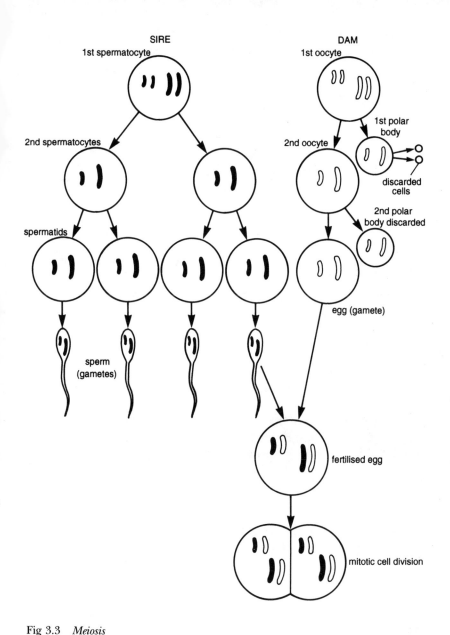

Fig 3.3 *Meiosis*
Cell division leading to formation of gametes (sperm or egg). It shows the
halving of the diploid number of chromosomes to the haploid number – only
1 member of each homologous pair of chromosomes goes into any one
gamete cell. This is followed by fertilisation which restores the diploid number
of chromosomes. Representation restricted to 4 chromosomes in 2
homologous pairs: the paternal chromosomes are shown as solid symbols; and
the maternal chromosomes as open symbols.

all the sperm or all the eggs from a particular individual (depending on its sex) will have the same (haploid) number of chromosomes but *not*, in normal farm livestock, the identical complement of genes.

Fertilisation – restoring the diploid number

When a sperm and an egg meet and fuse together, fertilisation of the egg is said to have occurred. The sperm and the egg each contribute their haploid number of chromosomes to the fertilised egg, called a zygote. In the zygote, there is the set of chromosomes derived from the sperm (the paternal chromosomes) and the homologous set of chromosomes from the egg (the maternal chromosomes). The zygote now has the normal, diploid number of chromosomes characteristic of each species.

Then the zygote cell divides by the process of mitosis retaining the diploid number of chromosomes in each daughter cell. Cell division continues in that way (Figure 3.2) for the whole of the development and life of the animal (except in the formation of gametes).

Sex determination

Mammals

One of the pairs of chromosomes in the cells is concerned with sex determination. In **female** mammals, that pair consists of two similar homologous chromosomes – called the X chromosomes. In **male** mammals the two members of that chromosome pair are different: one is like the X chromosome of the female but the other is usually a much shorter strand and is called the Y chromosome. When egg cells are formed by the ovaries of the female, each egg receives an X chromosome (though which member of the pair is again a matter of chance). In sperm formation, the X and the Y chromosomes go their independent ways and half the sperms formed will contain the X and the other half the Y chromosome (Figure 3.4). Again, it is a matter of chance whether an egg is fertilised by an X-bearing or a Y-bearing sperm. When fusion of egg and sperm has taken place, the fertilised eggs with two X chromosomes (XX) will develop into females and those with one X and one Y chromosome (XY) will develop into males.

Birds

In birds the same principle applies, but the situation is reversed because the female is the sex with the two different sex chromosomes (in this case called ZW) and the male the sex with the two similar sex chromosomes (ZZ). (In some species of bird the female has one Z chromosome but the second sex chromosome is missing. The male is thus ZZ as before, but the female Z/−. The mechanism of sex determination lead-

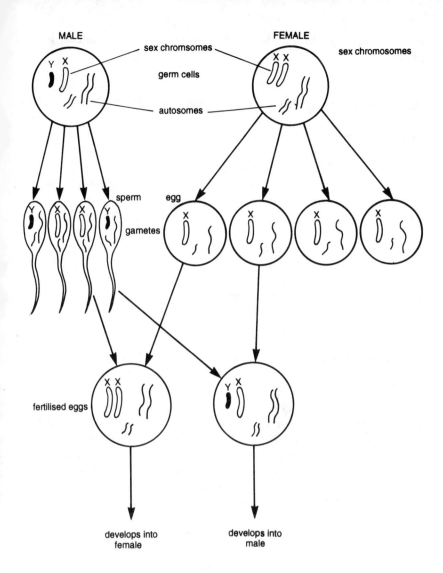

Fig 3.4 *Chromosomal sex determination in mammals (XY for male, XX for female)*
The X chromosome is shown as a long open symbol and the Y chromosome
as a short solid symbol. The male germ cell produces two kinds of sperm –
either with X or with Y chromosome. The eggs carry only the X chromosome.
At fertilisation, it is chance whether an egg is fertilised by an X-bearing sperm
or a Y-bearing sperm. It is, therefore, chance which sex is produced.

ing to half the chicks born being male and the other half female is the same.)

3.2 Genes and characters – genotype and phenotype

The chromosomes contain **genes** – the units of heredity – which act along with the environment to determine the characteristics of animals.

A gene is a segment of DNA; and DNA is concerned with protein synthesis. Proteins are made up of biochemical structures called polypeptides, of which there are many different kinds. One or more polypeptides make up each of the many different proteins which exist. Each polypeptide, in turn, is made up of a sequence of different amino acids, the biochemical building blocks.

The segments of DNA, the genes,

- start the process of protein synthesis by providing the codes
- for selecting different amino acids and
- for controlling the sequences in which different amino acids are built up into polypeptides.

In this way, each segment of DNA determines the manufacture of particular polypeptides. The proteins, made up from the polypeptides, are involved in all the functions which allow an animal to develop from the time of fertilisation onward, to grow, to reproduce and to perform.

The joint action of all the genes and of the environment, when expressed by the animal, is called the **phenotype** of the animal. The genes which contribute to the phenotype make up the animal's **genotype**.

Because chromosomes occur in pairs, so do genes. Some genes have large effects on the characters they affect, so that a single pair of genes will effectively determine a particular characteristic of an animal. In such a case it is possible to infer the genotype from looking at the animal (for example if a cow has horns, its genotype for that characteristic is immediately known, in example 3E).

There are other genes which have small effects in respect of any one characteristic of an animal. Many such genes may act together to exert their influence on a characteristic.

In addition, the environment may have a large influence. For example, an animal that is fed well is likely to be larger than a similar animal that is half-starved – quite apart from any differences between the two in their complement of genes for size.

When environmental (non-genetic) factors have a substantial effect on a trait, it is not possible, with any degree of accuracy, to infer the genotype (for example for body size) from the phenotype of an individual animal.

Mutations, alleles, homozygous and heterozygous individuals

Genes are located at particular points along each chromosome corresponding to locations along the strands of DNA. The genes at each such point, **locus** (plural: loci), affect a particular character. Over thousands of years slightly different forms of each gene have arisen by a process of change (**mutation**).

Mutations occur as a result of changes in the segments of DNA, through mistakes which sometimes happen when DNA replicates itself. When such a change occurs in the sex cells (where gametes are formed), the altered form of the gene is passed to future generations in the same way as the original gene.

These different forms of the gene are called **alleles**. There can be several such alleles of a particular gene (**multiple alleles**) in the population of animals, but any individual animal can have only two of them – one on each of the two members of a pair of homologous chromosomes, at the same locus. The different alleles of a gene produce slightly different biochemical actions and they have, therefore, a somewhat different effect on the character over which they exert full or partial control.

Homozygous and heterozygous

When the same allele is present on each member of a pair of homologous chromosomes, the individual is said to be **homozygous** for that allele. If the two alleles of the pair are different in kind, the individual is said to be **heterozygous**. (For purposes of illustration, if one of a pair of alleles be called A_1 and the other A_2, homozygous individuals might then be either of type A_1A_1 or of type A_2A_2 and heterozygous individuals would be of type A_1A_2.)

On an evolutionary time scale, mutation is the most important mechanism for creating and maintaining genetic diversity. For the relatively short time span over which most of our livestock breeds have been refined by selection and breeding, mutation must be assumed to counteract some of the forces which reduce variation.

Dominant, recessive and additive gene action

The alleles of any one pair may behave in three possible ways in relation to each other (dominant, recessive or additive) depending on the relative power of one allele over the other in its influence on the character.

Dominant and recessive alleles

The action of one of the alleles may dominate development to the exclusion of the other.

*One allele, let it be called C_1, determines the white, whilst the other, C_2, allows the
development of a coloured (non-white) face. The allele for white, C_1, is dominant
in the development of the character: therefore a genotype C_1C_2 will appear white in
the same way as the genotype C_1C_1. Only the genotype C_2C_2 will have a coloured
(non-white) face. Thus, C_1 is said to be* **dominant** *to C_2. Conversely, C_2 is* **recessive**
to C_1.

Example 3A is of some practical interest because Hereford bulls are
most frequently used for crossing with breeds which have coloured faces.
The crossbred offspring will then all have white faces (provided the
genotype of each Hereford bull was C_1C_1) and it is easy to infer that
Hereford bulls have been used to produce the crosses (Figure 3.5).

By convention, the dominant allele is usually denoted by a capital
letter, C, and the recessive by the corresponding small letter, c – thus,
the heterozygote would be written as Cc.

Although in example 3A of Hereford face colour the white is completely dominant over the coloured face there are other situations where
the dominance of one allele over the other may be only partial.

Overdominance
A situation where the performance of the heterozygote is superior to
that of either of the two homozygotes is called **overdominance**. This is

Fig 3.5   *Hereford × Friesian cross bullocks with white faces*

rare in relation to individual pairs of alleles at a locus. It has more relevance in relation to overall animal performance.

Additive gene action

Two alleles may be equal in power so that the phenotype of the heterogygote will be half-way between those of the two homozygotes.

EXAMPLE 3B   ADDITIVE GENE ACTION

*In a certain breed of poultry there are two different alleles affecting the colour of plumage: one allele produces black plumage when present in the homozygous state, B_1B_1; and the other produces white plumage when homozygous, B_2B_2. However, the heterozygote, B_1B_2, has blue plumage – the true Blue Andalusian fowl. The action of alleles B_1 and B_2 are said to be **additive** in relation to each other.*

3.3   Mendelian rules

The discovery how characteristics are inherited and transmitted is attributed to Gregor Mendel who lived in the nineteenth century and published his work, based on plants, in 1886. Two rules emerged from his work:
* The rule of **segregation**
* The rule of **independent assortment**.

Rule 1: Segregation

The first rule says that it is a matter of chance which of the two alleles of a pair goes into any one gamete.

It is again a matter of chance which sperm fertilises which egg cell.

It is important to note that while body cells (with the diploid number of chromosomes) may have two copies of the same allele or one copy of each, the gametes are always 'pure'. They always contain only *one* or other of the possible alleles of any pair. Thus, in the example 3A of Hereford cattle face colour, a gamete can only carry either C_1 or C_2 (C or c).

It follows that in any individual, one allele (of any given pair) comes from the father and the other from the mother – *never* both from one parent.

EXAMPLE 3C   OFFSPRING RECEIVE ONE ALLELE FROM EACH PARENT

Example 3A relating to the white face colour of Hereford cattle will now be taken

27

a stage further (using the convention of designating the dominant allele C and the recessive allele c. Thus: CC individuals will produce only C gametes; and cc only c. However, the heterozygous Cc will produce two types of gamete – C and c (in equal number).

The following combinations can occur, depending on which type of sperm meets which type of egg at fertilisation:

    C meets C to give CC
    c meets c to give cc
    C meets c to give Cc.

The mating of heterozygous animals (Cc) to other heterozygotes gives the following possibilities:

			Cc male	
			Male gametes	
			C	c
Cc female	Female gametes	C	CC	cC
		c	Cc	cc

Thus, out of the 4 possible combinations, 2 are homozygotes and 2 are heterozygotes. In the example chosen, C (white-face allele) is dominant to c (allele for coloured face), therefore, the heterozygotes (Cc) will have white faces. The ratio of white to coloured faces will be 3:1 – although there are 3 different genotypes for face colour in the ratio of 1:2:1.

When the heterozygous type is mated back to one or other of the two homozygous types it is called a **backcross**.

EXAMPLE 3D A BACKCROSS (IN HEREFORD CATTLE)

The heterozygote, Cc, – assume it to be the male – will again give rise to gametes of 2 types (C or c) while the homozygotes can give rise to only one type of gamete each. The following are the possible matings:

		Cc male	
		Male gametes	
		C	c
Female gametes			
[from CC female]	C	CC	cC
[from cc female]	C	Cc	cc

Both types of backcross result in only two genotypes of offspring in the ratio of 1:1 – one a homozygote and the other a heterozygote. But because in this example the C allele is dominant, the heterozygotes have a white face – even though they are not true breeding in this respect. Only the genotype cc, with the double dose of the recessive allele actually has a coloured face.

Rule 2: Independent assortment

The second of Mendel's rules relates to the inheritance of more than one pair of genes – provided they are on different chromosomes.

The rule is that the members of different pairs of alleles (when on different pairs of chromosomes) segregate independently of each other when the gametes are formed.

EXAMPLE 3E INDEPENDENT SEGREGATION OF 2 PAIRS OF ALLELES

Two simple traits of cattle are the white or coloured face of Hereford cattle (used in the examples 3A, 3C and 3D) and the polling allele which leads to absence of horns in cattle. The allele for the polled condition, P, is dominant to the allele for the presence of horns, p. The genes affecting absence or presence of horns are carried on a different pair of chromosomes from those for face colour.

As before, and for purposes of the present example, the alleles affecting each trait can be present in the homozygous or in the heterozygous state.

Because each trait behaves independently of the other, the gametes can be of 4 possible types (depending on the genotypes of the animals giving rise to them): PC, Pc, pC, and pc.

These 4 types of gamete would be produced by animals which are heterozygous for both traits (PpCc). If the double heterozygotes are mated to each other, the combinations of possible matings would be as follows:

			PpCc male			
			Male gametes			
			PC	Pc	pC	pc
		PC	PPCC	PPcC	pPCC	pPcC
PpCc female	Female gametes	Pc	PPCc	PPcc	pPCc	pPcc
		pC	PpCC	PpcC	ppCC	ppcC
		pc	PpCc	Ppcc	ppCc	ppcc

From the 16 possible combinations:

- *9 of the resulting offspring combine in their genotype at least one copy of P and one of C. Because of the dominance involved, all these will be polled with white faces (but only one of these, PPCC, true breeding in respect of both traits at the same time).*
- *A further 3 individuals combine at least one P with cc and will be phenotypically polled with coloured face.*
- *A further 3 combine pp with at least one C and will, therefore, have horns with a white face.*
- *Only 1 of the 16 individuals will, by chance, have the double dose of each of the recessive alleles (ppcc) – it will be horned with coloured face and true breeding in that respect. Only for this genotype will it be possible to infer that only one kind of gamete will be produced, pc, simply by looking at the phenotype of ppcc animals.)*

Ratios

It should be noted that, in the foregoing examples, *the ratios of the different genotypes are the ratios expected on average, when large numbers of matings are made.* The observed ratios may differ when only small numbers of animals are involved, because of the chance element in which allele of a pair appears in any one gamete and which sperm fertilises which egg. The chance effect can be likened to that found when tossing a coin with a head and a tail side. Over thousands of throws there is an equal chance of seeing heads or tails. But with a small number of throws, the ratio of heads to tails can differ greatly.

3.4 Other concepts of inheritance

Gene interactions

Genes which are on different chromosomes are independent of each other only in respect of their transmission. They often have joint effects on the development of the traits of an individual. Additive action is one possibility, similar to that referred to for pairs of alleles. What is considered now is an interaction leading to a masking of the effects of one gene (at one locus) by the actions of another (at another locus). Such interactions are called **epistasis**.

EXAMPLE 3F EPISTASIS – MASKING EFFECT

The allele for albinism controls an absence of colour production. Although itself recessive to the allele allowing pigmentation to proceed, when the albino allele is present in the homozygous condition, aa, it will suppress the pigmentation of hair and skin. This action is irrespective of the other colour genes which may be present and which would otherwise have resulted in variously coloured individuals.

Epistasis can manifest itself by the complete masking of the effects of one gene pair by those of another (as in albinism). Another effect is a modifying one, where the joint effects may in certain combinations produce something new.

EXAMPLE 3G EPISTASIS – MODIFYING EFFECT

For some of the combinations of rose comb with pea comb in poultry, both independently inherited traits, give a new type – the walnut comb – caused by epistatic gene interaction.

Linkage

Genes situated on the same chromosome are said to be **linked**. Such genes do not segregate independently – hence, Mendel's first rule does not apply to them. The characteristics controlled by such linked genes, therefore, tend to occur together.

Crossing-over and recombination

The different genes linked on a chromosome may be close to each other along the length of the chromosome, or further apart. Immediately prior to the cell division (meiosis) which leads to the halving of the number of chromosomes, the two homologous chromosomes of each pair come into close contact with each other and exchange segments. Linkages, therefore, may be broken and new ones created. The chances of this occurring are greater if the linked genes are far apart on their chromosome than if they are close together.

The process of **crossing-over**, therefore, leads to a **recombination of genes** affecting different traits and is one mechanism for maintaining genetic variability in a population.

Sex linkage

Sex linkage is a term that refers to genes which happen to be located on the sex chromosomes (see also section 3.1). The X chromosome has been found to contain a number of such genes with effects on the animal. Because of the short length of the Y chromosome, such genes are found there only very rarely.

A particular interest in sex-linkage arises because any gene on the X chromosome of mammals will then appear in its 'pure' form in the male

– since the corresponding allele on the Y chromosome is generally absent. Thus, the male will always express the character influenced by such a gene. If that effect is harmful, the male will show it.

EXAMPLE 3H   HAEMOPHILIA – SEX-LINKAGE IN HUMANS

The allele for haemophilia (which prevents the normal clotting of blood at a wound, thus allowing bleeding to continue) is carried on the X chromosome in humans. This allele is recessive to its allele which allows normal clotting of blood.

If the mother carries both the normal alleles, all her sons (and daughters) will be normal.

If, however, she is a heterozygote (carrying both the normal and the haemophilia-causing allele), half her sons will be affected by haemophilia, even though she appeared normal in respect of her own ability to clot blood. Daughters will be affected by haemophilia only in the rare cases where both her X chromosomes carry the recessive allele. A haemophiliac female must have received one of her X chromosomes from a haemophiliac father and the other from either a rare haemophiliac mother (double recessive) or, more probably, by a mating of an affected male to a carrier mother (heterozygote).

In poultry, the position of the male and female is reversed in respect of sex linkage (page 22). (For more details, see *Poultry* in *The Tropical Agriculturalist* series.)

Sex limitation

Sex limitation refers not to a mode of inheritance but to the expression of traits when dependent on sex. Thus, only females produce milk even though the male carries – and transmits – genes affecting milk production. Milk production is an example of a sex limited trait.

Genotype-environment interaction (G × E)

Hereditary and environment was dealt with in chapter 1. In the present context, G × E refers to the observation that sometimes genes express themselves, in their action on the trait, differently in one environment than in another. For example, genes causing photo-sensitivity to strong sunlight, as found in some breeds of sheep, do no harm in areas where strong sunshine does not occur for prolonged periods.

3.5   *Gene (allele) frequency in a population (herd or flock)*

Thus far, consideration has been given only to the genes carried by individuals. In respect to the genes for horns, an individual Hereford animal may be either pp, Pp, or PP (the first allowing the formation of horns and the last two both appearing polled).

However, in a large herd of Hereford cattle there may be some animals of each of the three different genetic types for horns. For instance, assume that breeders have produced a polled type of Hereford over many generations by introducing the allele for polling into what was, originally, a breed with horns. After several generations of selection for this trait, the majority of animals may well appear polled, but some of these will still be heterozygotes, Pp in respect of the alleles affecting polling. Some of the recessive homozygotes, pp, animals with horns, may also still occur.

EXAMPLE 3I CALCULATING GENE FREQUENCY IN A HERD OF CATTLE

Assume a herd of 100 Hereford cows in which it is known that 45 are homozygous polled, PP, a further 50 are heterozygous, Pp, but look polled, and the remaining 5 have horns, pp.

Since any one gamete contains only one of the alleles, these numbers of the three genotypes produce (proportionately)

- *90 gametes with the P allele derived from the PP homozygotes (45 + 45)*
- *50 gametes with the P allele from the heterozygotes (50)*
- *60 gametes of type p derived from the heterozygotes (50 in number) and from the 5 individuals with horns.*

In total this provides gametes a ratio of 140 with P and 60 with p.

Expressed more conventionally the proportion of P:p is therefore 7:3 and the allele frequency of P is said to be 0.7 and that of the recessive allele, p, is 0.3 (out of 1).

Predicting genotype frequency

The concept of gene frequency is useful because it allows *predictions* to be made about future genotypes.

Note What is really an indication of the frequency of the different alleles of a gene, has been called 'gene frequency' when 'allele frequency' might be less ambiguous. This has been done only because 'gene frequency' is the term used in all standard text-books on this subject.

EXAMPLE 3J PROCEDURE TO PREDICT GENOTYPE FREQUENCIES

If the cows from the herd used in example 3i were mated at random (in all possible combinations) to bulls with the same frequencies of the P and p alleles (0.7 and 0.3 for P and p respectively), the genotypes of the next generation can be predicted.

The procedure is to multiply the frequencies of the two alleles in all possible combinations – just as was done earlier in respect of the individual gametes from animals of specified genotypes. Thus:

		Proportion of male gametes	
		0.7P	0.3p
Proportion of female gametes	0.7P	0.49 PP	0.21 pP
	0.3p	0.21 Pp	0.09 pp

The expectations, from these data, are that for every 100 offspring there would be, on average:
- *49 homozygous polled individuals, PP*
- *42 heterozygous polled individuals, Pp*
- *9 individuals with horns, pp.*

Constancy of gene frequency

In populations where there is no genetic selection to favour one genotype over another, it is often assumed that the gametes produced are able to combine in all possible ways ('random mating'), as in example 3J. Under those circumstances the frequencies of the alleles (P and p in example 3J) remain the same from one generation to the next – provided also that there is no mutation and no migration of animals into or out of the population.

However, in example 3J, the alleles have become distributed somewhat differently as between homozygotes and heterozygotes than they were in the original herd from which the frequencies were calculated. The new proportions of genotypes, and associated phenotypes, arising from random mating – are said to be in **equilibrium**.

The rule of unchanging gene frequency is often referred to as the **Hardy-Weinberg law**, after its discoverers. Formally expressed it states that the gene frequency will remain unchanged in a large, random breeding population, in the absence of selection, mutation or migration.

Changing the gene frequency

To continue with the example of the polled condition and the presence of horns, there are only two ways in which changes can be made.
i) If it is intended to increase the proportion of polled animals, and especially those which are 'pure' for polled, PP, the obvious step is to cull the cows with horns because they must be homozygous for the recessive allele.

ii) The more complicated, procedure is to find a way of identifying the heterozygotes – the carriers of the recessive allele which are not shown up by their phenotype. As far as the bulls are concerned, which would be mated to the cows, individuals with horns would be avoided, and, if possible, only PP bulls would be used.

Checking up on the heterozygotes can be done by making **test-crosses**. This involves mating the animal being tested (for example a bull which looks polled but could be a heterozygote) to animals known to be double recessives – the animals with horns in this example. If from among a reasonable number of offspring of such matings, say 8, there are no offspring with horns, it is reasonable to assume that the bull is most probably homozygous for polled, PP. However, the occurrence of even a single offspring with horns from a polled-looking bull shows that he is heterozygous for the polling character, Pp.

EXAMPLE 3K   REDUCING THE FREQUENCY OF A RECESSIVE ALLELE IN A HERD

Assume that the 5 cows with horns in example 3ı were culled. The gametes from the remaining cows would then be in the ratio of 140 with P (45 + 45 + 50 as before) but only 50 with p. The frequency of the allele P would then have changed to 0.737 (140/190) and that of p to 0.263 (50/190).

If a large group of cows with these frequencies of the two alleles were then mated only to PP bulls, the following is the result (by multiplication as before):

		Proportion of male gametes	
		1.0 P	0.0 p
Proportion of female gametes	0.737 P	0.737 PP	0
	0.263 p	0.263 Pp	0

In the new population of calves:

1 *Frequency of P allele (two P alleles from each PP individual plus one from each Pp individual)*
   $= (0.737 + 0.737 + 0.263)/2$
   $= 0.869$
2 *Frequency of p allele (one p allele from each Pp individual)*
   $= (0.263)/2$
   $= 0.131.$

Without some deliberate process of selection it is difficult to eliminate a recessive allele from a population, especially when the recessive allele has a low frequency. The lower the frequency, the more difficult it becomes. Discarding the double recessive animals (the animals with horns in this example) has a small effect, but more of the recessive alleles are retained in the heterozygotes where their presence cannot be detected by visual means. Testing the heterozygotes might be practical for bulls – if the characteristic is really important – but it is not likely to be practical or economic for females.

The above discussion applies to alleles which are completely dominant in action over their partner. When dominance is incomplete, the heterozygote can be identified from the phenotype because it is different from each of the two types of homozygote. Creating a recessive type, for example to obtain only individuals with horns from a mixed population, is easy because the phenotype (with horns) indicates the genotype (pp) exactly.

4 Quantitative genetics

4.1 Different kinds of trait

Qualitative

Traits for which inheritance is usually controlled by only one or two pairs of genes with large effects on the trait were discussed in chapter 3. Such traits are often referred to as qualitative traits, because they usually differ in *kind*, for example horns or no horns, white face or coloured face and albino or pigmented, rather than in degree.

   While it may be relatively simple and instructive to follow the segregation of a pair of genes with large effects, as in the segregation of colour genes of pigs (Figure 4.1), this becomes impossible, or at least imprac-

Fig 4.1   *F2 crossbred litter displaying the segregation of genes controlling pigmentation, Meisham/Large White pigs* (photograph by courtesy of the AFRC Roslin Research Institute, Edinburgh)

tical, if large numbers of genes are involved. Also, for traits controlled by many genes and concerned with the animal's productivity, the consequences of segregation can no longer be seen because the different classes become more or less continuous.

The complexity increases when the number of genes involved increases. With a single locus and 2 alleles, 2 types of gamete and 3 possible genotypes can result. With 2 independent loci involved (2 pairs of genes each with 2 alleles) the possible number of gametes is 4 with 9 different genotypes. Examples of this type for 1 and 2 loci were shown in chapter 3. The corresponding numbers for 4 loci is 16 different gametes and 81 different genotypes, and for 10 loci 1024 different gametes and 59049 different genotypes. In general:

n = number of gene pairs with just 2 alleles

2^n = number of possible gametes

3^n = number of possible genotypes.

The number of possible combinations goes up very greatly with an increase in the number of genes considered.

Thus, when large numbers of genes are involved, as in the total genetic make-up of animals, the total number of possible combinations becomes astronomically large. That is why no two animals in nature are

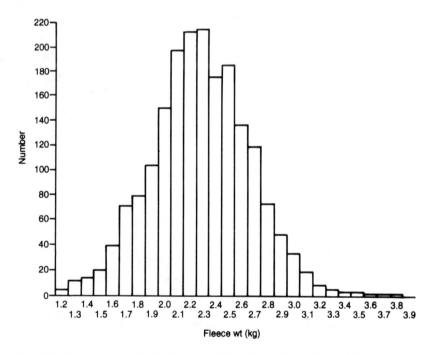

Fig 4.2 *Histogram showing the frequency distribution of clean fleece weight of some 1907 Australian Merino rams* (data by courtesy of B. J. McGuirk)

exactly alike in all respects except those which have developed from a single fertilised egg, e.g. identical twins.

Quantitative

Quantitative traits tend to differ among animals in *degree* rather than in kind. Most production traits are of this type. If the number of animals is large enough and the productivity of individual animals is plotted as a **frequency distribution**, such as a histogram, the distribution becomes continuous between the extremes. This frequency distribution often takes on a bell shape and approaches what is called a **normal curve** (chapter 5). In such a distribution there are a few animals at each extreme – very low and very high performing – but the largest proportion are near the middle of the distribution with a performance not far from the average. This is illustrated in Figure 4.2 by the fleece weights of a large number of Australian Merino rams, and in Figure 4.3 by the daily milk yield (in the early part of first lactation) of the heifers in a high-yielding herd. Figure 4.2 is based on much the larger number of observations and, therefore, approaches the expected shape of the normal curve more closely than Figure 4.3.

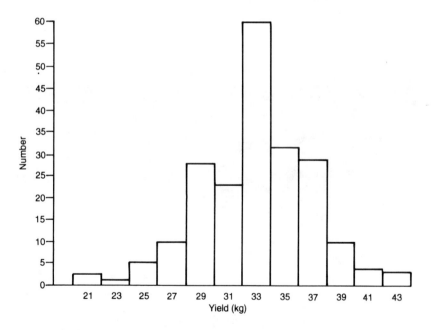

Fig 4.3   *Histogram showing the daily milk yield (adjusted for season of calving, etc.) in weeks 2–12 of first lactation of Holstein–Friesian females in the Genus/MOET nucleus herd* (data by courtesy of B. J. McGuirk and *Genus*)

The performance of some important traits, however, is distributed differently.

Distributions, with a large preponderance in the low classes, e.g. 1 offspring, and a small number in the higher classes have a long tail to the distribution and are called **skewed**.

EXAMPLE 4A SKEWED DISTRIBUTIONS

The distribution of the number of calves a cow has in a year would show that some cows have none, a large number have one and a tiny number have twins.

In sheep, where twins are more common, or in some breeds of goat where twins are quite frequent, the distribution of litter size (including some triplets and the rare larger number) would be more spread out, but still not a normal distribution pattern.

Such traits can generally be regarded as quantitative rather than qualitative, because many pairs of genes are involved. Often these traits may be controlled by an underlying characteristic which is more continuously variable. For example, there is greater and more continuous variability in ovulation rate, which sets limits to the number of young that can be born at a parturition, than there is for litter size itself. Similarly, levels and pulses of hormones control ovulation rate.

Quantitative traits are usually influenced by the action of many genes each with relatively small effects. Most production traits (e.g. meat, milk,

Fig 4.4   *Merino ewes and lambs*

40

work and litter size) which are measured by the performance of animals, come into this category. A small number of genes with large effects on economically important traits have been discovered and will be referred to in later chapters. But these cases tend to be exceptions. Many genes act together and in association with environmental factors produce a wide and more-or-less continuous range of performance, which is referred to as **variation** in performance.

All factors not directly related to the genes are generally referred to as factors of the environment of the animal. This includes all external influences on the animal, starting with the uterine environment of the developing fetus and continuing with nutrition, climate, aspects of management, disease challenges and so on. The effects of some of these environmental factors are identifiable when they affect many animals in similar ways. Other environmental influences have individually small effects and may vary from animal to animal.

From the foregoing it follows that the total effect of all the genes affecting one or more traits, the genotype, cannot be identified from the animal's performance, its phenotype. But for some traits the genes have a more powerful effect on performance than for others.

The principles of Mendelian genetics (section 3.3) do not stop just because many genes, each with small effects, influence a particular trait. However, these principles have little practical value in constructing genetic improvement programmes for such traits. How to deal with variation in the performance of production traits, for purposes of genetic improvement, is the subject of what follows in this chapter.

Compound traits

Many of the traits affecting the production of livestock (the meat or the milk output, etc.) are themselves complex combinations of component traits (chapter 1).

EXAMPLE 4B MEAT PRODUCTION FROM SHEEP – A COMPOUND TRAIT

The improvement of meat output from sheep would involve consideration of the following:
- *reproductive ability of the ewe*
    - *i) frequency (and regularity) of breeding*
    - *ii) conception rate (fertility)*
    - *iii) litter size at lambing (prolificacy)*
- *Lamb survival (and health)*
- *Ewe survival (and health)*
- *Maternal performance (ewe behaviour, milk production, etc.)*
- *Growth rate of the individual lamb*

- *Carcass characteristics*
- *Feed conversion efficiency (maternal and lamb).*

Meat production from sheep is thus defined as a **compound trait** made up of many components. The importance to be placed on any one of the components, in the overall meat production system, will differ greatly from one situation to another. In some cases it will be poor reproductive ability of the ewes (or a component of that reproductive ability) which sets the greatest limit on the total output of the flock. The path to overall improvement will then be to improve the regularity or frequency of lambing, or, under very good conditions, encourage the production of twins rather than single lambs. In another set of circumstances lamb numbers may already be adequate but individual growth of the lambs may be poor. This in turn could arise from poor feeding (the amount of milk produced by the ewe might be an important factor). Poor individual growth could also arise from an innately poor ability of the lamb to grow.

Examining traits in this way is essential for success in breeding programmes, because it allows the genetic pressure for improvement to be applied where it will do most good.

4.2 Variation

Variation in performance is the key to making genetic change. If all animals were identical in their performance – in the expression of a trait – there would be no way of choosing some in preference to others.

Genetic variation can be inferred from:
- Differences among breeds
- Differences among crosses of breeds
- Differences between crosses and pure breeds
- Part of the differences among individuals in a group.

For the differences to be meaningful in *genetic* terms, the comparison of breeds or of individuals must be made in a common environment – preferably on the same farm, the same feeding and management system, and so on. It is best if the (genetically) different groups are kept together as a single unit. At least, the comparisons must be set up in a way that makes it possible to separate genetic from non-genetic influences contributing to differences in performance (cf. chapter 1).

Apportioning variation – in general

First it is necessary to measure the performance characteristics of large numbers of individuals. This will show variation in performance and create a distribution of values. The next step is to attribute that variation to the part due to heredity and that due to the environment. After that it is possible to split up the variation due to these two broad categories into further components (described in more detail below).

Apportioning variation – *in more detail*

The total (phenotypic) variation in performance (for example, milk yield) can be thought of as made up of the following parts:

(1) $V_P = V_G + V_E + V_{GE}$
where

V_P = phenotypic variation (total)
V_G = variation due to action of genes (genotypic)
V_E = variation due to environmental factors
V_{GE} = variation due to the interaction or association of genetic (G) and environmental (E) factors.

Sub-dividing the genetic variation (V_G)

The genetic part (G) can be divided further. The components of the genetic variation mirror the three classes of genetic action (chapter 3).

Normally, the most important class comprises the **additive** effects of genes (A). Some have *plus* (positive) and others *minus* (negative) effects on the overall performance of a trait. In the case of additive gene action, the offspring will be expected to be mid-way in performance between the levels of its two parents, or parent breeds. (This is the average expectation for many individuals from many pairs of parents. The performance of any individual animal may be below or above that average.)

There can be systematic deviations from that additive model. One form of deviation arises from the action of dominance (section 3.4) whereby one of the pair of alleles has an effect which masks, or partially masks, the action of the other. For traits influenced by many pairs of genes, each with possibly quite small effects, it is not feasible to calculate the deviations from additive action separately for each locus (single pair of genes). But at the level of the *variation* in the performance of the trait (for example milk yield) the **dominance deviations** (D) can be calculated as an overall effect.

A further cause of deviation can arise from interactions among genes which are not members of a pair but still have a joint effect on a particular trait. At the individual gene level this action was called **epistasis** (section 3.4). By analogy, the deviations which are attributable to such effects arising from many genes are called **epistatic deviations** (I). There are methods of analysing data on animal performance which give an estimate of the relative importance of epistasis as part of the overall variation in the performance of any one trait. Thus:

(2) $V_G = V_A + V_D + V_I$
where

V_A = additive genetic variation
V_D = variation due to the action of dominance
V_I = variation due to the action of epistasis.

Replacing the V_G in the earlier equation (1) by the three components of the genetic variation shown in equation (2), gives the following representation:

(3) $V_P = V_A + V_D + V_I + V_E + V_{GE}$

In this way, variation in performance can be considered as that due to various kinds of gene action, the action of the environment and associations or interactions between genetic and environmental factors. The procedure for splitting up variation into components is described in section 4.4.

Environmental components

One more sub-division is conceptually useful. The environmental effects (E) can be looked upon as composed of external influences which animals have necessarily in common and others which they may share if they happen to be together, or not share if they are separated.

EXAMPLE 4C COMMON ENVIRONMENTAL INFLUENCES

1 *Piglets in a litter are born and brought up together under the influence of their mother. Quite apart from the genes which the piglets inherited from their mother (half of which the piglets share, on average), the piglets also share the environment provided by their mother. This common environmental effect stays with the piglets throughout their life, making them more alike than they might otherwise be, although its importance usually declines the older they become.*
2 *The age of the mother is a specific example of such an effect. Young mothers, when they have their first offspring, generally provide a less good uterine environment (and less milk later on) than older dams.*
3 *The sex of the animal (male or female – or castrate) is another feature which affects the performance of many traits and is regarded as an external influence on them.*

Other effects of environment are the general factors affecting performance, for example feed, management practices, the occurrence of disease and its prevention or treatment, climate, season of the year, and so on. Moreover, different sets of influences on the animals will arise throughout life and the effects of particular kinds of influences may change from one time to another, for example there may be more rainfall in one year than in another with differing effects on production.

Any of these various environmental influences may be shared by groups of individuals, at least for a time. If so, the impact of these influences can be estimated from their average effects on individuals. For example, some lambs may be weaned early and others late. Provided the two groups are alike in all other respects, any *average* difference in, for example, the weight of the lambs at six months old would be due to the difference in age at weaning.

Some environmental effects may be more or less permanent during the life of the animal, others may have more short-lived effects. All may change in their importance with time. The size of the environmental effects, therefore, is not constant and needs to be estimated for each occasion at which the performance of animals is assessed and comparisons are to be made.

Genotype-environment interaction (G × E)
See chapter 1, page 4 and chapter 3, page 32. They arise if, for example, two breeds differ in their performance by more in one environment than in another.

4.3 *Heritability*

The term heritability is used to describe the strength with which a quantitative trait is inherited.

In terms of splitting up the variation in performance, as described above, it is the ratio of the additive genetic variation (V_A) to the total (phenotypic) variation (V_P). The symbol for the term **heritability** is always h^2 (*not* h), thus:

(4) $h^2 = V_A/V_P$.

This ratio is normally expressed as a proportion (out of 1) or as a percentage.

Putting expression (4) into words:
• Heritability is the proportion of the total (phenotypic) variation among individuals in a population which is due to the additive effects of the genes.

It is also a measure of the extent to which relatives resemble each other or, more specifically, the extent to which offspring resemble their parents.

Heritability can also be defined as:

- *the proportion of the superiority of parents above the average of their contemporaries which is passed, on average, to their offspring.*

Some textbooks refer to the above as 'heritability in the narrow sense'. They then use the term 'heritability in the broad sense' to indicate the proportion of the total variation (V_P) which is due to all genetic influences derived from the genotype (V_G). This represents the degree of genetic determination of a trait. However, *in this book*, the term *heritability*, when used alone, *will imply the 'narrow' sense.* That is the sense in which it is most often used by animal breeders and in relation to breeding values (section 5.5).

Table 4.1 gives some estimates of heritabilities for different species and traits from studies undertaken in the tropics. It can be seen that the heritability estimates are variable. They differ among traits indicating that some are more strongly inherited than others. For convenience, the estimates for different traits can be grouped into low, medium, relatively high and very high categories indicating how easily a trait might be changed by selection. (Selection is the process of choosing superior animals as parents of the next generation, chapters 5 and 6.) *The higher the heritability, the better selection should work.*

Heritability estimates around or below 0.1 can be regarded as low, those between 0.1 and 0.3 as medium, between 0.3 and 0.4 is relatively high and above that very high. The estimates shown in Table 4.1, from the tropics, agree quite well with corresponding estimates from elsewhere. It is a general finding that:
- Traits associated with reproduction and survival have low heritabilities.
- Milk production and early body size traits have medium heritabilities.
- Adult size and various quality traits are in the high heritability classes.

Heritability estimates should be regarded as a *useful guide* and never as an absolute truth. The large range of the estimates for most of the traits illustrates this point.

Differences in heritability estimates for any one trait can arise because genetic variability may differ from one breed or population to another, or because the heritability estimates are derived from animals kept in different environmental conditions. For instance, if the management and nutrition of a group of animals is particularly uniform, the heritability estimates from them are likely to be higher than estimates from an otherwise similar group kept in less uniform conditions.

To illustrate these possibilities the estimates for milk yield shown in Table 4.1 have been sub-divided according to the type of breed from which the estimates were made. It is probably not a coincidence that, on average, the heritability estimates for the types of cattle with a crossbred foundation are higher, suggesting greater genetic variation, than those within the purebred groups. Also, the estimates based on exotic breeds

Table 4.1   Heritability (h²) estimates from the tropics (based on publications from 1984–1990)*

Traits	Number of studies	Average h²	Range of h²
Cattle			
Milk yield (single lactation, mostly 1st)			
Indigenous breeds (I)	13	0.25	0.11–0.48
I × E crosses	14	0.33	0.12–0.54
Exotic breeds (E)	6	0.25	0.15–0.34
Fat percentage	4	0.26	0.09–0.41
Lactation length	14	0.29	0.06–0.51
Age at 1st calving	15	0.30	0.01–0.69
Calving interval	21	0.12	0 –0.40
Service period	7	0.09	0.01–0.18
Services per conception	3	0.05	0.03–0.08
Calf mortality	3	0.05	0 –0.09
Birth weight	31	0.27	0 –0.48
Weaning weight	34	0.18	0.02–0.51
Adult weight	11	0.33	0.02–0.79
Weight gain (birth–weaning)	14	0.14	0.02–0.34
Weight gain (post-weaning)	4	0.26	0.13–0.38
Various body dimensions	13	0.31	0 –0.62
Buffalo			
Milk yield (lactation)	11	0.35	0.19–0.67
Fat percentage	2	0.30	0.22–0.37
Lactation length	2	0	
Adult weight	2	0.62	0.35–0.88
Sheep and Goats			
Milk yield			
lactation	7	0.38	0.20–0.53
test day	4	0.21	0.14–0.31
Birth weight	10	0.18	0.03–0.43
Weaning weight	12	0.34	0.08–0.62
Adult weight	12	0.39	0.11–0.72
Fleece weight	6	0.36	0.17–0.57
Fleece quality traits	8	0.49	0.13–0.72
Number lambs at birth	7	0.14	0 –0.49
Litter weight at birth	3	0.06	0 –0.12

Table 4.1 – *continued*

Traits	Number of studies	Average h^2	Range of h^2
Pigs (swine)			
Number piglets at birth	8	0.12	0 –0.39
Number piglets at weaning	6	0.16	0.02–0.34
Litter weight at birth	4	0.20	0 –0.31
Litter weight at weaning	5	0.15	0.03–0.20
Post-weaning weight gain	4	0.32	0.13–0.76
Backfat thickness	3	0.57	0.40–0.88
Various body dimensions	6	0.60	0.51–0.71

* A number of smaller-scale studies are omitted from the summary of
published results.

are less variable than the others, suggesting both a greater uniformity of
the breed types involved and of the management conditions under
which these breeds are kept.

The method by which the heritability is calculated (from relationships
among individuals – see below) can also affect the estimate. Thus, heritability estimates have to be looked at critically in relation to the conditions to which they apply.

• A heritability estimate provides guidance for predicting the likelihood
  of success in achieving genetic change. In practice the results may be
  better or worse.

4.4 How to estimate the different parts of variation in performance (genetic and environmental)

The essential feature is always to compare groups of animals which share
some things in common but not others. For example, the difference
between a group given a high plane of nutrition and one given a low
plane would be an estimate of the effect of *nutrition* (high minus low) –
provided the groups are alike in all other respects (such as breed, age
range, representation of the sexes and so on.). Similarly, the difference
in performance between young cows and old cows would be an *age*
difference – other things being equal.

Genetic differences can be estimated in a similar way. If two different
breeds are kept together as part of a single herd or flock and treated alike,

any difference in performance between the two breed groups will represent a real genetic difference. However, the two groups must be large enough to be representative of their respective breeds and must have animals of similar age, sex, stage of lactation and so on. The same principles would apply when comparing groups of different crossbred types.

Variation among relatives

Similar considerations to those for comparing groups apply when estimating the importance of genetic variation *within* a breed group. Individuals must be compared on a common basis. This is achieved by choosing animals which are alike in age, sex, treatment and so on, or by correcting their records to a common basis (examples 2E and 2F). The genetic information comes from comparing the variation in performance among relatives with the variation among less related or among unrelated individuals.

Twins

Twins have more of their genes in common than animals which are not twins. (Identical twins have all their genes in common: 'ordinary' twins share half the genes they received from their parents.) Thus, comparing the *difference* in performance between members of twin pairs with the *difference* between pairs of non-twins gives an indication of the extent to which heredity has, on average, made the twins more alike. If the twins were found to be no more alike to each other than any two other individuals, it would indicate that heredity had no influence on that particular trait. Conversely, if the members of twin pairs were very alike in a particular trait, but other individuals were very different from each other, it would suggest that heredity strongly influenced the chosen characteristic.

Twins are not, however, often available for this purpose. They also suffer from the disadvantage that they share the common uterine environment of their mother and, usually, a common early upbringing, not shared by other individuals. Twins may be more alike because of these early-life experiences and not only because of common inheritance. It is, therefore, more usual, and better, to obtain estimates of genetic variation from other types of relationship.

Offspring and parents

The performance of offspring can be compared with the corresponding performance of their parents – either one or both. The performance of the offspring and their parents must be compared at the same age or stage, for example weight at 1 year-old or milk yield in first lactation.

Since these events occur in different years for the different generations, account must be taken of this fact. Some years may be much better than others in their effects on the productivity of the animals. Appropriate corrections must, therefore, be made for the effects of year before offspring and parent performance can be properly compared.

Full sibs

Full sibs have both parents in common (if they were people they would be called full brothers or sisters). They share, on average, half the genes from their parents. In species such as pigs where several piglets are born in a litter (the piglets are full sibs), the variation in performance among piglets within the litter can be compared with the differences arising among unrelated litters. Piglets in a litter, however, share a common maternal environment which will make the piglets of the litter more alike than they should be for purely genetic reasons.

Half-sibs

A comparison which can usually avoid common environmental effects arises from the relationship of paternal half-sibs – animals with the same father but different mothers, for example offspring from a bull used on many cows. Half-sibs share, on average, one-quarter of their genes. Therefore:

- The variation that arises *within* groups of half-sibs includes three-quarters of all the additive genetic variation in the whole population.
- The variation *between* groups of half-sibs includes the remaining quarter of the additive genetic variation.

Comparing the between sire component of variation (×4) with total variation then provides an estimate of heritability.

When many sires, each with a reasonable number of offspring, are compared in this way, good estimates of heritability arise. Twenty or 30 sires with 10–20 offspring each might be a realistic target.

In a similar way, the variation arising within half-sib groups can also be compared with that arising within groups of full sibs, because the proportion of shared genes differs for the two kinds of sib.

Selection response

Heritability can also be estimated from the response to the process of selection. Selection involves the choice of animals as parents of the next generation which differ in performance from the average of their contemporaries (chapter 5). The proportion of that difference which is found in the next generation – the offspring – is a measure of heritability.

Further detail

Details of the actual procedures for these estimations will be found in more advanced textbooks under headings which include: offspring-parent regression, sib and half-sib analysis, analysis of variance (ANOVA) and 'realised' heritability (from selection).

4.5 Correlated traits

Many characteristics of animals are not independent of each other – they tend to change together. This relationship is called a **correlation** and can be expressed in statistical terms to denote the strength of the relationship (between 0 and 1). The relationship among traits can arise because specific genes can affect more than one trait (genetic correlations) or because particular factors in the environment affect more than one trait (environmental correlations). The existence of such correlations has an important effect on breeding programmes (chapters 5 and 6).

5 Selection I: Background

In the context of livestock improvement, **selection** is the process of choosing some individuals in preference to others as the parents of the next generation.

Selection is the basic method used both by nature and by humans to change the attributes of animals. Before embarking on a programme of livestock improvement it is important to define the objectives clearly. To make a breeding programme succeed:

- The objectives must be realistic (attainable).
- There has to be a commitment to allow a reasonable period of time (several years usually) for selection to work.

5.1 *Objectives*

The general objective is likely to be the improvement of overall productivity, for example in meat or milk output, draught power or wool production, or various combinations of these. (So as not to complicate the discussion, it will be assumed for present purposes that the efficiency of production, as defined in chapter 1, will be improved at the same time). Many of these production traits can usually be broken down into components (chapter 4). One or other of the component traits may be a major limitation on overall productivity. A decision will need to be made whether it is more effective to select on the overall productivity or on an important component.

5.2 *Genetic consequences of selection*

When some animals are chosen in preference to others as the parents of the next generation, it means that the genes of these selected animals are preferred. This has the effect of changing the frequency of the alleles carried in that population (section 3.5) – those with good effects on the trait are chosen at the expense of alleles with less good effects.

In respect of most production traits which generally show continuous variation, selection works on the genes with additive effects. Such genes are the main cause of resemblance between relatives.

The term selection can also be applied to relatively simple traits, such as the presence or absence of horns.

EXAMPLE 5A SELECTION FOR A SIMPLE TRAIT

Selecting for the absence of horns (the polled condition) in a breed of cattle predominantly with horns is a way of increasing the frequency of the allele for the polled character at the expense of that for horn formation (a calculation is shown in example 3K).

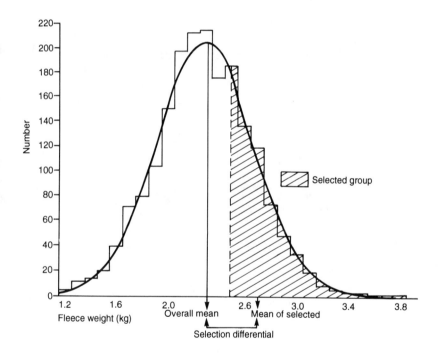

Fig 5.1   *Selection differential (S)*

The average of the clean fleece weights (kg) of rams with fleece weights of 2.5 kg or above (approximately the best third) are compared with the average fleece weights of some 1907 Australian Merino rams. Mean of selected (2.69 kg) – Overall mean (2.28 kg) = Selection differential (0.41 kg).

(normal curve superimposed on the distribution of Figure 4.1; data by courtesy of B. J. McGuirk)

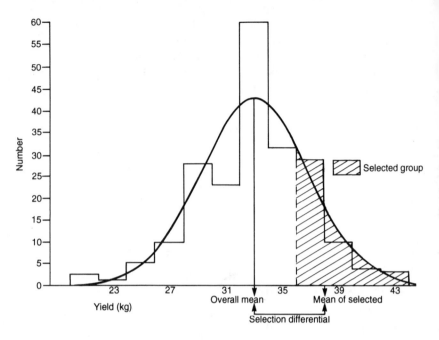

Fig 5.2   *Selection differential (S)*

Yield of the best 30% of cows compared with the average of all 205 cows.
Mean of selected (38 litres) – Overall mean (33 litres) = Selection differential
(5 litres).

(normal curve superimposed on the distribution of Figure 4.2; data by
courtesy of B. J. McGuirk and *Genus*)

5.3   *Factors affecting selection progress*

In general, there are three principal factors affecting the rate of improvement of quantitative traits which is achieved by selection:

1   Selection differential (S) – the average superiority of the selected parents relative to their contemporaries (in the herd, flock, or population).

2   Heritability (h²) – the proportion of the superiority of the selected
parents which appears in the offspring (section 4.3).

3   Generation interval (symbolised by the letter l) – the time interval
between successive generations in which selections can be made. It has
an important bearing on the rate (speed) of genetic improvement.

Selection differential (S)

Underlying the use of the selection differential is the concept of the continuous, normal distribution (page 58).

Figures 5.1 and 5.2 show distributions of fleece weight and milk yield (the same as shown in Figures 4.2 and 4.3) with the top-performing animals separated off – as they would be if they were selected to become the parents of the next generation.

Average fleece weight of selected rams (Figure 5.1) = 2.69 kg
Average for all rams = 2.28 kg
Selection differential = difference between the two means
$$= 2.69 - 2.28$$
$$= 0.41 \ kg$$
Daily milk yield of selected females (Figure 5.2) = 38 litres
Overall average = 33 litres
Selection differential = 38 – 35 = 5 litres

Because, in farm livestock, fewer males are usually needed for breeding than females, the selection differential is generally higher (better) for the males. Sometimes that difference can be very large, as when one bull can be made to serve potentially thousands of cows through artificial insemination.

Averaging selection differentials
When considering the individual herd, flock or the system as a whole, the selection differentials from the two sexes have to be averaged as shown in the example 5c.

1 *Choosing female replacements from dams*	
Average of selected dams (best 50%)	*1720 kg*
Average of herd	*1400 kg*
Selection differential (for females)	*320 kg*
2 *Choosing male replacements from dams*	
Average of selected dams (best 5%)	*2224 kg*
Average of herd	*1400 kg*
Selection differential (for males)	*824 kg*

3   *Average selection differential = (320 + 824)/2 = 572 kg*

It is necessary also to consider the selection differential on the sire side, if that is known. This involves, corresponding to the above example, the difference, from the average, of sires chosen as fathers of females and sires chosen as fathers of male replacements. In this way there are 4 separate selection differentials to make up the average instead of the 2 used in example 5c.

Heritability (h^2)

It is useful to have an estimate of the h^2 for the trait to be changed in order to predict the likely progress from selection. It is preferable if this estimate is made from the population considered for selection, before selection has started. This, however, is often impractical because the appropriate records are not available. That being so, a published estimate from a similar kind of population kept under similar conditions would be the next best thing. Some examples of heritability are given in Table 4.1 (page 47–8).

Generation interval (I)

Generation interval is defined as the *average age* of the parents when their offspring are born – or, more strictly, those offspring which are used to replace the parents. The genetic changes which occur as a result of selection, happen only when one generation is succeeded by the next. The speed with which generations follow each other, therefore, affects the annual rate of improvement. The shorter the interval the faster the improvement – if other things are equal.

The generation interval is affected by the age when the animals first start to breed. It is also influenced by the interval between successive parturitions and by the number of offspring born on each occasion which survive to breeding age. The earlier in the life of the parent its offspring are born, the closer parturitions follow each other and the more offspring per parturition, the sooner the number needed as replacements is reached and hence the lower the generation interval.

Poor feeding and environmental stress will adversely affect all of these attributes. It is difficult, therefore, to generalise about the length of the generation interval.

Since generation interval affects the rate of genetic progress from selection, it is an advantage to shorten it as much as possible consistent with other requirements, for example the need for replacement animals or for adequate information on performance.

Table 5.1 Generation interval – typical values in tropical countries

Livestock	Generation value (years)*
Cattle	4–7
Goats	3–5
Sheep	3–5
Pigs	2–4

* For the *average* (not the first) age of parents when the offspring that replace them are born.

The average generation interval incorporates 4 separate intervals (corresponding to those for the selection differential). These are the intervals:
• between the sires and their sons and daughters respectively, and
• between the dams and their sons and daughters.

The generation interval is usually greater for female parents, because they are kept to produce offspring for several years, than it need be for the males of the species. However, though males do not usually have to be used for several years, they often are retained until they are quite old.

EXAMPLE 5D CALCULATION OF GENERATION INTERVAL

Cows in a herd have offspring for the first time at 4 years-old and for the last time at 10 years-old. The cows calved every second year (at 4, 6, 8 and 10 years-old), then the average age of the cows when their offspring are born is 7 years-old. (It is assumed that all the female calves born to these cows are needed as replacements.) Bull calves are kept only from 4-year-old cows.

Female replacements are kept from sires aged 5 years on average, but bull replacements are chosen from sires not until they have had numerous daughters (to show their merit) – average age 8 years.

The four separate generation intervals are:

Dam to daughter	=	*7 years*
Dam to son	=	*4 years*
Sire to daughter	=	*5 years*
Sire to son	=	*8 years*
Total	=	*24 years*
Average	=	*6 years*

The average generation interval could be significantly reduced if young bulls were used as sires.

Other useful concepts

Before describing other concepts used to estimate past and likely future breeding progress, it is necessary to note the assumptions which underlie some of the calculations.

Distribution of observations

It is usually assumed that most continuously variable traits of livestock follow the kind of pattern shown in relation to fleece weight and milk yield (Figures 4.2, 4.3, 5.1 and 5.2). There are a few animals at each extreme, good and bad, and increasing numbers towards the middle of the range, giving a bell-shaped distribution – the **normal distribution**,

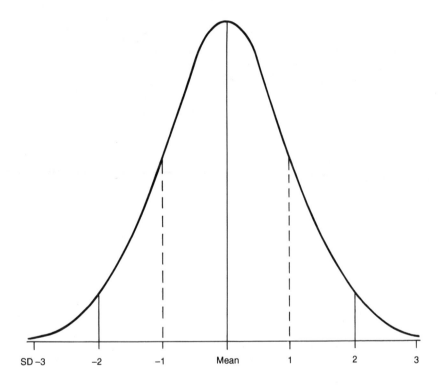

Fig 5.3   *Normal distribution*

Three standard deviations (SD) are shown on each side of the mean. The area enclosed by 1 SD each side of the mean includes 68% of the total number of animals contributing to the distribution, 2 SD each side includes 95%, and 3 SD includes a little over 99%.

shown formally in Figure 5.3. It has a number of useful statistical properties and these are widely used in animal breeding. Usually, the larger the number of animals measured the closer the observations follow the normal curve (compare the fleece weight distribution Figure 5.1 with the milk yield distribution of Figure 5.2). Even when the distributions do not follow the normal curve *strictly*, the statistics derived from the normal curve apply *approximately* in many cases.

There are other kinds of distribution which are not continuous in the above sense, i.e. not normal, (page 40). Animals will be either alive or dead, so that survival, as a trait, has only two classes. Other characteristics may have a vast majority in one class alone – **categorical distribution**.

EXAMPLE 5E CATEGORICAL DISTRIBUTION

In the tropics, the vast majority of ewes lambing will have 1 lamb, a small number may have 2, and triplets or larger litters are very rare.
The distribution of lamb numbers is categorical and is often skewed.

Different statistical rules apply to such distributions, but these will not be described here. However, if the original units of measurement are changed, using a **statistical transformation**, it is often possible to turn a non-normal distribution into a normal one for purposes of statistical analysis. For example, a skewed distribution with a long tail towards the top end might be transformed to normality by changing the original units into logarithms. There are many possible forms of transformation to suit different situations.

Measures of variation
In general, variation can be expressed in different ways, for example the difference between:
- the best and the worst performers,
- the yield of the top or bottom half of all the animals,
- the best and worst quarter of all the animals.

The normal curve allows the amount of variation which exists for the observations to be described in a particularly useful way. When the distribution of performance follows, even approximately, a normal distribution, the best measure of variation is given by the **standard deviation** (SD), because it takes account of the scatter of the values around the average (Figure 5.3). The standard deviation, when related to the normal curve, has the advantage that each SD accounts for a fixed proportion of the animals in the distribution.

As seen in Figure 5.3:
- 1 SD either side of the average performance (the mean) accounts for 68% of the animals

- 2 SD above and below the mean accounts for 95%
- 3 SD for more than 99% – or nearly all the animals.

This last fact is useful if the individual values needed to calculate the SD are not available but the range of values is known: an approximate estimate of the SD is the difference in yield between the poorest and the best few animals and dividing by 6 (since 6 SD cover 99% of the whole distribution).

Components of the selection differential

The selection differential is very important for the progress that can be made by selection. However, the magnitude of the selection differential is not likely to be known at the time when decisions have to be made whether to use selection as a method of livestock improvement. The selection differential can be predicted from two other pieces of information:

- the *proportion* of females and males which it is necessary to retain as parents of the next generation, and
- the amount of *variation* present for the trait under consideration.

Proportion selected

The proportion selected is usually limited by the particular circumstances of the herd or flock (or larger population) being improved.

EXAMPLE 5F DIFFERENT PROPORTIONS OF FLOCK SELECTED

If, in a flock of sheep, it were possible to obtain all the necessary female replacements from only half the ewes: the best 50% can be used to supply the future female breeding stock; and the offspring from the rest are sold for other purposes.

On the other hand, since relatively few rams are needed to serve the ewes, the males kept for breeding might be chosen from the best 5% of those born.

Thus, the intensity of selection can be said to be greater in the case of the males than the females (in this example).

It is a statistical convenience that for relatively normally distributed traits the **intensity of selection** (symbol i) can be derived directly from the *proportion* selected. The corresponding figures can be looked up in tables prepared for the purpose (e.g. Falconer 1989, Appendix Table A) or, less accurately, from the graph in Figure 5.4.

The figures for intensity are given in units of standard deviations. Thus, if the best 1% of animals are selected, they will be, on average, 2.67 SD above the mean of all the animals in the distribution. Some other examples are: the best 5% = 2.06 SD; 30% = 1.16 SD; and 50% = 0.80 SD. If, in practice, it is possible to cull only the poorest 10% of the breeding

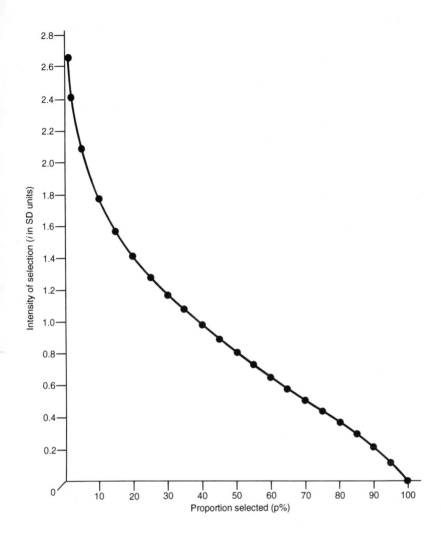

Fig 5.4   *Intensity of selection (i in SD units) corresponding to different proportions of total population selected* (p%)

The graph is drawn for a population of very large size. When the number of animals in the population is small, for example 10 or 20, the selection intensity is lower for any given proportion selected, but that reduction in i is particularly marked when the proportion selected is low. For example, when 10% of a very large population is chosen, $i = 1.76$; when 2 are chosen from 20 (10%), $i = 1.64$; and when 1 is chosen from 10 animals (10%), $i = 1.54$. When the proportion selected is high, the population size makes less difference in absolute terms. For example, if 50% are retained in each case, $i = 0.80$, 0.77 and 0.74 selected from very large numbers, 20 and 10 respectively.

females, the 90% retained would be a little better than the average – by approximately 0.2 SD units.

Variation
The amount of variation in performance is important. If there is little variation, the performance of the animals selected as superior may be only a little above the average. If there is a large amount of variation in performance, the same proportion of selected individuals will be much more above average.

If the variability of the population is known in SD units and the proportion to be selected has been decided, the *superiority of the selected group* above the mean of their contemporaries (the selection differential) is:

Selection differential (S) = selection intensity (i) × phenotypic standard deviation (SD)

EXAMPLE 5G USE OF SD TO DETERMINE SELECTION DIFFERENTIAL

Assume growth rate of lambs to be the criterion for selection. The average growth = 100 g/day; and the best 40% of the lambs are selected.

1 **Standard deviation 30 g** *(Figure 5.5a)*
The selected lambs should then be 0.97 × 30 = 29 g/day better in growth than the average of 100 g, where 0.97 is the selection intensity corresponding to choosing the top 40% (Fig 5.4).
i.e. Average growth of the selected 40% of the lambs should be 100 + 29 = 129 g/day.
Similarly, if the best 20% were chosen, the selected lambs would have gained, on average, 142 g/day (for a proportion of 20%, i = 1.40).

2 **Standard deviation = 15 g** *(Figure 5.5b)*
The best 40% of the lambs would then be 0.97 × 15 = 14.5 g/day better than the average of 100 g. The average daily gain of the selected group would be 114.5 g. If the best 20% were chosen, their average growth rate would be 121 g/day.

5.4 *Genetic progress from selection*

Only the genetic part of any observed (phenotypic) superiority of the selected parents is passed to the offspring. Hence the response per generation (R) to selection will be the product of these two factors:
Response = Selection differential × Heritability

$R = S \times h^2$

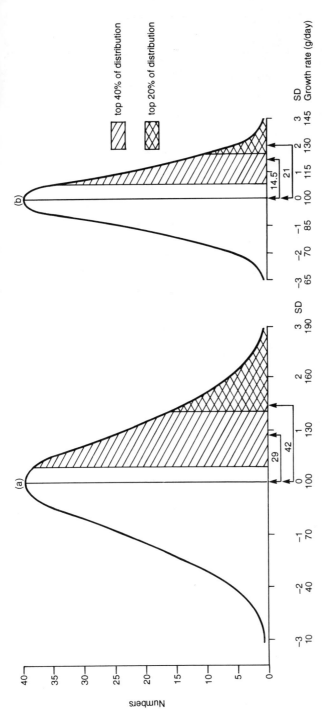

Fig 5.5 *Two distributions showing different amounts of variation and effect on selection in growth rate of lambs (a) SD = 30 g/day, (b) SD = 15 g/day*

Variability in a population effects the selection differential. The two normal distributions shown are for growth rate of lambs with an average of 100 g/day: (a) shows high variation – SD of 30 g/day; (b) shows low variation in rate of gain – SD of 15 g/day.
(i) If the top 20% of animals are selected, average daily gain of the selected animals (a) 142 g and (b) 121 g with selection differentials 42 g and 21 g respectively.
(ii) If the top 40% are selected corresponding figures are (a) 129 g and (b) 114.5 g with selection differentials 29 g and 14.5 g.

63

Since the selection differential (S) is itself the product of the intensity of selection (i) and the phenotypic variation (in SD units), the response to selection can be expressed as:

Response = Selection intensity × Standard deviation × Heritability

$R = i \times SD \times h^2$

Rate of progress

The **annual rate** of progress is usually of greater economic importance than the progress in each generation. The genetic consequences of the selection can take place only when selected parents have offspring. That is when genes with inferior effects are replaced by some with better effects. If the same parents are used repeatedly for many years, the only additional benefit is that more offspring are born to the selected parents; but there is no further genetic change – no further change in gene frequency.

EXAMPLE 5H   AVERAGE GENERATION INTERVAL AND ANNUAL RATE OF PROGRESS

Contrast the herd in example 5D, average generation interval = 6 years, with a second herd in which the cows start calving younger and calve more regularly and where the bulls are also used younger, average generation interval = 4 years.

Over 12 years:
- *In the first herd there have been effectively only 2 generations (12/6 = 2).*
- *In the second herd 3 generations have passed (12/4 = 3).*

If other things are equal, the second herd with the shorter generation interval will make the faster genetic progress.

An estimate of the annual rate of response to selection is provided by the Response (per generation) divided by the Average generation interval.

Annual $R = R/l = (i \times SD \times h^2)/l$

Separate consideration of males and females

Normally, a much smaller proportion of the males is needed than of females (as parents of the next generation), also, male and female parents, are likely to be used for a different number of years. Therefore, the two sexes require separate consideration when trying to predict the annual rate of progress.

Response to selection = Selection differential for male (S_m) + Selection differential for female (S_f) / 2 × Heritability.

$$R = [(S_m + S_f) / 2] \times h^2$$

For completeness, the following equation repeats the earlier process of re-writing the selection differentials $(S_m$ and $S_f)$ in terms of selection intensity (for males (i_m) and females (i_f)) and the SD:

$$R = [(i_m + i_f) / 2] \times SD \times h^2$$

Finally, introducing the generation interval (L) separately for males (L_m) and for females (L_f) gives the following:

Annual $R = [(i_m + i_f)/(L_m + L_f)] \times SD \times h^2$

EXAMPLE 5I CALCULATING ANNUAL RATE OF RESPONSE TO SELECTION

Assume the objective is to improve the 6 month-old weight of lambs. Average weight = 20 kg; SD = 4 kg, and h^2 of the trait = 0.3 (assumed). Rams are selected from the top 5% and female replacements from the best 50% of the flock. Generation interval between rams and both their sons and daughters = 2 years, and between dams and their sons and daughters = 5 years.

Substituting the appropriate figures in the equation (from Reference Tables or Figure 5.4) i for 5% = 2.06, for 50% = 0.8):

$$
\begin{aligned}
\text{Annual } R &= [(i_m + i_f)/(L_m + L_f)] \times SD \times h^2 \\
&= [(2.06 + 0.8)/(2 + 5)] \times 4 \times 0.3 \\
&= (2.86/7) \times 4 \times 0.3 = 0.49
\end{aligned}
$$

Therefore the rate of progress will be just under 0.5 kg/year. If this rate were maintained for 10 years the average weight of lambs at 6 months-old would have risen from 20 kg to nearly 25 kg.

5.5 Breeding value

The term **breeding value** (BV), as applied to individual animals, provides a prediction of their genetic worth. At its simplest, it is the difference (deviation) between an individual's performance and the average performance of its contemporaries multiplied by the heritability:

BV = Deviation of individual performance from average of contemporaries × h^2.

(The deviation of an individual from the average is similar in concept to the selection differential discussed earlier in relation to groups.)

The term, breeding value, is often used in connection with dairy bulls whose genetic merit has been evaluated on the basis of the milk yield of their daughters. Equally, the idea can be applied to individual animals in a herd or flock.

Because an animal passes on only half its genes to its offspring it passes on only half its 'breeding value'. This half is often called the **transmitting ability**. Transmitting ability is an estimate for an individual of how much of the difference in its performance, above or below that of its contemporaries, it is likely to pass to its offspring.

Confidence

It is also necessary to consider the degree of confidence which can be placed on the recorded superiority in performance of an individual relative to its contemporaries and how that confidence can be increased.

For example, if a cow is weighed once this provides an estimate of her weight. If she is weighed again even a short time later, her weight may be somewhat different – perhaps because she has eaten or drunk in the interval.

Any one weight is only an estimate of the 'real' weight. The 'real' weight might be considered as close to the *average* of many weights – so that random fluctuations in weight, from one occasion to the next, will become unimportant.

Taking repeat records on an animal increases the confidence which can be placed on the measurement – random errors or, for example seasonal effects, are removed or their influence diminished. Animal breeders refer to this as affecting the **accuracy** of the observations. The same principle applies to pooling records from different years, for example successive calf or lamb crops, or the yield in successive lactations.

The extent to which accuracy is increased by repeat measurement depends on the **repeatability** of the trait. This is a measure of how an animal, measured on any one occasion, will repeat its performance during its lifetime. In statistical terms, repeatability is the correlation between records and is expressed as a proportion from 0.0 (zero repeatability) to 1.0 (complete repeatability).

EXAMPLE 5J DIFFERENT REPEATABILITY OF DIFFERENT TRAITS

1 *The colour of an adult cow is unlikely to change: one observation gives as much information as many (repeatability is 1.0).*
2 *Birth weights of the successive calves of a cow may differ a great deal (low repeatability, perhaps 0.2).*

3 *For birth weight, the average from several calf crops would provide a more accurate (reliable) estimate of that cow's capability relative to other cows.*

Repeat observations

The formula for calculating the extra accuracy from repeat observations is:

$$k/[1 + (k - 1)t]$$

where k = number of records
      t = repeatability of the trait.

Table 5.2 shows the effect of repeat observations on accuracy for traits of high (0.8), medium (0.4) and low (0.2) repeatability (wool quality, milk yield and birth weight respectively might be the examples).

Table 5.2   Effect of repeat observations on the accuracy of records for 3 levels of repeatability, relative to a single observation

Number of observations	Repeatability (t)		
	0.8	0.4	0.2
1	1	1	1
2	1.111	1.429	1.667
3	1.154	1.667	2.143
4	1.176	1.818	2.500
7	1.207	2.059	3.182
10	1.220	2.174	3.571

The examples of Table 5.2 illustrate that the first one or two extra records increase accuracy appreciably, but further extra records give a diminishing return. The example also shows that the advantage of extra records is relatively much greater when the repeatability of the trait is low than when it is high.

Calculating the Breeding Value

The idea of accuracy of observations can be introduced to the calculation of the Breeding Value. Thus, now:

$$BV = [kh^2/(1 + k-1)t] \times \text{Average deviation of animal}$$
$$\text{from its contemporaries}$$

The multiplication of the accuracy factors (examples shown in Table 5.2) by the heritability (in the formula above) is sometimes called the

confidence factor which can be placed on the deviation in performance of the individual from the average of its contemporaries. Table 5.3 shows the confidence factors for a trait with a heritability of 0.2.

Table 5.3 Confidence factors for a trait with heritability of 0.2 and repeatability of 0.4

Number of observations	Confidence factor
1	0.200
2	0.286
3	0.333
4	0.367
7	0.412
10	0.435

Table 5.4 Example of calculating Breeding Values for three cows (assume $h^2 = 0.2$, repeatability = 0.4)

	Difference from contemporaries (kg)		
	Cow A	Cow B	Cow C
Data			
Lactation 1	+ 32	+ 30	− 10
Lactation 2		+ 20	+ 20
Lactation 3			+ 32
Calculations			
Total difference	+ 32	+ 50	+ 42
Average difference	+ 32	+ 25	+ 14
Confidence factor (c.f.)	0.200	0.286	0.333
Breeding Value (av. diff. × c.f.)	+ 6.4	+ 7.2	+ 4.7

- *On lactation 1 alone cow A would have been chosen because of her small advantage over cow B and her much better yield than cow C.*
- *Lactation 2 shows cow B still to be above average – but, because cow A had only one lactation, no information is available to show whether cow A might have maintained her advantage in a second lactation.*
- *Therefore, from the available information, cow B has slightly the better genetic superiority. Cow C improved in milk yield relative to cow B in later lactations, but not enough to make her the best choice.*

Disadvantages of repeat records

Attention has been drawn to the benefits of repeating observations in terms of extra reliability. Disadvantages relate not only to the extra work involved, but to the fact that it may delay decisions about which animals to select. It could, therefore, increase the generation interval. A balance always has to be struck between the speed of selection and the accuracy of selection.

In Table 5.4, the balance has to be between (a) a poorer estimate of genetic worth for milk production and a relatively short generation interval (when using just the first lactation), compared with (b) a more accurate estimate of genetic worth for milk production but with a long generation interval (when using the records of several lactations).

5.6 *Use of relatives to assist individual selection*

Attention has been drawn to the use of animals which are related in different ways in the estimation of heritability (chapter 4). These relationships can also be used to assist the process of genetic selection.

Relatives share genes. They, therefore, provide information about the genetic worth, the breeding value, of an individual to which they are related. If an individual's own performance (a performance test) is supplemented by information on relatives it will increase the accuracy of the genetic assessment of the individual (page 79).

Records from relatives may also be the only information available to indicate an individual's genetic merit.

EXAMPLE 5K INFORMATION *ONLY* AVAILABLE FROM RELATIVES

1 *A bull does not produce milk: its breeding value for milk production can only be assessed on the basis of the performance of relatives – for example (and most commonly) the milk yield of his daughters (a progeny test).*

2 *Improvement of carcass quality has been limited, in the past, because relevant information could not be obtained until the animal had been slaughtered – that prevented information on carcass quality being available until after the animal had been used for breeding. Carcass information could, however, be obtained from relatives and applied to the animal under consideration. (Scanning equipment is now available for use on live animals to provide information closely related to carcass composition. The use of relatives is, therefore, no longer as important for this purpose.)*

3 *Estimation of the expected breeding value of a young animal – records of the performance of its parents or grandparents can be used (pedigree information).*

The three main classes of relatives of an individual which provide additional information about that individual's genotype are **parents**, **offspring** and **sibs**. Other relationships include grandparents, cousins, uncles, aunts, nephews, etc.

Parents

Traditionally much attention has been paid by breeders to **pedigree**, that is to say, to the information on the ancestors of an individual. Originally, pedigree information was used simply to provide a record of ancestry for purposes of identification and registry in, for example, a herd book. Records on the performance of ancestors became fashionable later.

Such performance records from the ancestors can provide useful information about the potential genetic worth of the individual in question. This is especially so before the animal is old enough to give useful information of its own. An estimate of a calf's potential for milk yield, for example, could be based on the milk yield of its mother until such time as the calf is grown up and can be milked.

Note about using pedigree information – an animal inherits:
- Only half its genes from each parent.
- Only one-quarter of its genes from each grandparent.
- A further halving of its genes for each generation back beyond the grandparents.

Parents never provide as much information about the breeding value of an individual as that individual's performance itself would provide. Distant ancestors of an individual provide even less good genetic information about that individual's breeding value – certainly when it comes to productivity traits.

Progeny

Individuals pass half their genes on to their offspring. If there are many progeny, their average performance will give a large amount of information about the genotype of the parent, and possibly perfect information. For traits of low or moderate heritability, 4 or 5 progeny will give as much information about the breeding value of their parent as that parent animal's own performance would. For more highly heritable traits the equivalent number of progeny might be around 10.

Progeny information is especially useful when individuals cannot provide information about themselves, or when very accurate information about an animal's breeding value is needed (for example, for widespread use through artificial insemination).

Progeny testing also has a special value for traits which are only weakly inherited. Many offspring will represent many samples from the geno-type of the parent and thus give a good picture of the parental genotype.

The principal disadvantage of progeny testing, apart from the cost, is that the parent tends to be quite old before the records on the progeny have been collected. Progeny testing, therefore, increases the length of the generation interval which, in turn, reduces the annual rate of im-provement which could otherwise be made. Much effort in devising effective selection programmes goes into trying to minimise this prob-lem.

Sibs

The same principles as for progeny apply – the more sibs an animal has the more information is provided about the genetic merit of that animal. However, even for traits of relatively low heritability it needs quite a large number of full sibs, and an even larger number of half-sibs, to equal the value of a performance test. For traits of high heritability, sibs do not provide as much information as the individual does about itself. When information from sibs or half-sibs is added to the information from a performance test, the sib information can be valuable in increasing the accuracy of an estimate of a breeding value.

Use is most commonly made of **half-sibs** – animals with the same father but different mothers. The advantage of half-sibs is that they may well be contemporaries of the animals being judged (born and perform-ing at or around the same time and kept under the same conditions). The use of half-sib information is, therefore, less likely to require correc-tion for environmental differences and, also, less likely to prolong the interval between generations.

EXAMPLE 5L VALUE OF HALF-SIB INFORMATION IN SELECTING INDIVIDUALS

Assume a cow, which is well above average in her herd, is being considered for that reason as a potential mother of a future bull needed for breeding. This cow has a number of half-sisters in the same herd.
1   *If these half-sibs are also above average it would be a good sign in favour of the cow under consideration.*
2   *If the half-sibs are no better than average, or even below, it would cast doubt on the merits of the cow as a future mother of a bull; the cow's own superiority may be more a matter of luck or good feeding than of good genes.*

In a breeding programme the best practice is to combine all the available information from the individual and its relatives into a single estimate of genetic merit (chapter 6).

5.7   Number of traits

One trait or more than one

Everything has been discussed (so far in chapter 5) in terms of a single trait or a single criterion for selection. This may not be appropriate in some situations. Although farmers have a tendency to want to improve 'everything' – and in consequence often end up by improving nothing – there can be legitimate reasons for paying attention to more than one trait.

EXAMPLE 5M   SELECTING FOR MORE THAN ONE TRAIT

1   *Some farm animals, for example cattle in the tropics, are kept for more than one purpose (e.g. milk, meat and draught). Overall merit will depend on the right amount of attention to each trait – even though the selection programme may give priority to one of the traits.*

2   *Many traits (compound traits) are made up of several components. Attention may have to be given to more than one of these.*

3   *Many traits are inter-related so that changes made in one will produce changes in others.*

Numerical considerations

It is a general rule, that the more traits are used in selection the less progress can be made *in any one* of them.

Table 5.5 shows how the inclusion of different numbers of traits affects the selection which can be applied to any one of the traits (each trait is given equal importance and the traits are assumed to be genetically uncorrelated).

Table 5.5   Minimum proportion of population from which the best for *any one* trait would need to be selected to supply 5 breeding animals from a flock of 100 (Different numbers of traits given equal importance and (genetically) unrelated to each other.)

Number of traits selected	Population needed for any 1 trait (%)*	Selection of 1 animal from *approx.*:	Selection Intensity per trait (SD)
1	5	20	2.063
2	22	5	1.346
3	37	3	1.020
4	47	2	0.846
5	55	<2	0.720

* % population needed for selection of each trait = $x^{1/n}$, where x = proportion, n = number of traits.

- *As the number of traits is increased so the selection intensity for any one trait is reduced quite dramatically.*
- *If one of the traits was 6 month-old weight, SD = 4 kg (as in example 5I), the 5 animals needed could be chosen from the top group averaging 8.3 kg heavier than the mean of their contemporaries – if weight were the only selection criterion (selection intensity × SD).*
- *If 5 separate traits were included in the selection process, the choice on 6-month weight would have to be restricted to a part of the flock which is only 2.9 kg heavier than the population average. Selection of 1 animal in 20 would be replaced by 1 animal from (less than) 2.*

It is of great importance to include in a selection process only those traits which are essential to the performance of the animal. If unimportant things are included ('fancy points') they simply dilute the effectiveness of the selection for the essential things.

However, it is often necessary, in practice, to pay attention to more than one trait at a time. The main aim of livestock improvement is to increase the efficiency and hence the profitability of animal production – several traits are likely to contribute to that profitability. The way in which traits are combined for purposes of selection (chapter 6) can have a large effect on the overall rate of progress that is made.

Correlated traits

Many aspects of production are inter-related. When one trait is changed, others may change as a consequence. These other traits may get better or worse even if no direct attention is paid to them in selection. These traits are said to be correlated.

Such a correlation, can arise, or partly arise, from changes in the environment. For example, animals that are fed better than others are likely to give more milk but are also likely to grow better. Because milk yield and body size *both go up or down together,* they are then said to be **positively correlated**. Improving the milk yield, however, often leads to poorer milk quality (less fat and protein content) if nothing is done about it. Milk yield and milk quality are then said to be **negatively correlated** because *as one increases the other declines* (as in example 2B).

Such correlations among traits also arise (or partly arise) because some genes affect more than one trait – sometimes by influencing some underlying process which is common to more than one trait. A physiological reason might be that some hormone, itself controlled by genes, affects more than one trait. In a more practical example, animals with a better efficiency of food conversion might perform better in a number of other ways – they may grow better, give more milk or be healthier.

- **Genetic correlations** arise for genetic reasons.
- **Environmental correlations** arise for environmental reasons.

- **Phenotypic correlations** are the total correlations arising from all causes.

In a selection programme it is necessary to take account of the correlation among traits. This is so whether it is desired to change a correlated trait or not. Sometimes, the aim is to improve both the trait which is the principal object of selection as well as the correlated trait. Often, the aim is to improve the principal trait but not to allow others to change. For example, it may be desirable to improve milk yield without also increasing the size of the animal, as that would increase its feed requirements even more. These considerations are relevant to selection methods (chapter 6).

Indirect selection

Selection on a correlated trait, called indirect selection, can sometimes be considered with advantage in place of direct selection on the principal trait. These advantages can occur if the correlated trait can be observed earlier in the life of the animal, or if the actual performance trait, which is the ultimate objective of improvement, is difficult to measure.

EXAMPLE 5N INDIRECT SELECTION USING A CORRELATED TRAIT

1 *If larger animals are wanted, perhaps because they produce more power for work, it would be useful not to have to wait until the animals are mature before they are chosen. Weight at one or two years of age might then be regarded as a trait correlated with final size, but with the advantage of much earlier selection.*

2 *Carcass quality, or the lean meat content of the carcass, cannot be assessed in absolute terms without killing the animal, but ultra-sonic scanning (see Figure 10.2) would provide correlated information and at an earlier age.*

3 *Litter size can only be observed once at every parturition – and that relatively late in the animal's life. But, ovulation rate, which sets a limit to litter size and is a correlated trait, can be measured repeatedly and hence more accurately, and somewhat sooner, if the facilities and necessary skills are available.*

4 *First lactation yield is used almost universally as the criterion of a cow's merit for milk production, even though lifetime production is often the aim of improvement.*

Whenever a component part of a production characteristic is the selection criterion it represents a form of indirect selection for the overall production trait. It is selection by use of a correlated trait.

If indirect selection is to be the more effective, the following has to apply:

$$r_A h_y > h_x$$

where:

r_A = the genetic correlation between the two traits

h_y = the square root of the heritability of trait y (the secondary trait)

h_x = the square root of the heritability of trait x (the primary trait)

These conditions are likely to be met only when the heritability (h^2) of the secondary trait is fairly high and the genetic correlation between it and the primary trait is also high. However, this alone does not take account of any potential advantages from reducing the generation interval through indirect selection.

There is another potentially beneficial role for the use of correlated traits in selection. Some traits, such as milk or egg production or litter size, are expressed only in the female of the species, yet the male also carries the genes for these traits. Some research, in various parts of the world, is, therefore, aimed at finding criteria in the male (for example the levels or pulses of certain hormones) which might be correlated with the female performance. These correlated traits could then be used to choose among males and thus help to improve the rate of progress in the selection for female characteristics.

5.8 *The effect of selection on inbreeding and variability*

Selection involves choosing only some of the animals in a population as parents of the next generation. Selection produces changes in performance by changing allele frequencies – choosing some alleles in favour of others.

A consequence in future generations is the increased chance that animals which are related (even slightly) will be mated to each other. For this reason and because the frequencies of alleles have been changed, some of the heterozygocity present in the population at the start will be lost. That is to say: at individual loci where there were two different alleles at the beginning there is an increasing probability that only one allele will be present in the homozygous state.

What is happening is called inbreeding (chapter 9). A consequence of inbreeding is to depress performance, called **inbreeding depression**. The more intense the process of selection the greater the inbreeding caused. The depression caused can be very slight or much more serious depending on a number of different factors. Benefits from selection in improving performance can therefore be reduced by the inbreeding. Selection procedures can be chosen which will slow down the rate of inbreeding.

A related consequence of selection is that some of the genetic variability present at the start is lost. This reduction in variability due to selection has not, in the past, caused much concern in respect of quantitative traits. With increasing opportunities for more intense selection, helped by new technology, it is, however, a matter to be borne in mind so that genetic changes made now do not prevent further changes in the future. The opportunities for selection in the future must be kept open because the circumstances of livestock production may change.

Such potential drawbacks to selection are almost never reasons for not selecting for improvement. They are only *possible* complications which need to be considered when deciding on the objectives for selection and on the actual procedures to use.

5.9 *Conclusions on selection*

Genetic selection changes the performance of livestock. (Some examples of the rates at which this happens will be given in chapter 6.) Provided a trait is heritable, the more intense the selection the greater the changes made. The more quickly the generations are made to follow each other the faster the progress will be. The two possible risks are inbreeding depression and reduction in variability.

6 Selection II: Methods, schemes and rates achieved

In order to put selection into practice it is useful to consider three other points: the information available on which to base selection, whether to select for more than one trait, and the most appropriate procedure for selection.

6.1 *Methods*

Individual and family information

When selecting animals from a large population (e.g. a large herd), there are likely to be different **families** of animals within that population. These could be:

- half-sib families – usually sire families which are the offspring of the same bull but with different mothers making up each family;
- full-sib families – animals sharing both parents, for example the piglets in a normal litter.

There are only three ways of selecting animals (but there can also be combinations of these):

- Individual selection – on the basis of their own performance irrespective of their family (or mass-selection).
- Family selection – by choosing the best families as a whole and rejecting the others (also called between family selection).
- Within family selection – by choosing the best individuals from each family.

The three methods of selection are illustrated in Figure 6.1 in relation to an imaginary population of 36 animals divided into 6 families of 6 individuals each.

Individual selection

The simplest method is to choose animals on the basis of their own performance. Comparing individuals on the basis of their own performance is often called **a performance test**.

In most situations, individual selection, irrespective of family, is the best procedure as it takes account of all the additive genetic variation that is present in the population.

The information on the performance of the individual can often be supplemented by information from its relatives – those, like its parents, which are part of its pedigree, its sibs or half sibs, or its progeny. This introduces elements of family selection.

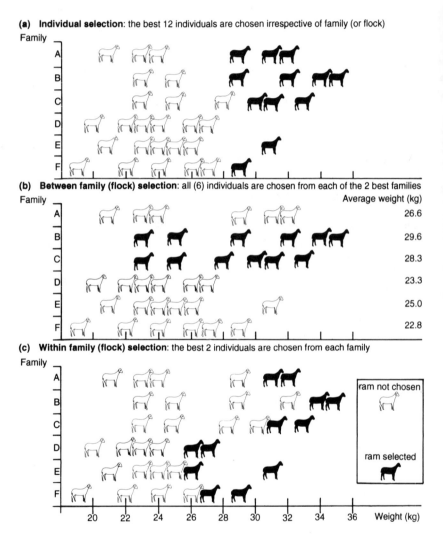

Fig 6.1 *Methods of selection – an example of selecting 12 rams on yearling weight from 6 families (or flocks) each with 6 rams to choose from: (a) individual selection, (b) between family selection, (c) within family selection*

Family selection

Selection is on the average value for the family (the family mean) and takes no separate account of individuals. Whole families are chosen or rejected. This has advantages over individual selection when:

i) the heritability of the trait under selection is low;

ii) resemblance among family members is not high on account of a common environment; and

iii) the family size is large.

Under these circumstances, the observed mean value for the family can come close to the genotypic mean. The larger the number of individuals in the family the better this estimate will be.

Family selection is not efficient when common environmental factors make the members of a family very alike. If that happens, families would appear to differ but it would be for environmental reasons, whereas the object of selection is to differentiate for genetic reasons. For instance, the piglets of a litter would be alike when very young because of the maternal environment provided by the sow which they share: this resemblance might swamp any resemblance the piglets may have because of the genes they also share.

Selecting whole families is likely to reduce the number of families represented among the parents of the next generation. For any given selection intensity, family selection would therefore increase the rate of inbreeding (chapter 9) compared with individual selection.

Progeny testing and **sib testing** are both special forms of family selection. As noted (pages 70–71), they have a special value when the trait in question cannot be measured directly in the individual.

Both progeny testing and sib information, as well as information from other relatives such as parents, can supplement the information from the individual itself and thereby improve the accuracy with which the individual's breeding value can be assessed. This can be especially useful when the heritability of the trait under consideration is low. Each offspring carries a sample of half the genes of the individual and so with many offspring the breeding value of the individual can be assessed with accuracy – but at the cost of making the generation interval longer (example 5H). Similar arguments apply to the use of information from sibs or half-sibs except that this information is often available earlier than that from progeny.

In the selection of individuals, the observations from the relatives have to be given the correct weighting. These weights depend on the closeness of the relationship. The closer the relationship the higher the weighting. This reflects the fact that close relatives share more of their genes than less close relatives. For instance, an offspring carries half the genes of one parent, a half-sib shares only a quarter of its genes with the individual being judged. The information from the relatives is best incorporated into an **index** (page 82) which summarises the animal's breeding value and then allows the animals to be ranked in order, from best to worst.

Within family selection

When choosing the best individuals from each family, within family selection is taking place. This procedure retains at least one representative of each family for the next generation. It is most useful when differences between families are mainly due to differences in environment (possibly because different families have been treated differently). In that case there may be more chance of finding the genetic differences within the family, for example among the sibs which make up the family.

EXAMPLE 6A WITHIN FAMILY SELECTION

Selection for the early growth of piglets (before weaning):
- *Each piglet in a litter shares the common maternal environment provided by the sow which will tend to make the piglets in the litter alike.*
- *Differences between litters in the growth rate of the young piglets could, for the same reason, arise because of the different mothering abilities of the different sows rather than the innate ability of the piglets to grow.*
- *Selecting on individual piglet growth irrespective of family would tend to favour piglets from litters where the sow has provided particularly good conditions.*
- *Under such circumstances, selecting the best-grown piglet(s) from within each litter will at least exploit any genetic differences within that litter for early growth in piglets.*

Retaining at least one member from each family for the future can also be helpful in reducing problems from inbreeding (chapter 9).

Selecting more than one trait

The aim of selection, in practice, should be to improve the efficiency and profitability of the farming enterprise. Therefore, it may be necessary to pay attention to more than one individual trait. The more traits that are selected the less the progress which can be made in any one of them (Table 5.4). Since many traits are inter-related (correlated), however, changes produced in one trait may lead to changes in other traits (page 73). These correlated changes can be desirable or undesirable depending on the direction and strength of the correlation.

Each individual trait is not, however, of equal importance to the overall goal of improvement. The separate, component traits will differ in the economic importance they have for overall profitability of the animal or the animal enterprise. The traits will also differ in the strength with which they are inherited (measured by the heritability). Therefore, for a given selection intensity there might be more change in one trait than in another. Finally, the extent to which the traits are genetically correlated with each other must affect the decisions about the selection procedure to be adopted.

There are three methods of including more than one trait in a selection programme:

1   Tandem selection where one trait is improved to the desired level first, followed by the next trait, and the next, and so on.

2   Independent culling levels whereby a particular performance level is set separately for each of the traits, and no animal is selected for breeding if it falls below these levels in any of the traits;

3   Index selection whereby the traits are combined to provide a single criterion of overall merit, often the economic merit. This is usually closer to what farmers really want.

With selection on an index, deficiencies in any one trait can be compensated for by outstandingly good performance in other traits, an option which is not open in the method of independent culling levels.

Tandem selection

The poorest option in the long term, although it is quite widely used in practice, is tandem selection. (For instance, farmers may want to improve the conformation of their lambs and only when that is considered satisfactory might they decide that growth rate needs improvement too.)

It is nearly always better to set the objectives right in the first place and, if more than one trait *must* be improved, to select the different traits together at the same time.

Independent culling levels

The intention in combining the traits and fixing culling levels for each should be to ensure that the profit from the *overall* performance is improved. To arrive at the separate culling levels involves calculating the relative importance of the separate traits and takes account of their heritabilities, inter-relationships and economic values (see index selection page 82). This process can be quite complicated. Once determined, however, the culling levels can be simply applied to the records of the animals.

It is possible for farmers, simply, to set their own levels, on the basis that they do not want animals to fall below a certain standard in respect of any one trait. But that procedure is unlikely to give the best result overall.

Although, in theory, the use of independent culling levels is not as good as combining traits in an index, there are some situations which lend themselves well to this approach. These are when each trait is normally culled at a different stage of the animal's life and when the number of traits is small (2 or 3). It may also be that the number of animals available for initial selection is large and that it would simply be too costly to keep them all until the later criteria for selection are known.

EXAMPLE 6B SELECTION BY INDEPENDENT CULLING LEVELS FROM TRAITS AT
DIFFERENT AGES

Assume that it is desirable to improve both growth rate and milk yield or other aspects of maternal performance.
- *The information on growth rate of an individual becomes available before that on its milk yield or other maternal characteristics.*
- *Therefore, selection on growth may already have been done by culling animals which fall below a certain level, before the mothering qualities or milk yield are known.*

Index selection

The greater the number of traits involved, the more efficient the use of an index becomes relative to independent culling levels.

To be fully effective, an index requires knowledge of heritabilities and of genetic correlations among the traits. These genetic correlations are rarely known with accuracy and are difficult to calculate – rough estimates may have to do.

The **economic values** of the different traits also need to be known, or guessed at, for inclusion in an index (as also in determining independent culling levels). These are the monetary value of a unit of change in each trait. This is also often difficult to determine – especially so when not each of the products is actually sold for cash. Thus, the exercise can require many assumptions about the economic value of genetic change in each trait.

The object is to give each trait in the index the weight (relative importance) necessary to maximise the profitability of the genetic improvement. Without good statistical and computing back-up, index selection involving many traits may not work well – but sometimes an uncomplicated index of 2 or 3 traits is all that is required and is relatively simple to use.

Comparison of selection by independent culling levels and an index

For purposes of this illustration (Figure 6.2, example 6c), the two traits

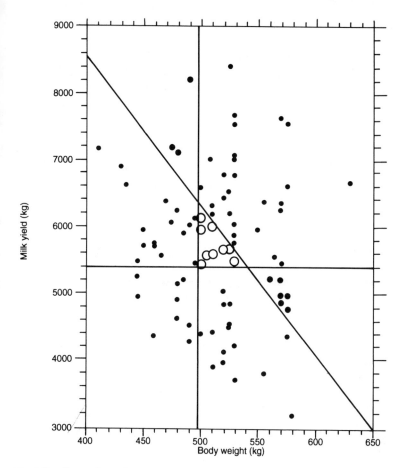

Fig 6.2 *Comparison of selection on an index with selection by independent culling levels*

The traits are first lactation milk yield and body weight at first calving in a high-yielding herd of Holstein-Friesian cattle. The two traits in this herd are not correlated with each other. The requirement is to retain the best 50% of the cows on a combination of the two traits – for purposes of illustration only.

When using independent culling levels, the *vertical line* shows the culling level for body weight and the *horizontal line* that for milk yield. No animal is then chosen with weight or milk yield below these levels.

The *diagonal line* shows the division using index selection when the two traits are given equal importance. Note that with index selection 3 cows are kept which are very good on milk yield although below the culling level of the other method for body weight (*top left triangle*).

Similarly, 6 cows of high weight are included although they would have been rejected on milk yield by the other method (*bottom right triangle*). Index selection, however, rejects 9 cows which are not outstanding on either milk yield or body weight although above the culling levels of the other method (*central triangle*).

chosen, body weight at the time of calving and milk yield in the first lactation, have been given equal importance. In the absence of data derived from the tropics, example 6c is based on a Friesian herd in Scotland – however, the principle is not affected. (The example does *not* illustrate the selection procedure actually used in this particular herd.)

EXAMPLE 6C PRINCIPLE OF INDEX SELECTION COMPARED WITH SELECTION ON INDEPENDENT CULLING LEVELS

See Figure 6.2. It is assumed that 50% of the females are needed for breeding: therefore, the poorest half can be culled. The two traits are virtually uncorrelated in this herd.

Independent culling levels: the best 70% in respect of each trait are kept. The poorest 30% culled: (in Figure 6.2) (a) all females (to the left of the vertical line) below 500 kg are rejected on body weight and (b) all the females (below the horizontal line) below 5400 litres are rejected on milk yield.

- *Therefore, 50% of animals kept for future use are those of 500 kg body weight or over provided they also yielded more than 5400 litres milk (top right-hand square of Figure 6.2).*

The procedure for applying an index is simplified by giving equal importance to the two uncorrelated traits. Hence, the females selected are those above the diagonal line in Figure 6.2. In many situations the two traits chosen would not be given equal importance in selection. Genetic considerations and the farming circumstances might dictate that less importance be given to body weight and more to milk yield – or vice versa: the principles involved are the same as shown.

Computers in a selection programme

The aims of modern animal breeding practices are:
- To make the best use of the total available resources.
- To obtain the best return from any changes.

Only with the help of computers are the most efficient selection procedures likely to be used. Investment in computers and in the software for appropriate statistical techniques is likely to be cost-effective, at least in large-scale operations.

Selection environment

Whenever possible, selection of breeding stock should be carried out in the same kind of environment as that in which the offspring of these animals are intended to perform. If this cannot be done, often the next best choice is to select in an environment which is *worse* than that in which the animals (or their progeny) will later perform (example 6D).

Though correct in principle, this may not be possible in practice in the tropics where the normal conditions are already harsh for the animals. If even poorer conditions are created, the animals may not have enough offspring, and early enough in life, to make selection effective. There are, however, other situations where it would be sensible to consider selection under the poorer of conditions (subject to the limitations on reproductive rate). For example, where feed supply is uncertain, animals will often be given supplementary feed: rather than select under the good conditions of constant supplementary feeding it may be better to select animals in the absence of supplementary feeding.

This is the opposite of the popular perception that to select successfully, animals must be induced to express their genetic potential to the full (e.g. make the animals yield as much as possible by feeding them as much as possible). The reason for not doing this is that genetic improvement made by selecting under good condition may not then show up (express itself) under the normal commercial system of production – the normal, poorer environment. Thus:

- Selecting for high milk yield under excellent feeding conditions and with good health and management practices is very likely to increase the yield under those conditions, but these selected animals may not show any genetic superiority if they have to produce milk under poor conditions of feeding and management.
- An analogous situation is seen in the often disappointing performance of imported, exotic breeds in the tropics (created in excellent conditions, but poor when transferred to the harsher conditions of smallholder farming in the tropics).

There is also some experimental evidence that selecting for what may appear to be the same trait actually produces a different result if the selection is done under different environmental conditions.

EXAMPLE 6D SELECTING UNDER DIFFERENT ENVIRONMENTAL CONDITIONS

In Australia, selecting for growth under intensive feeding conditions increased the animals' appetite: they ate more and grew faster.

Selection under poorer feeding reduced the animals' maintenance requirements for food. The animals then used more of the feed that was available, above the needs of maintenance, for growth.

The latter would be a more desirable route to better growth if feed is in short supply.

More experimental results, as in example 6D, are needed before it is possible to be sure about the best procedure to adopt in each case – but the example illustrates the point that the environmental conditions under which the selection is carried out can have an important bearing on the results.

Choosing the appropriate environment for selection is a way of avoiding the problems of **genotype-environment interaction** (G × E). In the present context, it would mean that the difference in performance between two selected strains (or more than two) in one environment is not the same as the difference in another environment. Sometimes, this is not too serious, but it would become so if the size of that effect was very large or even led to a change in the ranking of the selected strains in the two environments (as was shown for breed crosses in Figure 1.1).

Selecting animals in the environment in which the offspring will be used avoids this problem altogether because there is only one environment. If that cannot be done, the choice of the best environment in which to select can be determined, formally, by regarding the performance of animals in each environment as two different traits which are correlated with each other. The best environment in which to select, is then determined by the genetic correlation between the two traits and the amount of variation shown in each environment.

How to monitor progress from selection

It is very important to find out whether a breeding programme is making the changes which were hoped for.

Because selection usually has to continue for several years, non-genetic factors can change apart from the genetic merit of the animals. There may be 'random' differences between the years over which the selection process takes place, for example the weather, the feed supply or the disease incidence. There could also be systematic changes through an improvement in feeding and management over the years. Any such changes could easily be confused with any genetic changes that have been made.

There are several methods by which the genetic changes can, however, be monitored. The best way is to keep a control group of **unselected animals** (the original animals before the improvement process started) alongside those in the selection groups. Both the selected and the unselected (the **controls**) will be subject to the same environmental effects from year to year, but the difference between them will be a measure of the success or failure of the selection effort.

Other forms of control are less satisfactory but may be cheaper or less demanding.

One possible way is to compare the performance of the selected animals with **commercial animals** which may not yet have much (or any) of the blood of the selected stock. As stressed for other comparisons of different genetic groups, it is important to make the comparison with the animals of the two types (selected and commercial) under the same conditions.

Two other possible procedures depend on the use of 'preserved' material – frozen semen or frozen embryos. Either or both of these can be stored from time to time from the animals in the selection programme, starting with the original unselected population. At intervals, animals from these earlier generations can be recreated and compared with the animals at the latest stage of improvement. **Frozen semen** is the cheaper to use and the least demanding. The disadvantage is that the semen, when used to fertilise the females available in later years, ends up in showing only half the genetic change that has occurred.

Frozen embryos can be transferred in later years to recipient animals. The animals which are born as a result will show up the whole of the genetic difference between themselves – representing an earlier generation – and the animals of the then current generation. The penalty attached to this procedure is the high technical sophistication required and the consequent costs.

6.2   *Selection schemes*

A selection scheme provides the framework for putting the various selection methods into practice. A balance has to be made between:
• the costs of any particular scheme and
• the expected rewards.

Compromises are usually necessary between the theoretically desirable and the practical.

Selection works most effectively when large numbers of animals are involved, but recording the individual performance of large numbers of animals can be very costly. The compromise, made in many schemes, is:
• to concentrate most effort on a proportion of the total population
• to use other herds or flocks to exploit the genetic improvement made in the group on which most effort has concentrated and
• to multiply the genetic improvement for the benefit of the general population.

Generally, expert advice is useful before embarking on a large-scale breeding scheme. Choice of scheme and the procedures to be adopted will be affected by the particular circumstances of the region, country or district and by the wishes of the farmers and, often, their governments. All that is intended here is to refer briefly to some of the most common forms of organisation and to recent developments affecting them.

Breed structure

Historically, breeds of livestock became organised into hierarchies of breeders as some became more popular than others. This trend was particularly apparent in breeds supported by Breed Societies. These helped the tendency of some herds or flocks to become more important to the breed. The Societies maintained and published pedigrees of the animals and information about the herds or flocks. The more enlightened Societies also published performance records on the animals.

The hierarchy involved a top group consisting of a relatively small number of breeders who relied largely on each other for their male and female replacement stock. This group also supplied the bulk of the breeding males to a next tier of flocks or herds which then multiplied any genetic improvement in the top tier – but also, occasionally, spread any genetic defect which may have arisen in the top tier. When males from the top tier are used to produce sons and daughters in the next tier – the multiplier group – any genetic gains made in the top tier are halved (because the sires pass on only half their genes to each offspring). But

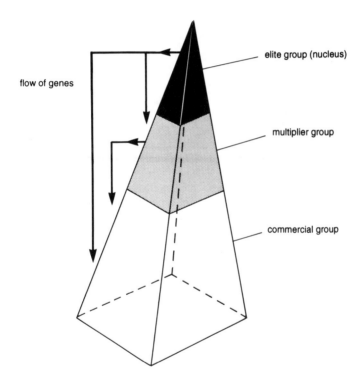

Fig 6.3   *Breed pyramid (or breed hierarchy)*

The elite (or nucleus) group is at the top, the multiplier group in the middle and the commercial group of herds or flocks at the bottom. The flow of genes is predominantly from the top downward, thus, genetic improvement made in the top group is spread downward.

large numbers of such animals can be produced.

The multiplier group in turn supplied breeding stock, males in particular, to the next, genetically lower, tier of commercial producers. This, again, halves any genetic gains made in the tier above. The flow of genes, both good and, on occasion, deleterious, was thus predominantly from the top to the bottom of what is often illustrated by a pyramid of flocks or herds (Figure 6.3).

The advent of artificial insemination, particularly in the dairy cattle breeding of much of the 'western' world, has broken down much of this formal structure but only by replacing one top group of animals by another. This has been accompanied by a much stronger emphasis on performance as the criterion for being at the top – not merely a fashionable pedigree and 'good looks'. Artificial insemination has also greatly increased the speed of the gene flow from the top to the bottom, often by simply eliminating the need for the middle tier of multipliers. Similarly, breeding companies, with their generally scientific approach to breeding and their larger resources, have taken on much of the role of the breeders formerly at the top of their breed pyramid.

The principle of the **breed pyramid**, the genetic hierarchy of breeders, has more than historic interest. Hierarchies still exist wherever some herds or flocks are more popular than others. But, it is also recognised that, for practical reasons, genetic improvement needs to proceed more rapidly in some sections of an animal population than in others and that this improved group has the greatest genetic influence on the breed as a whole. This has led to the development of schemes which have a nucleus herd or flock of genetically superior animals at the centre of their activities.

Nucleus – Group breeding schemes

These were pioneered in New Zealand and Australia, but successfully adopted in many countries. For such a scheme, at its simplest, a number of flock (or herd) owners agree to co-operate by deciding on common breeding aims and by pooling their animal resources. The key of each scheme is the creation of a **nucleus** flock (or herd) from the best of the breeding females of each participating flock (or herd) (but see page 91 for an alternative).

Schemes with conventional nucleus

The agreed selection programme with all necessary recording is carried out in the nucleus flock usually located on the farm of one of the co-operators, but this could also be an institutional or government farm. The size of the nucleus flock must be large enough to make selection effective and to avoid undue inbreeding.

1 *If 5 breeders with equal sizes of flock co-operate, each might contribute to the nucleus the best 20% of their breeding females (as judged on the selection criteria).*

2 *If 10 breeders co-operate, each might contribute their best 10%, and so on for differing numbers.*

Initially, the males are chosen from among the co-operators, or possibly introduced from elsewhere, but thereafter bred in the nucleus.

The best males are retained and used in the nucleus: the co-operators also receive males from the nucleus for use in their own flocks. The co-operating breeders may hope to receive much of their income from the sale of breeding males for use in the rest of the population of animals outside the scheme.

A group breeding scheme involves detailed recording of performance in the nucleus – at least for the traits contributing to the selection aims. However, since other characteristics of the animals may also change indirectly, perhaps as an unforeseen consequence of the main selection, it is a good idea to monitor other traits as well. While less recording is usually done in the other co-operating flocks, some is necessary to provide a measure of the progress being made by selection, to identify superior females which might be transferred to the nucleus flock (if it remains open – see below) and to persuade purchasers of breeding stock of the merits of the animals they are buying. The side benefit of the recording is that it provides information to assist good animal management.

Open or closed nucleus

If the selection scheme goes according to plan, it is likely that, after a few generations, the animals in the nucleus will become genetically superior to any outside. If, however, the nucleus remains closed to all outside blood – whether from the co-operating flocks or from others – inbreeding may arise with deleterious effects. Also, the nucleus would not benefit from the introduction of exceptionally good animals which may occur in the co-operating flocks, or elsewhere.

It is wise to keep the nucleus open to the introduction of animals – at least for some generations. This is usually done by an annual introduction of the very best of the breeding females from the co-operating flocks. These females have to compete, in terms of their performance, with the females already in the nucleus. As a result of the comparison, they either remain there, in place of some of those from the nucleus, or they are culled if found to be not good enough. These introductions

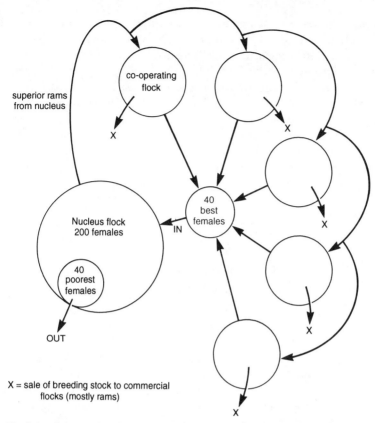

superior rams
from nucleus

co-operating
flock

40
best
females

IN

Nucleus flock
200 females

40
poorest
females

OUT

X = sale of breeding stock to commercial
flocks (mostly rams)

Fig 6.4   *Open nucleus breeding scheme – an example of a group breeding scheme with sheep*

The nucleus flock was set up from the best of the females from the participating flocks. Thereafter, each year, the poorest females (40 in the example) are culled from the nucleus flock and replaced by an equivalent number from the co-operating flocks taking the best (8 females) from each. The best of the rams are used in the nucleus flock and the next best in the co-operating flocks.

can increase the rate of genetic improvement in the nucleus – most especially in the early years of the scheme – but also reduce the rate at which inbreeding accumulates. Figure 6.4 illustrates an open nucleus scheme after it has been set up and is operating.

Group breeding scheme without (conventional) nucleus by use of reference sires

One of the main benefits from co-operation among breeders is that the animal population directly involved in a selection programme is enlarged compared to that available to each individual breeder. In order to know whether a ram (for example) used in one flock is genetically better than a ram used in one of the other co-operating flocks, it is necessary to have some sort of link between the flocks. This can be done by using what has been called **reference sires**. These sires leave offspring in several, possibly all, of the co-operating flocks. The offspring of the reference sires can then be compared with the offspring of any other rams used in the same flock. Thus, the best males in the whole of the group breeding scheme:

• can be identified, with the help of appropriate statistical programmes;
• can become available to the scheme as a whole; and
• can be used to breed the next generation of males.

This procedure could then be an alternative to having a separate nucleus flock to produce the best sires (page 98).

Nucleus – Centralised breeding schemes

The principle is similar to that described above (page 89), in-so-far as a nucleus is created. The nucleus is supported by an organised method of supplying superior breeding females to the nucleus and organisation is needed for testing the males bred in the nucleus.

Such schemes have been recommended for dairy cattle breeding on a national scale, though not widely used in a formal way. They have been more extensively used in pig and poultry breeding – although here, breeding companies have taken over the role formerly occupied by national bodies and breeders' co-operatives.

For dairy cattle, the schemes for genetic improvement in use for several decades have used a principle which is akin to having a nucleus, though without the formal structure associated with nucleus herds. The schemes differ in detail from country to country but they generally have four elements in common:

• Mating of young bulls to cows in milk-recorded herds to produce a number of test daughters for each bull – with each bull used in many herds so that the daughters are spread over many herds. The bulls are then compared on the basis of the yield of their daughters (progeny test). The average performance of the daughters of each bull used in a herd is compared with the performance of the daughters of all the other bulls in the same herd (called a **contemporary comparison**). Then by use of special computer programmes the results are accumulated over all the herds in which such comparisons have been made (with appropriate weighting for the number of daughters involved for each bull). (For example, in the UK, some 150 young bulls were mated annually to approximately 300 cows each to produce about 60 lactating daughters per bull spread over 30–40 herds.)

- The young bulls are removed from service until the progeny test is complete – or semen from them is stored.
- The best of the bulls (by this time no longer young, or represented only by conserved, frozen semen) are then selected and mated in turn to selected, high-yielding cows in farmers' herds to produce the males for the next generation of young bulls to be tested.
- The selected bulls are also used widely to breed female herd replacements.

It must be added that such large-scale dairy cattle improvement schemes as described above were made possible only by the advent of artificial insemination which allowed large numbers of bulls to be used widely over a large population of cows. These schemes also relied on milk recording of all the cows in the many herds participating in the scheme (the example from the UK given above involved 45 000 cows). Thus, the conditions for such schemes do not generally exist in most countries of the tropics.

Proposals have been made from time to time to restrict the mating of the young bulls to specified herds and to test them in only a restricted number of herds. This, it was thought, would provide more control over management and recording and, thus, improve the efficiency of selection – compared with assessing the bulls across a very large number of herds, with only a very small number of daughters of those bulls in each herd.

Testing of all animals in a single large group, or testing station, has gone largely out of favour because the management and general environment of these stations has not been sufficiently close to that of the commercial farms where the animals, or their offspring, are to be used. The costs of such centralised testing has also been found to be high. Centralised testing, when it was fashionable, was applied particularly to traits which could be measured directly in the individual (performance testing), such as growth rate or fatness.

In many developing countries where recording of performance is not widespread, centralised testing may yet have a role to play for some traits – especially those that lend themselves to performance testing. It is important, however, that the ranking of the animals on merit at the testing station is relevant to the ranking which would apply on the commercial production holdings (in technical terms: genotype-environment interactions must not make the results from the testing station irrelevant to the needs of farmers).

From studies carried out a number of years ago, it was found that, in relation to dairy cattle, the correlation between station performance and performance on commercial farms was poor and that under those circumstances the high costs of testing on a centralised station were not justified.

Nucleus – Multiple ovulation and embryo transfer (MOET)

Developing countries of the tropics generally lack the widespread farm recording of animal performance which has supported national selection programmes, especially for dairy cattle. New opportunities have been created for genetic improvement by the combination of multiple ovulation and embryo transfer (MOET) to increase the reproductive rate of chosen females in a self-contained nucleus herd or flock. The idea was first developed into a breeding scheme in the early 1980s and is now being tried in a number of countries, either on its own or in conjunction with more conventional schemes.

The MOET scheme is a method of selecting, principally males but also females, at an earlier age than in conventional schemes. It pays particular attention to the performance of the dams of the animals to be selected and to any other female relatives that are available. Initially applied to the selection of dairy bulls, MOET schemes are also applicable to the selection of beef bulls and to that of sheep, goats, or species where the number of offspring per breeding female at any one parturition is not high.

Basically, a MOET breeding scheme sacrifices accuracy in selection in favour of a great reduction in the generation interval to achieve similar, or better, annual rates of genetic improvement than conventional procedures involving progeny testing. Two forms of scheme were proposed for dairy cattle:

- An adult scheme with a generation interval of less than 4 years (under European conditions).
- A juvenile scheme with a generation interval of possibly less than 2 years.

EXAMPLE 6F MOET IN DAIRY CATTLE

In dairy cattle, the principle is to create a nucleus herd of very superior cows in terms of their yield (or whatever criterion is chosen).

*These cows (**donor cows**) are then mated to the best possible bulls (from within the scheme after it has started) and superovulated.*

*The fertilised eggs are transferred to **recipient cows** which give birth to the calves.*

In an adult scheme, with milk production as the example, selection of replacements takes place after the first lactation.

- For a female, selection is based on information on her own performance, that of her full- and half-sibs and on the performance of her (genetic) dam (the cow from which the fertilised egg was taken) and older female relatives.
- For a male the information is the same, except that there is no

94

information (if milk yield is the criterion) from the individual itself.

In the juvenile scheme, because selection takes place much earlier, information is restricted to that from the dam and the dam's and sire's female relatives. All available information is combined into an index.

The adult scheme (originally proposed by Nicholas and Smith 1983) was based on 64 selected donor cows, expected to produce 4 male and 4 female progeny each on average. The whole scheme was based on a herd of 512 cows of which half are in their first lactation and the others in their second. The rate of genetic gain from an adult scheme was expected to be at least equivalent in rate of genetic progress to that from conventional progeny testing schemes (though less than that from a juvenile scheme – but see below) and with some additional *advantages*:

- Recording and selection restricted to the relatively small number of cows specified (instead of the many thousands of a conventional scheme).
- Selection could be based on additional criteria, such as efficiency of food conversion and not only yield, which cannot normally be measured in a large population.
- Indirect (physiological) criteria of milk yield measured on the young bull progeny might increase the efficiency of selection.
- Since only one bull calf is chosen from each selected dam, there are opportunities for selecting that calf from among the several born to the dam on the basis of, for example, his growth rate (or the physiological criteria referred to above).

Disadvantages were noted to be:

- A more rapid rate of inbreeding occurs than in conventional schemes. This arises from the very restricted number of males and females used in the scheme. In a juvenile scheme inbreeding is even more rapid and can increase to the point where a juvenile scheme may not be an acceptable long-term option.
- There is the possibility that the environment of the MOET herd was out of keeping with that of the commercial production herds (see page 4 for genotype-environment interactions).
- High technology is required for successful multiple ovulation and embryo transfer.
- The efficiency of the scheme is reduced by the fact that donor cows ovulate a variable number of eggs rather than the theoretical 8 each, used for the original calculations, and not necessarily with an equal sex ratio of offspring – some donor cows become under-represented in the scheme and others over-represented.

To reduce the problem of inbreeding, the nucleus could be kept open or the selection procedure could be otherwise modified, but at the cost of some of the potential rate of genetic progress. In many countries the skills and facilities needed to run a successful MOET scheme are lacking.

In those situations it is a matter of judgement whether the potential rewards from a MOET scheme are sufficient to justify creating the necessary technical sophistication.

Population screening

Population screening is not a breeding scheme in itself but an aid to genetic improvement. It can be practised even in the absence of on-farm recording and has, therefore, much to offer in the tropics and in developing countries.

Population screening is a way of searching for the exceptionally good in the population as a whole, in order to accumulate a group of superior breeding stock. This stock, after it has been tested and found to be genetically elite, can become the nucleus of a breeding programme.

There are two main reasons why it may be a good idea to involve the whole of a population of animals in the search for superior genetic material:

1 Increasing the size of the population used for selection

Even in countries where recording of animal performance occurs and pedigrees of animals are kept, the process of within-breed selection is usually limited to a relatively small section of the animal population. This excludes exceptional animals which may be found in the rest of the population and which could be the carriers of particularly useful genes – genes which occur in the population in only low frequency. This could include major genes – those with individually large effects on a trait.

2 Circumventing a lack of adequate records

In many countries, the absence of adequate recording of animal performance in a sufficient proportion of herds or flocks places an obstacle in the way of starting selection programmes.

A possible solution, which has now been adopted successfully in a number of countries, is to screen large populations of animals, by whatever means possible, in the search for individuals which are genuinely *extreme* in some aspect of their performance.

EXAMPLE 6G POPULATION SCREENING FOR ANIMALS OF EXTREME PERFORMANCE

If the criterion of extreme were that the animal's performance in the chosen trait had to be 3 or more standard deviations above the average, it would mean that only about 1 animal in 1000 would be expected to be that good. Such animals, depending on the variability of the trait, may be twice as good as the average, or even better.

The approach to identifying such animals may have to be, in a sense, 'old fashioned' – based on a mixture of subjective assessment, the opinion of farmers and their neighbours and whatever measurements or observations can be made on the spot. Since the animals being sought are rare, by definition, they will have to be sought over a wide area and a large population. Differences in conditions in which the animals are kept will influence the performance. The important thing is, therefore, that the animals chosen should *stand out* from among their contemporaries in their immediate vicinity.

EXAMPLE 6H EXTREME PERFORMANCE IN ANIMALS

Reproductive performance in sheep is used for illustration:
1 *A ewe is likely to be outstanding if she has had twins repeatedly and annually in a flock where twins are a great rarity and ewes do not have lambs regularly.*
2 *In a flock where twins are relatively common, an outstanding ewe might be the one that has produced triplets or better more than once and twins for the rest of the time.*

Having identified superior animals by enquiry and inspection and negotiated their acquisition, the chosen animals can be transferred to a single location, perhaps an institutional farm. There, they can be kept under controlled conditions alongside a random sample of contemporary animals and their performance recorded. If they repeat their allegedly high performance – or are at least much better than the average of their contemporaries – they can go for further assessment and into the creation of a nucleus flock.

'Proof' of the genetic superiority of the selected animals will come only when it is found that their progeny are superior to the average. If the animals obtained by the initial screening fail to perform well they are disposed of. It must be assumed that their previous good performance was a chance occurrence or due to exceptional treatment, or that perhaps it was based on inadequate information.

It has sometimes been suggested that the accuracy of reports of exceptionally good animals will be improved if final agreement to purchase an animal (at a price which provides an incentive to sell) is not made until the further tests have shown the animal to be superior when recorded alongside contemporaries. Incentive can also be provided by promising the farmer concerned some benefit from the genetically superior stock which will be produced – perhaps a ram or use of a ram.

Several reports of successful screening and the accumulation of superior animals into elite flocks have come from a number of countries. So far, all are in respect of superior reproductive performance in sheep (Timon 1987). This is perhaps not surprising since it is easier to verify the presence of a large number of lambs with a particular ewe, than, for example, exceptional growth rate. (Such growth should be reflected in the body size at a given age, but it may be difficult to establish age sufficiently accurately, or to discover whether special feeding could have contributed to exceptional growth.) There is, however, no reason why this approach should not be tried for traits other than litter size, even if more of the chosen animals turn out to be not as good as hoped for and then have to be rejected.

Sire referencing

The name **reference sire** is given to a male which has progeny in several herds or flocks alongside the offspring of other males. This can be done deliberately to compare the performance of the offspring of the reference sire with the performance of the offspring of other males used in the same herds or flocks. The reference sire then provides a *link* through which to compare the genetic merit of all sires used in these herds (by the performance of their offspring) even those not used alongside each other.

EXAMPLE 6I REFERENCE SIRE

Assume 3 herds and 4 males (A, B, C, D). Sire A is used in all the herds, sires B, C, and D in one of each of the herds.

Sire A provides a link whereby the merits of B, C, and D can be compared with each other as well as with sire A.

For the most effective use of this system, a statistical programme, such as BLUP (best linear unbiassed prediction) is needed to make allowance for differences between herds which may affect the difference in performance between the reference sire and the others used in each herd. An application of the system was described earlier in relation to group breeding schemes.

It is not necessary to use each reference sire (or more than one reference sire) in every herd, although this has statistical advantages, but it is necessary to ensure that there is a link across all herds.

EXAMPLE 6J LINK ACROSS HERDS BY REFERENCE SIRES

See example 6i: if sire A were used in only 2 of the herds, alongside B in one and C in the other, there would still be a statistical link if sire B was used alongside sire D in the third herd.

The principle can be and is being applied across wider areas and can in fact be applied across national frontiers and regions.

EXAMPLE 6K INTERNATIONAL LINKS BY REFERENCE SIRES

- *Some dairy bulls leave progeny in many countries, through the distribution of frozen semen, and provide a link to other bulls used in those countries.*
- *An organisation called Interbull has been set up in Sweden for the purpose of publishing the results of such evaluations.*

The system is not good at estimating genotype-environment interactions and if these are truly important may give less good information about the relative merits of different males than if they were used directly alongside each other. Nevertheless, the system has much to recommend it where conditions across herds or flocks are fairly similar as in a group breeding scheme.

An anxiety expressed by some geneticists is that international comparisons involving dairy bulls may lead to too great a use of a small number of bulls across the world (the 'best' bull in the world!). This could lead to a loss of genetic diversity, arising partly from a concentration on a small number of breeds, or strains from within those breeds, and partly from an increased opportunity for inbreeding which itself has harmful effects on productivity (chapter 9).

Reference breeds

A further extension of the idea of referencing would be to use a particular breed or breeds in many places or many parts of the world as a baseline against which to compare other breeds. For example, the worldwide use of the Large White breed may fulfil that role for pigs. It is important to make sure that the same type or strain of a breed is used everywhere for the purpose of reference – preferably animals derived from a common source. Again, the resultant comparisons may not be good for estimating genotype-environment interactions, unless this is built into the comparisons.

It is necessary, therefore, to be careful when interpreting the results on the relative merits of two breeds which are not themselves compared directly with each other, but only through the common link supplied by a third breed.

Sire circles

The use of sire circles is not a breeding scheme in the sense of selecting animals for improved productivity. It is, however, a sensible method for spreading to farmers the benefits of genetic improvement made elsewhere, and of reducing risks from inbreeding in the herds or flocks involved.

The idea was pioneered in Norway. There it involved co-operation among flock owners in the purchase and use of rams. There is no reason why the idea of ram circles should not be applied in other species of farm livestock. In the scheme, a number of males, which are considered to be superior, are held in joint ownership. Depending on the size of the flock, one ram (or more than one) is used in each of the participating flocks, but only for a year. The male is then moved to the next flock in the circle of owners for use there, also for a year, and so on. The rams are replaced before any ram can return to the flock in which he was first used. The particular merit is that it avoids inbreeding.

It would be an easy matter to extend the practice of a sire circle into a sire referencing scheme if more than on sire is used in a flock at any one time.

6.3   *Rates of progress from selection in practice*

EXAMPLE 6L   RESULTS OF A SELECTION EXPERIMENT

See Figure 6.5. It shows a representative Scottish Blackface (hill) sheep from each of two lines selected over a period of more than 20 years – one line for short cannon bone (leg) length of lambs at 8 weeks-old, the other line for long cannon bone

Fig 6.5   *Sheep of short cannon bone selection line (left) and long cannon bone line (right)* (from A. F. Purser, 1980, photograph by permission of the AFRC Roslin Research Institute, Edinburgh)

length. The experiment was carried out by the late A. F. Purser, of the (then) Animal Breeding Research Organisation, on a large, unimproved hill farm in Scotland.

One of the purposes was to establish systems of recording and selection under what were very poor environmental conditions. Cannon bone length was adjusted for body weight so that the two lines would remain roughly the same in that respect. Cannon bone length was found to have a high heritability (0.5) but very low variability and for the latter reason progress was slow at little over 0.5% per year in each direction.

By the end of the experiment:

1   *The difference between the 2 lines in cannon bone length was 25% as seen in Figure 6.5.*

2   *Significant correlated changes had occurred – the short-legged lambs were fatter at the same liveweight, as had been predicted from the much earlier work of the late (Sir) John Hammond who had shown an association between cannon bone length and carcass quality.*

3   *The long-legged females had, on average, (a) slightly more lambs at birth, (b) lower lamb losses (in spite of the larger lamb numbers), and (c) produced slightly heavier lambs by the time of slaughter.*

4   *In consequence, the lamb meat output of the long cannon bone line was, by the end of the experiment nearly 25% higher than that of the short cannon bone line.*

This experiment demonstrates, in terms of direct and correlated changes from selection, the principles of selection (chapter 5) with the added thought that it was carried out in poor farm conditions – although the trait chosen for experimental purposes is not one which would normally be chosen in practical improvement schemes.

Sadly, there is little published information on comparable results of selection programmes in practice, as distinct from the experimental situation, especially in the tropics. One can speculate as to the reasons. It is possible that some schemes do not move beyond the point of planning, or are given up after a short time. It may also be that those undertaking improvement schemes in the field are not attuned to the work involved in analysing and publishing results. Failed attempts at selection may also be forgotten about rather than publicised – and so the lessons from failure, although important, cannot be learnt.

It is often noted that there have been large annual increases in milk yield per cow (between 1.5% and 2.5%) in parts of Europe and North America where selection programmes have been applied over recent decades. In contrast, it is noted that in, for example, Africa as a whole there has been no corresponding increase. Similarly, rates of improvement in meat output per cattle beast have, over the same period, been much lower in Africa than in Europe in particular (for details see FAO

Production Yearbook 1990). However, it would be incorrect to attribute all of the improvement in Europe or North America to genetic selection – arising among other things from progeny testing in conjunction with artificial insemination schemes. Other practices have also changed over that period. Methods of management and feeding have improved and there have been changes in the breed composition of the national cattle populations. Genetic selection within breeds has played only a part.

A review by C. Smith (1984) tabulated some examples of rates of genetic change from breeding programmes practiced in the USA, New Zealand and some European countries. For growth and carcass traits, annual rates of improvement (as a percentage of the mean) were: pigs 1.80; sheep 1.2%; beef cattle (yearling weight) 0.3%. For sex-limited traits, rates of response were: pig litter size 1.5%; sheep litter size 2.9%; dairy cattle milk yield 1.0%. The high rate of improvement recorded for litter size in sheep is unexpected and in this case due to a situation akin to population screening where extreme animals are chosen. More conventional selection for litter size in sheep has been found to give lower rates (around 1%).

Nearly all the rates achieved in practice were found to be a little lower than those obtained in long-term selection experiments and these in turn slightly lower than theoretically possible. A commonly quoted example of this loss of selection efficiency relates to dairy improvement schemes, where the progress achieved generally falls below that possible. It is usually found in such cases that animals which should have been kept because of their merits for milk yield were rejected on grounds of conformation or health – thus making the selection pressure on milk yield alone effectively less intense. However, the important message from the published results is that the rates of progress achieved accumulate into very significant and economically important amounts of extra production over a period of years.

From the point of view of genetic improvement by selection, animal populations in the tropics suffer disadvantages because of a lack of recording and of precise knowledge of some of the genetic parameters which are needed if breeding schemes are to be fully effective from the start. The infrastructure needed to distribute the genetic gains from a selection programme is also often inadequate. Livestock populations in the tropics have, however, a great advantage in showing a wide range of variation in performance which is the essential pre-requisite for success.

7 Crossbreeding I: Background theory

The breeds native to particular countries or localities are often well adapted to the local conditions – climate, nutrition, disease exposure and so on. The breeds are rarely thought to be perfect in all respects and improvements in productivity are desired. Improvements in feeding and management will often, on their own, bring about an increase in the productivity of the animals. However, changing the genotype, by making changes to the breed
- will often improve productivity, and
- may make better use of any extra feed and improved management that can be provided.

One of the most rapid ways of making a genetic change is to introduce some of the characteristics of a new breed by crossing it with the indigenous breed. The most popular way is to use males of the new breed either directly, or its semen by means of artificial insemination.

Before discussing some of the practicalities it is important to understand the actual genetic consequences of such crossbreeding. This will help to answer three important questions about a crossbreeding scheme:
- How much of the blood of the new breed should be introduced?
- What proportion of a given herd or larger population can be, or should be, crossed?
- What crossbreeding strategy would optimise these two factors?

7.1 Basic genetics – a reminder

The production characteristics of animals are usually controlled by many genes acting together. To make the genetic consequences of crossbreeding easier to understand, they can be illustrated, in the first instance, by reference to single pairs of genes. The concepts were described in Chapter 3. It was seen that for any one pair of genes, the two alleles present in the cell may be the same (**homozygous**) or different (**heterozygous**). The two alleles are likely to differ in the strength of their effect on the characteristic they are helping to control. The effects of the two alleles may be **additive** (that is, the heterozygote may be half-way in its performance between the performances of the two different homozygotes), or one allele may be **totally** or **partially dominant** in its effect over the other (and the performance of the heterozygote the same as, or closer to, the performance of one of the homozygotes). When more than one pair of genes is involved, the second pair may influence the action of the first (**epistasis**).

7.2   Different breeds

Genetic differences between breeds in their outer appearance and their production characteristics have arisen because different breeds have usually been developed in different localities and by breeders with different aims. Most of the world's well-known breeds have been developed over the past two centuries – though some much more recently than that. Many breeds have also been developed from different foundation stocks originating even further back in time.

It is a basic presumption of animal breeders that – for at least a proportion of the genes carried by breeds – different breeds are likely to carry alleles (affecting the same trait) in different frequencies, possibly to be homozygous for different alleles. Crosses between different breeds are likely, therefore, to have a larger proportion of heterozygous gene combinations than the pure breeds contributing to the cross.

Usually, breeds which have been developed in very different areas, and often for different purposes, will differ more, in this genetic sense, than breeds with similar function derived from the same region. Thus, *Bos indicus* (zebu) breeds will be expected to differ more from *Bos taurus* breeds (e.g. European cattle breeds) than zebu breeds from each other. For more precise purposes, however, the genetic differences between breeds and their value in crossbreeding have to be discovered by direct comparison of the performance of the cross relative to the performance of the breeds contributing to the cross. The result cannot be predicted accurately in advance.

Characterisation of breeds in terms of their performance (chapter 2), special genetic features, health and distribution, is important as a basis for breeding programmes and conservation (chapter 11). Computer programmes have been developed to assist in the process of characterisation (Faugere and Landais 1989; Matheron and Planchenault 1992; Planchenault and Sahut 1990).

Comparing breeds

Differences in performance between breeds can be assumed to be *genetic* in origin, but only if the number of animals involved is adequate and if different breeds are compared under the same conditions. This rarely happens in developing countries, especially in the tropics and sub-tropics, and particularly when one of the breeds under consideration is an exotic.

For *valid* breed comparisons, the numbers of each breed sample must be large enough to be representative of the animals in the breed as a whole and not merely of one or two herds or flocks. For traits such as body size, wool production or milk production, 60 animals per breed might be adequate, but a much larger number than that (perhaps 200–300) would be needed to detect real differences in traits which are not highly heritable (e.g. reproductive rate). The reasons for comparing different breeds under identical conditions of feeding and management should be self-evident: if one breed is treated better than the other, the difference between them in their performance will be due, in part, to feeding and management and not only due to any genetic differences between the breeds.

7.3 Additive genetic effects – in crossbreeding

The first expectation from crossing two breeds, if the conditions ex-plained above are met, is that the performance of their progeny will be **half way** between the performances of the two parent breeds.

EXAMPLE 7A PERFORMANCE OF CROSSBRED – ADDITIVE GENE ACTION

Post-weaning growth: Breed A = 100 g/day; Breed B = 140 g/day.

Expected post-weaning growth: crossbred = 120 g/day.

7.4 Heterosis – in crossbreeding

With crossbreeding there is sometimes a bonus of **heterosis** (also called **hybrid vigour**) which is measured as the *deviation* of the crossbred pro-geny performance (reciprocal crosses pooled, section 7.5) from the *average* of the two parent breeds. It occurs to differing degrees for different traits of the animals and for different breed combinations.

Heterosis arises mainly from the action of dominance at heterozygous loci: crossbreds are expected to have more heterozygous loci than the pure breeds contributing to the cross. The occurrence of heterosis is, therefore, *directly proportional* to the degree of heterozygocity.

Epistasis also contributes to the occurrence of heterosis but follows no easy rules.

Post-weaning growth: *Breed A* = *100 g/day*
Breed B = *140 g/day*
Crossbred = *132 g/day*
Average of breeds A + B = *120 g/day*
Difference (estimate of heterosis) = *(132 – 120)*
= *12 g/day*

Sometimes, the crossbred can be better than both the breeds used for the cross. The heterosis then arises from *overdominance* whereby the heterozygote is better, in its own right, than either homozygote (chapter 3). If farmers use for crossbreeding two breeds each of which is successful in the locality (for example two different indigenous breeds), they would want the crossbred to be superior to the better of the two breeds which was used for crossing. If it were not so, it would be more sensible for farmers to replace the poorer of the two breeds by the better. This can be done directly or by grading-up (chapter 8).

The proportion of heterosis in different crosses

The expression of heterosis is always at its maximum (100%) in the first cross between two breeds (F1). Varying amounts of the heterosis are lost in later generations of crossing (because some of the heterozygocity is lost).

Table 7.1 Percentage of heterosis in different crosses*

Generations	Any heterosis (%)
P × P = F1	100
F1 × F1 = F2	50
F1 × P = B	50
B × B	37.5
F2 × F2 = F3	50

* In respect of dominance alone.
P = parental generation represented by two different breeds.
F1 = first crossbred generation.
F2 = product of mating together F1 crossbreds (of same breed combination).
B = backcrosses – a crossbred mated back to one or other of the two pure breeds involved.
Note: backcrosses must *not* be called F2, F3, etc. – this is sometimes done but leads to serious confusion.

Comparing crosses with pure breeds

In comparing the average performance of crosses with the average of the pure breeds contributing to the cross, it is essential that the different groups are kept and compared under the same conditions (Figure 7.1). This is the same rule as for comparing different breeds.

7.5 Maternal effects

For the accurate comparison of crossbred performance with purebred performance, theory requires that the cross should have been made in both of the two possible ways:

1 Females of breed A (e.g. local breed) mated to males of breed B (e.g. an exotic breed); and
2 Females of breed B mated to males of breed A.

The two variants of (genetically) the same cross are called **reciprocal crosses**. Though, on average genetically alike, they differ because the two reciprocal crosses have had a different maternal environment: one from dams of the local breed (breed A), the other from dams of the exotic (breed B).

These maternal influences can be important for the offspring at the

Fig 7.1 *To compare pure breeds and crosses accurately, the different types should be managed as a single herd – photograph shows part of such a herd in Ethiopia* (photograph by author)

time of birth and, perhaps, up to the time of weaning. The importance of the maternal effect usually becomes less after that, but sometimes never disappears completely.

The effect on the offspring arises because different maternal environments may provide the fetus and, later, the new-born animal with different advantages or disadvantages at the start of life. One breed may supply the crossbred offspring with better nutrition even before birth and may have better mothering abilities thereafter. Locally adapted dams may give the newborn a better supply of antibodies in the colostrum than dams of a recently imported or exotic breed. Differences between reciprocal crosses are due to such **maternal effects** and are not uncommonly found in practice.

Therefore, when calculating the magnitude of heterosis by comparing the crossbred performance with that of the pure breeds, the effects of the maternal environment should be removed. This is done by taking the average of the two reciprocal crosses. Only then will the comparison of crossbred performance with the average of purebred performance be strictly valid.

7.6 *Finding the magnitude of the heterosis effect*

Difficulties

In practice, the theoretically desirable conditions for estimating heterosis

Fig 7.2 *Friesian-Holstein cow*

are often difficult to fulfil, especially if the crossing in the tropics involves a local breed and an exotic breed from another country or continent.

- Animals of the exotic breed are often absent – at least as females – or present in only small numbers.
- Even when the exotic females have been imported, for example Holstein-Friesian cows, it is not uncommon that they are kept in better conditions of feeding and management than the local cows. (Thus, as stated earlier, a comparison of the performance of well-treated Friesians with the performance of poorly-treated local cows on local farms would not be a measure of genetic differences alone.)
- The requirement for the presence of crosses produced from dams of both the local breed and the exotic breed is rarely met.
- It is unlikely that imported exotic females would be available in sufficient number for crossing with bulls of the local breed (or that those responsible for the importation would be willing to use expensively procured exotic animals in that way).

Thus, for one or more reasons, one of the reciprocal crosses is likely to be missing.

The most common situation is that records can be obtained from the females of the local breed and from crosses of the local females with males (or semen from males) of the exotic breed. This shows whether:

- the cross is better in performance than the local breed,
- that level of performance is acceptable and *economically viable.*

But, as already stated, it does not provide the *correct conditions* for estimating the magnitude of heterosis. No strict conclusions, therefore, can be drawn about the relative importance of additive and non-additive genetic variation, in the commonly-found situation. Approximations are possible if maternal effects are known to be unimportant or of little importance, as in some traits of adults (see also page 112).

Methods

Knowledge of the magnitude of heterosis is critical for correct decisions about crossbreeding strategies. If the (most direct and) most accurate method of estimating heterosis (by comparing the average performance of the two pure breeds with the average of the reciprocal crosses) is not available, comparisons of other stages of crossing can be used.

Different stages of crossbreeding achieve different proportions of the total achievable heterosis (Table 7.1). For any particular trait, the maximum heterosis is always achieved in the F1 generation. Thereafter, when first crosses (F1) are mated again – either among themselves or backcrossed – some of the heterosis is inevitably lost. What that amounts to in terms of lost performance needs to be known – but the fact that such a loss of performance occurs can be used to estimate the effect of heterosis (even if only approximately).

Fl compared with F2

An easy way of estimating heterosis is to compare the performance of F2 animals with that of F1 – at the same time and under the same conditions. The F1 and F2 have each received half their genes from one of the breeds (e.g. the local) and the other half from the other breed (e.g. the exotic). In terms of their gene complement (and the additive genetic effects) they are, on average, the same – but they differ in the proportion of the genes present in the heterozygous state. Thus, while the F1 expresses all of the achievable heterosis, the F2 expresses only half.

EXAMPLE 7C EXPRESSION OF HETEROSIS IN F1 AND F2

Holstein × Zebu cross milk yield
> *F1 = 2000 litres*
> *F2 = 1600 litres*
Difference = 400 litres = 50% of the heterosis
Therefore, estimate of the whole (100%) of the heterosis effect
> *= 800 litres.*
(For a possible complication from maternal effects, see page 112.)

The use of backcrosses

Backcrosses will differ from other crosses in the proportions of the two breeds involved.

EXAMPLE 7D ESTIMATION OF HETEROSIS IN A BACKCROSS

(3/4 Holstein 1/4 Zebu)
milk yield = 1700 litres

- *Similar to the F2 (Table 7.1): the backcross manifests 50% achievable heterosis for milk yield (half that shown by the F1).*
- *Different from the F2: the backcross has an extra 25% of Holstein blood.*
- *Therefore, the extra 100 litres of milk (1700–1600 litres) yielded by the backcross is due to extra 25% of Holstein genes (25% of the additive effect).*
- *From this, it follows that the whole of the additive effect – the effect of changing from the local breed totally to the Holstein – would provide an extra 400 litres of milk (there would be no heterosis from the pure Holstein at that stage).*

Note: the figures in examples 7C and 7D are hypothetical. There could well be situations where the milk yield of backcrosses is better or worse than that of F1 or F2.

Combining information from different crosses

By comparing F1, F2 and 3/4-bred Holstein yields, using the examples 7c and 7d (see example 7e), it was deduced that the full effect of heterosis was 800 litres of milk (achievable in the F1) and the whole of the additive genetic effect from the Holstein was 400 litres.

Note: Such a relatively small additive effect from the Holstein, as in this example, would simply indicate that Holsteins are not suitable, on their own, for that particular environment. The performance of Holsteins in that tropical environment bears no relationship to the potential performance of Holsteins in their temperate countries of origin.

EXAMPLE 7E EFFECT OF HETEROSIS ON MILK YIELD IN DIFFERENT CROSSES

The milk yield of different crosses can be worked out, from the yield of only the 3 crosses (F1, F2, and 3/4 Holstein), given in examples 7c and 7d.

F1 = 50% additive effect (200 litres) + 100% heterosis effect (800 litres) = 1000 litres above the local breed.

F2 = 50% additive effect (200 litres) + 50% heterosis effect (400 litres) = 600 litres above the local breed.

3/4-bred Holstein = 75% additive effect (300 litres) + 50% heterosis effect (400 litres) = 700 litres above local breed.

1/4-bred Holstein (backcross of F1 to local breed) = 25% additive effect (100 litres) + 50% heterosis effect (400 litres) = 500 litres above the local breed.

Pure Holstein = 100% additive effect (400 litres) + 0% heterosis effect (0 litres) = 400 litres above the local breed.

Local breed: It will be noted that in examples 7c, 7d and 7e, all the findings were calculated by reference to the local breed but without specifying its actual yield. In practice, this would normally be the first thing recorded. But it can be *deduced* from the information given in the above example: the yield of the F1 was given as 2000 litres and estimated to be 1000 litres above the level of the local breed's yield – the yield of the local breed must be 1000 litres. The same could be deduced from the F2 or 3/4 Holstein.

EXAMPLE 7F ESTIMATES OF ABSOLUTE MILK YIELDS (FROM EXAMPLE 7E)

    Pure local = 1000 litres

$$1/4\text{-bred Holstein} \;=\; 1500 \; litres$$
$$F1 \;=\; 2000 \; litres$$
$$F2 \;=\; 1600 \; litres$$
$$3/4\text{-bred Holstein} \;=\; 1700 \; litres$$
$$Pure\ Holstein \;=\; 1400 \; litres.$$

It is not difficult to add estimates for other kinds of crosses using this approach.

Difficulties with estimating heterosis

In practice, all the information and calculations rarely come together so neatly, and there are also three difficulties in the above approach.

Role of maternal effects

F1 animals have purebred dams (e.g. the local cows) whilst F2 and the backcrosses have crossbred dams (F1). F1 dams may, therefore, differ in their maternal performance from the local (purebred) cows partly because of the additive genetic effect from another breed and partly because maternal performance may itself show heterosis. Such heterosis would be seen if the F1s differ in their maternal performance from the *average* maternal performance of the two breeds contributing to the cross.

If a crossbred cow has a better (or worse) maternal performance than the local breed, this will affect the offspring – particularly at birth and in early life. Therefore, comparing F1 with F2 would measure not only half the heterosis but also would include a maternal effect. This sort of effect is far less likely to be important for traits measured later in life, such as milk yield, than for traits which appear early in life, for example birth weight or early growth of their calves. It should be noted that when comparing F2 performance with that of backcrosses, it is likely (or possible to ensure) that these two types are both derived from F1 mothers so that they share the same maternal environment.

Thus, in example 7c, the 800 litre effect of heterosis obtained by comparing F1 with F2 could be an *overestimate*, but probably not seriously so because the offspring are adults by the time they give milk themselves.

Possible contribution of epistasis to heterosis

The predictions, from comparisons of F1 with F2, are based only on the role of dominance in causing heterosis. As shown, half of the useful allelic interactions (resulting from dominance of the effect of one allele over that of the other) are lost between the F1 and F2 generations. But if epistasis (interactions among genes which are not alleles to each other) also contributes to heterosis some of this is also lost between the generations (but the amount is not readily predictable). Thus, F2 performance may be worse, compared to F1, than would be expected from the action of dominance alone. In theory, this puts a larger margin of error into the kind of comparisons and predictions made above.

Statistical efficiency
The third difficulty is that estimates of additive genetic effect, heterosis and maternal effects, made by comparing different classes of crossbreds, are not efficient in a statistical sense. They require more animals than do comparisons which include both the pure breeds and the two reciprocal (F1) crosses. However, the ideal methods for the comparison may not be feasible.

Conclusions on estimating heterosis

The intention of the comparisons among the different classes of crossbreds and purebreds is to build up a picture of the relative importance of additive genetic effects and heterosis effects – the effect, in example 7E, of adding Holstein genes to a local breed and the extra effect of crossing resulting from genes combining in a special way. Also, if necessary, the calculations provide an estimate of the importance of maternal effects – provided reciprocal crosses have been produced.

In spite of the difficulty of accurately estimating the relative contribution of dominance and epistasis to the expression of heterosis, an estimate of F2 performance relative to that of the F1 is a valuable and practical piece of information. It provides guidance on whether it is useful to mate crossbred animals to each other and to create new breeds from crosses.

The exercise illustrated above (examples 7C–F) provides one *part* of the answer to the first of the questions posed at the beginning of chapter 7 'How much of the blood of the imported (e.g. exotic) breed should be used?'.

7.7 Proportion of crossbred animals in herd, flock or population

Before final decisions can be made about the best breeding strategy, another matter needs to be considered: how widely can any benefits of crossbreeding be spread in a particular population?

The reason for needing to know how much heterosis arises from crossing particular breeds, is that the answers matter for the economics of choosing the best breeding strategy.

If heterosis is *absent* or negligible (this is likely for traits such as mature body weight, fleece quality or the percentage of fat in milk), a breed combination which meets the requirements of the farmers can readily be maintained by interbreeding the crosses. If there is no heterosis, there should be no loss in productivity from such interbreeding.

If heterosis is a *large* component contributing to the merit of a first cross (such as could occur in reproductive and survival traits and milk production), the interbreeding of the crosses would lead to loss of heterosis – this could amount to a large performance loss. If so, the question to ask is: would it be good policy to continually re-create first crosses (F1) in order to benefit from the heterosis?

EXAMPLE 7G   RE-CREATING F1s FOR HETEROSIS ADVANTAGE

The F1 crosses, example 7F, had the highest yield and better than any of the other crosses, or either of the two pure breeds – the local and the Holstein.

A strategy of only producing F1 crosses carries the penalty that only a proportion of the total population can be crossbred – perhaps no more than 1/3 of total.

This is because the local animals have to be kept as purebreds both to produce crosses and to reproduce themselves.

Therefore, the total population under consideration (irrespective of whether it is a single herd or the animals of a region) will be composed of a proportion (say 1/3) of good yielders (the F1s) and a larger proportion (say 2/3) of poorer yielders (the indigenous animals).

From figures in example 7F:
1/3 females in F1 = yield 2000 litres
2/3 females local breed = yield 1000 litres
Average yield for whole population of females = 1333 litres.

An alternative way of producing crosses may maintain a larger proportion of the population in the crossbred state. Even if individual crossbred animals yield less, on average, than the F1, it is still possible that the average yield for the whole population could be higher.

EXAMPLE 7H   F2 HERD FOR HETEROSIS ADVANTAGE

From figures in example 7F:
Whole population of F2 = yield 1600 litres.
Combination of F1 and purebred local cows = yield 1333 litres
Therefore, a large herd or population of a whole region, composed of F2 animals, could produce a large quantity of extra milk.

If heterosis is a *major* component in the performance level of the first cross, it also follows that simply introducing more exotic blood will not lead to further improvements in productivity. This is because gains from extra exotic blood will not make up for loss of heterosis.

If, in a particular situation, epistasis is an important contributor to the occurrence of heterosis, a further complication arises. F2 performance, then, could well be below the level expected from the loss of 50% of the heterosis seen in the F1 (the expectation based on the loss of useful dominance alone). This has been found in some trials in the tropics when crossing local breeds with exotics for milk production, though it has not occurred in *all* trials. If epistasis is found to play a significant role in the expression of heterosis in particular circumstances it would also influence a decision whether:

- to stay with F1 production (if, for example, almost no heterosis was expressed in the F2), or
- to consider more advanced crossing systems (if perhaps the effects of epistasis on loss of heterosis were small).

A physiological explanation of heterosis (?)

The figures in the hypothetical example of milk yield of different breeds and crosses (examples 7c–h) were chosen because they reflect a common experience in the tropics: that the optimum level for introducing exotic blood is around 50%, with the other half derived from an indigenous breed.

This is explained by considering the Holstein – although most highly-developed exotic breeds could be used as examples. The Holstein breed was developed and genetically improved in temperate parts of the world specifically for high yields under conditions of plentiful nutrition, good health care and excellent management. Its appetite, metabolism and the partitioning of nutrients for its various bodily functions are all geared to high yield under those conditions. In the tropics, many of these conditions are likely to be missing. Extremes of climate, disease risks and variable levels of nutrition provide an environment for which the breed was not originally intended and with which its genetic make-up interacts unfavourably. Thus, such cattle do not perform well in the tropics in their purebred state, and may not even survive. Experience has shown, however, that a Holstein-zebu crossbred will perform better than expected from the average performance of the two parent breeds (if they had really been compared together under the ordinary local conditions).

The F1 has extra milk potential derived from the Holstein parent but it also has enough of the genes from the zebu parent for good adaptability to the local conditions. It is this genetic resistance to the stresses of the environment which allows higher milk yield to be expressed.

For traits other than milk yield and indeed for other species of animal the same principles apply, although the details may differ from case to case.

Conclusions on proportion of crosses, heterosis and performance

When heterosis is important, the breeder has to decide what proportion of the whole population to maintain as crosses. In all situations it becomes a trade-off between the proportion of crosses in the population and the yield of the crosses.

7.8 The effect of stratification

If the indigenous purebred and the crossbred type can occupy different environmental niches, the problem of choice of breeding strategy is simplified because there is a natural place for both breeds (usually the local and crosses).

For instance, an indigenous pure breed of cattle, usually a dual- or triple-purpose breed, may perform adequately for small-holders while crosses may be more relevant for larger units supplying a city population with milk. To meet this situation, the local breed has to be prolific enough to reproduce itself for use as a pure breed, whilst still allowing a proportion to be set aside for crossbreeding.

In the case of sheep or goats, the details might be somewhat different.

In many countries, large migratory flocks still exist which utilise large tracts of natural vegetation. Crossbred sheep may be too demanding in their feed requirements for such conditions. However, in areas of mixed farming, where crop residues are available, a crossbred type of sheep or goat could be the more profitable.

The crosses could be produced by mating surplus females of the local breed in the migratory flocks and selling the crossbred progeny for further use in the mixed-farm flocks (providing, incidentally, another potential source of income for the herders of the migratory flocks).

Again, it is a pre-requisite that the local breed should be sufficiently prolific to produce both purebred and crossbred progeny without risk to the survival of the pure population.

An example of stratification is found in the sheep industry of the UK. Traditionally, hill breeds are bred pure on the hills for usually 3–4 years. When older, the sheep are moved to better land for crossbreeding.

The crossbred females are in turn mated to yet other types of ram to provide the generation of lambs slaughtered for meat. This final stage of the process takes place, normally, under even better conditions. This system optimises the financial returns for each class of sheep.

8 Crossbreeding II: Systems and examples

Only some of the more common systems of crossbreeding will be described.

8.1 *Grading-up*

Grading-up is the name given to continuous backcrossing using males of one breed, or a crossbred type, first on females of the breed which it is intended to grade-up and then on the succeeding generations of crossbred offspring which arise from these matings.

Grading-up to an exotic breed

In the tropics, grading-up is most commonly thought of in terms of using males of a breed imported from another country. Grading-up can equally be carried out using one local breed to replace another by continuous backcrossing. (In countries of temperate latitudes whole populations, particularly in dairy cattle, have been changed from one breed to another by this procedure.)

EXAMPLE 8A EFFECT OF GRADING-UP A LOCAL WITH AN EXOTIC BREED

A zebu breed is crossed with the Holstein; the first crosses are mated again to the Holstein; and so for every successive generation.

The proportion of Holstein blood (Holstein genes) increases from 0.50 to 0.75 to 0.875 to 0.9375 to 0.96875 to 0.984375 (note: the large number of decimal places are given only to show the progression – in biological terms they are quite meaningless).

After about 4 generations the crossbred animals are indistinguishable, for practical purposes, from pure Holstein.

The proportion of zebu genes becomes smaller and smaller until they effectively disappear.

Grading-up a local breed with an exotic breed in the tropics would only be suitable where the pure exotic, for example the Holstein, has been shown to do well. The aim of grading-up is that every further generation of backcrossing to the exotic would perform better than the generation before it. This rarely happens in the tropics (as also illustrated by examples later in this chapter).

In practice, grading-up would often be accompanied by improvements in feeding and management. It is important to ensure that the extra production obtained in this way is economically worth-while. The extra feed and health care which might be given (or needed to sustain the production of the higher grades) should not cost more than the value of

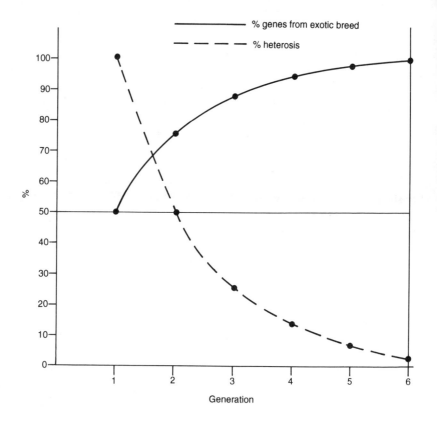

Fig 8.1   *Grading-up to an exotic breed*

The effects of grading-up a local breed by successive backcrossing to an exotic breed increases the proportion of exotic genes but the percentage of heterosis decreases in successive generations.

any extra milk or other products which might be obtained. (The problem of not confusing genetic improvements with those from nutrition and management was referred to earlier.)

The conditions for grading-up will not be right if heterosis is an important factor in the productivity of the first crosses (section 7.4). This heterosis is progressively lost in the process of grading-up until it disappears completely (Figure 8.1).

Because benefits are often seen from a first cross, this may give a false impression of the ultimate benefits of introducing a new breed in a more continuous way. Good performance from first crosses relative to the local breed must not lead blindly into grading-up. Careful investigation of the role of heterosis and the suitability of higher grades to the local conditions is necessary first.

Grading-up to 50% or 75% exotic

Continuous backcrossing, starting with a local breed, to crossbred males, which are either 50% or 75% exotic, will give animals at the end-point of the process, after 4 or 5 generations, that have the appropriate proportion (50% or 75%) of exotic blood. Use of such crossbred males is a more sensible approach when there is prior evidence that the *optimum* proportion of exotic blood is either 50% or 75% (as the case may be) for the conditions under which the animals have to perform. There is a further benefit from this procedure in terms of obtaining and retaining some heterosis.

With the repeated use of F1 males, first on females of the local breed and thereafter on successive generations of crosses, the proportion of the total heterosis in the offspring is *one half* – the same as for F2.

If 75% exotic males are used, initially on local females and thereafter on the successive generations of crosses, the proportion of heterosis expressed in the offspring starts at 75%, in the first generation, and then declines to and stays at approximately 40%.

The crossbred males needed for this purpose can themselves be produced by mating *selected* local females with exotic males. Thus, some advantage can be derived from choosing superior local females as the dams of the crossbred males used for this grading-up. (It would also be possible – although unusual in practice – to use exotic females as the dams and selected local males as the sires of the crossbred males.)

8.2 Continuous production of F1s

Two pure breeds are used repeatedly to produce only first crosses (F1s). In terms of the additive genetic effects, the F1 is half-way between the performance levels of the two parent breeds contributing to the cross. However, the F1 generation displays the whole of any heterosis which is achievable as a result of crossing two breeds.

Consideration will need to be given to the relative importance of the additive genetic and heterosis effects, and to the proportion of the population which can be maintained as crosses (section 7.7). This information will determine whether continuous production of F1 is a good policy.

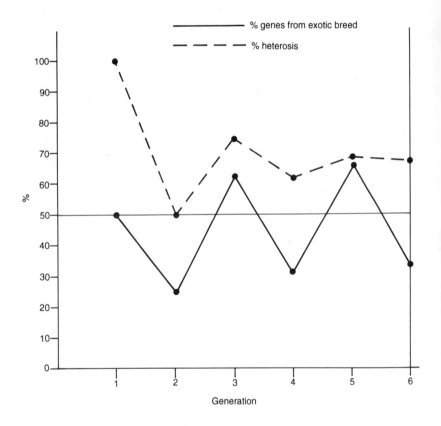

Fig 8.2   *Rotational crossbreeding of two breeds*

The effects of rotational crossbreeding with 2 breeds, a local and an exotic, are shown on the proportion of exotic genes and of heterosis in successive generations (using males of the exotic breed to produce the first cross, males of the local breed for the second cross, etc.).

8.3 *Rotational crossing*

Two or more breeds are used in rotation. The males are always purebred – one or other of the breeds involved. First one breed is used, then the next and so on until the sequence is complete. It then starts over again with the first breed used. The females to which the males are mated are purebred only for the first generation of mating. Crossbred females are used in subsequent generations.

Rotation of two breeds

Also called crisscrossing, the system of using two breeds in rotation produces the whole of the potential heterosis in the first generation, an F1, half in the second (first backcross) and variable proportions, between 2/3 and 3/4, in subsequent generations (Figure 8.2). Because after the first generation all the females are crossbred, there is also the benefit of maternal heterosis for traits where this is important.

Table 8.1 Rotational crossing using two breeds

Generation	Parents		Offspring	Genes (% from)		Heterosis (approx. %)
	Female	Male		L	E	
1	L	E	LE	50	50	100
2	LE	L	L/LE	75	25	50
3	L/LE	E	E/(L/LE)	37	63	75
4	E/(L/LE)	L	L/[E/(L/LE)]	69	31	62
5	etc.	E	etc.	34	66	63
etc.						

L = local breed; E = exotic breed.

As seen in Table 8.1, the breed of sire used last always provides half the genes of the next generation. After the first generation the proportion of that breed's blood (the breed of the sire used last) is greater than half because of the previous use of that breed. The performance of the crossbred offspring thus fluctuates between high and low points depending on the variable proportion of each breed contributing to each generation.

If the two breeds differ markedly in performance – as they might if one is an indigenous tropical breed and the other a temperate-region exotic breed – it could lead to an unwelcome fluctuation in yield among the generations. If the two breeds are similar in performance, successive generations of crosses would also be similar in performance, whilst benefiting from approximately 2/3 of the achievable heterosis. Some purebred females may have to continue to be bred pure to provide the males needed for the system. But the rest of the females, the vast majority, could be crossbred after the first generation. If purchased semen were used with artificial insemination, instead of live males, the whole of the female population could be crossbred after the first generation.

Rotation of three breeds

The males used are always pure and used in rotation, following the same principle as for crisscrossing.

Table 8.2 Rotational crossing using three breeds

Generation	Parents		Offspring	Genes (% from)			Heterosis* (%)
	Female	Male		L	A	B	
1	L	A	LA	50	50	–	100
2	LA	B	B/LA	25	25	50	50
3	B/LA	L	L/(B/LA)	63	12	25	75
4	L/(B/LA)	A	A/[L/(B/LA)]	32	56	12	62
5	etc.	B	etc.	16	28	56	32
6	etc.	L	etc.	58	14	28	84

* assumes heterosis (approximate figures) is only generated by the combination of local with exotic genes and not by the two exotics (A and B) with each other.
L = local breed; A and B = exotic breeds.

As seen in Table 8.2, the breed of the sire used last contributes half the genes of the progeny – in addition to what is present of that breed from earlier use. After many generations the contributions of the three breeds – to any one generation of offspring – settle down to the ratio of approximately 4: 2: 1, where the 4 parts come from the breed of the sire used last, and the 2 parts from the breed of the sire used immediately before that.

As far as heterosis is concerned, the proportion achieved in each generation is variable – especially if it is assumed that the two exotic breeds do not generate heterosis with each other but only in combination with the local breed.

It is likely, depending on the magnitude of both the additive and the non-additive genetic effects, that performance will be rather variable from one generation to the next. It is also important to keep good records of the breed of sire used on each occasion. It is unlikely that the breed composition of an animal will be apparent simply from looking at it – records are needed to determine which male should be used next on the crossbred female.

8.4 New breed formation (synthetics)

New breeds formed from two or more constituent breeds have, corporately, been called **synthetic breeds** by geneticists for many years now. New breeds can be synthesised from crosses combining breeds in virtually any proportion – first crosses or various backcrosses of two breeds, or combinations of more than two breeds.

The desired breed combination has to be determined – on the basis of the early performance of crosses and from an estimate of the importance of heterosis. The desired crossbred type is then inter-bred for several generations. Selection can and should be used alongside that process to improve the production characteristics.

Table 8.3 Examples of synthetic breeds

Livestock	Breed	Composition
Dairy cattle	Australian Milking Zebu	0.33 Sahiwal + Red Sindi/0.67 Jersey
	Jamaica Hope	0.8 Jersey/0.05 Friesian/0.15 Sahiwal
	Karen Swiss	Brown Swiss/Sahiwal
Beef cattle	Bonsmara	0.62 Afrikander/0.19 Hereford + 0.19 Shorthorn
	Chabray	0.62 Charolais/0.38 Brahman
	Santa Gertrudis	0.62 Shorthorn/0.38 Brahman
	Renitole (of Madagascar)	3-breed cross Malagasy zebu + Limousin + Afrikander
Sheep	Dorper	Dorset Horn/Blackhead Persian
	Katahdin	Virgin Island/Wiltshire Horn + Suffolk
	Perendale	Cheviot/New Zealand Romney
Goats	Boer	Local with European, Angora and Indian blood

Several of the well-established pure breeds of all species were originally developed from breeding stock derived from more than one breed or source.

Sheep breeds have, particularly many examples of this type: the Columbia breed derived from the American Rambouillet crossed with the Lincoln Longwool, and the even older Corriedale breed from the Merino with infusions of Lincoln and/or Leicester. Few people would now consider the long-established British Down breeds of sheep, used for meat production, as anything other than pure breeds (for example the Suffolk, Hampshire Down, Oxford Down and others) – and rightly so after a century or more of pure breeding. However, their origins owe much to the Southdown breed which was crossed with other native types in order to improve them. Also, many old-established breeds, particularly those with relatively small or declining populations, have had infusions from other breeds from time to time in order to improve performance or counteract inbreeding.

It is useful to note that a large number of breeds with national identities as part of their names were derived from common foundations. Selection with different aims in different countries and infusions of some local blood produced different strains from that single foundation.

EXAMPLE 8B ORIGINS OF NATIONAL HERDS

Many of the present strains of Friesian or Holstein cattle were originally derived from Dutch cattle.

Among pig breeds, there are many national variants of Landrace and Large White (also called Yorkshire).

The Landraces share German origins (itself infused with Large White) often through intermediate development of Landraces in other countries.

The various Large White (Yorkshire) types trace back to pigs from England.

Thus, the mixing of breeds to form new breeds and their further change into new types by selection has a long history – dating back long before the name 'synthetic' was coined for this purpose. For present purposes, the production of synthetics is put forward as an alternative approach to other forms of crossbreeding, or to straight selection within an indigenous breed in the tropics.

Characteristics of a synthetic

The breed composition of a synthetic will determine its initial performance. The additive genetic effects will reflect the proportions of each contributing breed. In addition, some heterosis is retained in these new breeds, depending on the degree of heterozygocity created by the combination of different breeds.

When two breeds (A and B) are combined, the proportion of heterosis retained in the synthetic depends on the starting point for interbreeding of the cross. This is shown in Table 8.4 (one of the breeds might be a local breed the other an exotic).

Table 8.4 Percentage of heterosis in synthetic breeds

Genes (% from)		Achievable heterosis retained in the synthetic (%)
Breed A	Breed B	
12.5	87.5	22
25	75	37
37.5	62.5	47
50	50	50

Larger proportions of breed A (62.5% and above) have exactly the same effect on heterosis as the equivalent proportions of breed B.

When more than two breeds are combined, the picture in respect of heterosis becomes more complicated. Local (*Bos indicus*) breeds in the tropics may generate substantial heterosis when mated to exotics (*Bos taurus*) but not when crossed with each other. Similarly, exotic breeds may produce little or no hybrid vigour when mated to each other.

If three breeds are used which generate heterosis from all their combinations, more than half of the achievable heterosis is retained. When heterosis arises from only two of the combinations (the exotic with the local), only a little above one third of the total achievable heterosis is retained in the 3-breed synthetic.

Non-allelic interactions (epistasis) can contribute to heterosis, as explained earlier (page 105). More of this epistasis is lost in the creation of synthetic breeds than in the rotational crossing using the same combination of breeds.

The potentially large advantage of the synthetic, apart from the opportunities for selection to improve the type, is the expectation of a more uniform level of production compared to the fluctuating levels, from one generation to the other, of rotational crossing.

8.5 Monitoring progress of crossbreeding strategy

It is important to monitor the progress of a crossbreeding scheme, just as it is in the case of selection. It involves contemporary comparisons of the various stages of the process, so that changes due to breeding are not confounded with (mixed up with) changes in the environment.

It is not unusual, over a period of time, for the system of feeding and management to change alongside the changes of breed type. A proper comparison can be achieved if, for example, the pure breeds are present at the same time as the F1 generation, or at least overlap in time, and have their performance recorded under the same conditions. Similarly, there should be overlaps between F1 and F2 and/or 3/4-bred or 1/4-bred; and 3/4-bred with 1/4-bred, etc.

It is also useful to have a **control** population against which to monitor progress from rotational crossing or the development of a new breed. Such a control population is the only secure way of distinguishing between genetic gains from the breeding policy and other changes which take place over time. Such comparisons are important:

- For evaluating the cost-effectiveness of a breeding scheme.
- For deciding whether changes to the breeding programme are necessary.

8.6 *Examples of crossbreeding results*

The purpose of providing examples of the results of crossbreeding is:
- To illustrate the principles of crossbreeding.
- To show that actual results may be more difficult to interpret because they do not always conform neatly to the theoretical pattern.

Sometimes good effects of crossbreeding on one trait are counteracted by less good effects on other traits. This also applies in the comparison of breeds – provided they are compared under the same conditions.

The examples used here are *not* intended as models of particular crossbreeding schemes to be followed. The principles involved in crossbreeding provide general guide-lines, but only specific trials will show which breeds and breed combinations suit particular circumstances.

Dairy cattle crossbreeding

Crossbreeding has been widely used to improve milk yield of cows in the tropics and there are many published results. However, a majority do not allow calculation of the importance of heterosis because both the parental breeds contributing to a cross are not present as cows, or there is no contemporary presence of several different generations of crosses (e.g. F1 alongside F2).

The results of one trial in India where a full set of comparisons were made (Table 8.5) show that:
- *Crossing the Brown Swiss with the Sahiwal led to a substantial improvement in milk production and that all the crossbred types gave significantly more milk than either the Sahiwal or the Brown Swiss.*
- *In practice, calculation of the additive genetic effects and of the heterosis effects from the different types of crosses only provides general guidance. (The results from the different crosses do not fall into a 'neat' pattern.)*

126

Table 8.5 Age at first calving and milk yields of Brown Swiss (BS) × Sahiwal crosses at NDRI, Karnal, India (number of lactations in brackets)

Breed group	Age at first calving (days)	Milk yield, first lactation, 305-day (kg)
Sahiwal	1211	1704 (471)
25% BS	930	3039 (10)
50% BS F1	908	3160 (98)
50% BS F2	1020	2579 (35)
75% BS	930	2670 (34)
Brown Swiss	1077	2355 (83)

Source: Taneja and Chawla (1978)

Calculation of additive genetic effects and heterosis
Assuming that all the different types were treated alike and kept under the same conditions), the following information in respect of the proportion of the additive genetic effects (A) and heterosis (H) is obtained from each of the different types:

Sahiwal (parent breed 1)   = m (base line yield)
Brown Swiss (parent breed 2) = m + 100% A
F1   = m +   50% A + 100% H
F2   = m +   50% A + 50% H
25% Brown Swiss   = m +   25% A + 50% H
75% Brown Swiss   = m +   75% A + 50% H

1   *Additive genetic effects – by simple difference:*
• *from the difference between the pure breeds (+651 kg)*
• *75%BS – F2 (+ 364 kg)*
• *F2 – 25%BS (– 1840 kg)*
• *75%BS – 25%BS (– 738 kg)*
(The average yield of the 25%BS group is based on only 10 lactations – see conclusion 2 below.)
2   *Magnitude of heterosis – difference between F1 and the average of the parental breeds (+ 1131 kg) and the F1–F2 difference (+ 1162 kg).*
Note that the differences between some of the classes provide estimates of only a proportion of the additive and heterosis effects. The figures given in brackets have been multiplied, where necessary, the give an estimate for the whole effect.

Conclusions (from Table 8.5)
1   The two estimates of the magnitude of heterosis are in surprisingly good agreement with each other.
2   The estimates of the size of the additive effect of Brown Swiss genes is far less good. This is because the 25%BS class had an unexpectedly high milk yield; taken at face value, this complicates the comparisons by suggesting a negative effect of BS blood because the 25%BS yield is

127

higher than that of the F2 and of the 75%BS groups, both of which have more BS blood than the 25%BS group – yet the same expected 50% of heterosis. However, the 25%BS average is based on only 10 lactations whilst all the other values are based on very much larger numbers. It would right, therefore, to pay little attention to comparisons involving the 25%BS group.

3 All the data can be combined simultaneously into a single estimate of the additive genetic and the heterosis effects, while also taking account of the number of lactations in each group. This leads to estimates of introducing the Brown Swiss into the Sahiwal of + 626 kg for the additive effect and + 1150 kg for the heterosis.

4 Irrespective of the method of calculation, the results from this trial in India suggest that the effect of heterosis was more important than the additive effect from the Brown Swiss. However, the milk yield from the F2, relative to the F1, was close to what would be predicted from the loss of 50% of the possible heterosis (in some other trials a relatively poorer F2 performance has been reported). Therefore, in this particular example from India, the creation of a synthetic breed could reasonably be considered since there are no apparent complications from epistasis. A decision would then depend on the proportion of F1 cows which can be maintained in the population relative to a population which is largely crossbred but showing a lower level of heterosis than the F1 cows.

Effects of the crossing on traits other than milk yield is also important. As shown in Table 8.5, age at first calving was earlier in the crosses than in the pure breeds, but the F2 was, as expected, poorer than the F1. The milk yield results were presented in terms of 305-day yield. That involved adjusting the records to the basis of lactations of that length even if, in reality, lactations were shorter. Such a procedure can be misleading if some breed types have many short lactations whilst others have long ones. Having short lactations could be associated with the breed type. However, in the particular example here, this complication did not appear to arise because the breeds did not vary greatly in average lactation length.

A second example, see Table 8.6, is taken from a study by Syrstad (1990) based on results of 54 published crossing experiments involving several different indigenous and several different exotic breeds. The purpose was to summarise the effect of increasing proportions of exotic blood and to find a genetic model to explain the results.

- *The results (Table 8.6) show that there was an increase in milk yield up to the F1 stage and that further additions of* Bos taurus *genes led to little further improvement.*
- *Cunningham and Syrstad (1987) estimated (from 46 of the 54 data sets) that the additive genetic effect of the* Bos taurus *genes was a little over 1000 kg of milk and the heterosis effect about 450 kg.*

128

Table 8.6 Lactation milk yield of cows in the tropics with varying proportions of *Bos taurus* blood

Bos taurus blood (%)	0	12.5	25	37.5	50 (F1)	62.5	75	87.5	100	50 (F2)
Milk yield (kg)	1052	1371	1310	1553	2039	1984	2091	2086	2162	1523
SE (±)	39	170	158	100	28	75	45	84	50	92

Source: Syrstad (1990)
Summary of 54 sets of data (weighted least squares means and standard errors). All groups except F2 were sired by purebred bulls.

- *The yield from the F2 class was, however, significantly lower than that of F1, in fact about 300 kg less than predicted if dominance effects alone were responsible for the observed heterosis.*
- *Epistasis was considered by Syrstad (1990) also to be involved, but to an extent which could not be accurately estimated.*

A cautionary note is required. There must be a possibility that in this and other studies the yield of the pure exotics and high grades (75% exotic and over) is overestimated relative to the yield of other classes, particularly the indigenous breeds and low grades (25% or less exotic). This would arise (as stated several times in this book) if exotics and high grades were treated better than the others.

Cow performance is only one aspect of herd productivity. Another relates to losses of animals from disease or death and the length of time it is possible to retain cows in the herd.

A review of the subject by L. P. de Vaccaro (1990), showed that

- on almost every criterion of survival, European cattle in the tropics, world-wide, did less well than their crosses with zebu;
- in terms of herd life, European cattle averaged only 2.9 lactations whilst crosses with 0–25%, 50–62.5% and 75–87.5% *Bos taurus* blood achieved 3.4, 6.6 and 3.9 lactations respectively.

The evidence, though not strictly interpretable in terms of heterosis, yet strongly suggests that heterosis is likely to be important for survival and herd life of cows in the tropics.

Vaccaro further showed that

- on average, purebred imported European cattle produced, in the tropics, only 0.74 heifer replacements (females alive at first calving) in their whole lifetime, and locally born purebred European cattle produced 0.98.

This suggests that purebred European cattle in the tropics will not, on average, replace themselves. While this is certainly not true in some of the more favoured herds or countries in these regions, there are other areas of the tropics where such cattle can only be maintained by continuous importation.

Table 8.7   Breed and crossbred means (reciprocal crosses pooled) for various traits of cattle in Zambia

Breed	Weight, 2.5 years (kg)	Weaning %	Weaning weight (kg)	
			Calf	per Cow*
Afrikander (AF)	339	51.4	174	89.4
Angoni (AN)	285	65.1	149	97.0
Barotse (BA)	311	53.8	163	87.6
Boran (BO)	329	64.5	169	109.0
Average of crosses				
AN × BA	302	61.8	158	97.6
AN × BO	312	69.1	160	110.6
BA × BO	340	65.9	173	114.0

Adapted from Thorpe, Cruikshank and Thompson (1980, 1981)
* Calf weaning weight multiplied by weaning percentage.

The results of crossbreeding from trials in Zambia (Table 8.7) provide a comparison of breeds kept under the same conditions and also provide some estimates of heterosis (F1 with reciprocal crosses pooled and compared with the average of the pure breeds contributing to each cross). The Afrikander breed was not involved in the crossing and is presented only for interest, showing that although it was the heaviest of the breeds here, with the heaviest calves, the calf production, in terms of weaning percentage, made it less desirable.

The amount of heterosis generated was not great in this trial, ranging from barely 1% (AN × BO) weaning weight per calf to over 11% (BA × BO weaning percentage). There is, as indicated earlier, a general expectation (usually derived from crosses of *Bos indicus* with *Bos taurus* breeds) that crosses of breeds which come from different origins will generate more heterosis than crosses of breeds with more of their origins in common. The Barotse (as well as the Afrikander) is a sanga breed, while both the Boran and the Angoni are zebu breeds (but all are of the *Bos indicus* type). The highest estimates of heterosis came from the Barotsi × Boran cross, in line with this expectation, but the Barotsi × Angoni cross gave, surprisingly, the lowest heterosis.

This example shows how important it is to do actual trials to test breeds and breed combinations for each set of circumstances and not to base an improvement programme on theoretical expectations alone.

Sheep crossbreeding

Reproductive capacity is often one of the main limitations on meat output from sheep. An example has been chosen to illustrate the effect of crossbreeding on these traits.

Table 8.8 Traits of two breeds and their cross in Morocco in two different seasons (parity >3)

Traits	Season 1 mated Oct./Nov.			Season 2 mated May/June		
	D'man	Sardi	F1*	D'man	Sardi	F1
Mating weight (kg)	28	45	35	29	45	34
Fertility (%)	95	95	98	89	62	95
Litter size	2.5	1.3	1.9	2.1	1.2	2.0
Total weight of lambs at 60 days per ewe mated (kg)	18	19	22	18	12	21

Adapted from Bradford and Berger (1988)
*Original data adjusted for age.

Results from Morocco on crossbreeding indigenous breeds of sheep (Table 8.8) illustrate that the crossing of two indigenous breeds can give a significant advantage in overall productivity because of heterosis. Also, they illustrate that the way in which heterosis arises can vary and that data have to be examined carefully.

Body weight of crosses (Table 8.8) showed no heterosis. In respect of fertility, it appears that a much smaller proportion of ewes of the Sardi breed conceived during mating season 1 than in season 2. Because the other breeds were not affected in that way, this demonstrates a genotype-environment interaction. It has also led to the manifestation of heterosis in fertility in season 2, because the relative failure of the Sardi to breed has reduced the average of the purebreds well below that of the cross-breds. In season 1, the three types of sheep were rather similar in fertility. Heterosis was not evident for litter size in season 1 but did arise in season 2.

When all aspects of performance, including lamb mortality and growth are combined into a single measure of performance, the crossbreds, in both seasons, produced more weight of lamb per ewe mated than either of the pure breeds.

The fact that the crossbred (in this example) performed better in important respects than either of the parental breeds, the D'man and the Sardi, represents, in genetic terms, overdominance (chapters 3 and 7).

131

Fig 8.3 *Angora goats*

Crossbreeding of goats

The great majority of goats in the tropics are kept for meat and milk but
fibre production (mohair, in particular, and cashmere at higher altitudes) has increasing importance in specific areas. Fibre traits do not
normally show much heterosis from crossbreeding, but breed differences in performance are important. Improvement of mohair production in Pakistan provides a useful illustration of successful grading-up.

Mohair is prized for long and very fine fibres. The results of continuous backcrossing for mohair production (Table 8.9) show that first

**Table 8.9 Grading-up fibre length and fibre diameter of local goats by
backcrossing to Angora goat, in Pakistan**

Breed group	Angora (%)	Fibre length (mm)	Fibre diameter (μm)	True Mohair (%)
Angora (A)	100	79.5	20.2	91
A × local (F1)	50	34.5	50.0	47
A × F1 (BC1)	75	57.1	25.3	85
A × BC1 (BC2)	87	77.5	20.2	90

Source: Ahmad and Kahn (1984)

132

crosses of the Angora with local goats produced much shorter and coarser fibres than the pure Angora. The first backcross improved both traits and the second backcross, resulting in goats which are 7/8 Angora, was very close in fibre length and fineness to the pure Angora.

This illustrates, for a trait expected to show little or no heterosis, that, within 3 generations, good mohair production can be built up from local goats crossed with imported Angora bucks.

Crossbreeding of pigs

Table 8.10   Litter size and weight at 21 days in various imported breeds and their crosses (reciprocal crosses pooled), in Korea

Imported breeds and their crosses	Number per litter	Heterosis (%)	Weight (kg)	Heterosis (%)
Landrace (L)	8.35		47.0	
Yorkshire (Y)	7.98		43.0	
Duroc (D)	6.94		38.0	
Hampshire (H)	7.04		39.2	
L × Y	8.36	2.4	46.6	3.6
L × D	8.30	8.6	46.1	8.5
L × H	8.04	4.5	46.6	8.1
Y × D	7.87	5.5	41.9	3.5
Y × H	8.06	7.3	45.0	9.5

Adapted from results of Park and Kim (1982) restricted to breeds and crosses represented by reciprocal crosses.
Heterosis expressed as a percentage of the average of the pure breeds contributing to each cross.

Some results from 5 pure breeds and their first crosses imported to Korea and maintained on a swine breeding farm are given in Table 8.10. They show that heterosis has made a useful, though small, contribution to production but that the estimates vary from one breed combination to another.

The average heterosis for litter size in these comparisons (but also including some not shown) was computed by the authors to be 1.4% at birth, 6.5% at 21 days and 6.9% at weaning at 30 days. The corresponding estimates of heterosis were 7.6% for litter weight at 21 days and 2.1% for individual piglet weight at 30 days. Table 8.10 shows, however, that for the two traits shown, different breed combinations varied in this respect.

9 Inbreeding

Inbreeding, the mating of related animals, is nearly always harmful in its effects. In most societies, marriage of close relatives is forbidden, so the bad effects to humans must be known. Yet it is not unusual for farmers to believe that inbreeding will fix good points of their livestock and improve them. This is far more often wrong than right. Inbreeding can also occur by chance. It is important therefore to examine the subject in some detail, even though it is *not* recommended as a general breeding practice for farm livestock.

9.1 *Occurrence of inbreeding*

Inbreeding occurs when two individuals which share an ancestor, or ancestors, are mated to each other. Mating animals to each other that are related by descent can be deliberate, by choice of the breeder, or accidental. Even animals mated together at random may have an ancestor in common. In a population of finite size, inbreeding to some degree can never be totally avoided – it can only be minimised. The chances of two animals sharing a common ancestor, especially a recent ancestor, are greater in a small population (where the number of ancestors is relatively small) than in a large population. Inbreeding is, therefore, more likely to occur in small, self-contained herds or flocks than in larger populations. For the same reason, inbreeding may arise at an undesirable rate when numbers in the parental generation are deliberately restricted, as in selection – especially because of the small number of males used as sires.

Inbreeding varies
- in magnitude (page 136) and
- in the rate at which it proceeds from one generation to the next.

The amount of inbreeding arising from a particular mating of two individuals depends on how closely they are related. In practice, the most recent ancestors of animals mated to each other have the greatest impact on inbreeding.

Inbreeding increases more if two animals sharing a father are mated to each other than if the animals share only a grandfather.

Sharing a grandfather causes more inbreeding than having only a great-grandfather in common, and so on.

Inbreeding accumulates in a population. In the long-term even the presence of more distant links in the ancestry of the two parents of an animal will lead to inbreeding.

Small numbers of males

Inbreeding can arise quite readily through the breeding practices in many countries. For example, it is not uncommon when importing bulls (or their semen) to a tropical country to restrict the importation to a relatively small sample of animals. These bulls are then used to serve a relatively large population of cows. It is very important in such an importation to make sure that the bulls (or some of them) are not related to each other. If the bulls are related through sharing recent ancestors, the chances of inbreeding are greatly increased when offspring of these bulls are, in turn, mated to each other.

If a relatively small number of bulls, or their semen, are used for several years, there is also a high probability that related animals will be mated to each other as soon as the first batch of daughters become old enough to be bred – perhaps after 2 or 3 years. Since records of matings in the form of pedigrees are rarely kept it is quite possible that some daughters of the imported bulls may be mated to their own father. It is even more likely that a cow might be mated, by chance, to a half-brother (a son of the same father as the cow but with a different mother).

It also appears to be the practice in sheep flocks and goat herds in some countries for a valued ram (or buck) to be followed by use, in the same flock, of a son of that animal. This practice leads to inbreeding – perhaps quite rapid inbreeding.

9.2   *Effect of inbreeding*

Inbreeding depression

Inbreeding is nearly always associated with an average **deterioration in performance** (inbreeding depression). For this reason, inbreeding should be avoided as far as possible (with the one exception of testing for genetic defects, page 146). The depression in performance is greatest for traits for which crossbreeding is most often beneficial; for example

135

for traits associated with reproduction and survival. However, inbreeding is also likely, on average, to lead to

- reduced growth rate and smaller body size (even at maturity)
- lower milk yield.

Inbreeding causes a **loss of heterozygocity**. The inbreeding depression in performance occurs because, when heterozygocity is lost, there is also a corresponding loss of any benefits associated with the action of dominance (in gene action) at heterozygous loci. Inbreeding is, in this sense, the direct converse of crossbreeding and the inbreeding depression the converse of heterosis. However, it is difficult to make any strict comparison between the magnitude of inbreeding depression and the magnitude of heterosis. The reason is that inbreeding depression occurs within a population, for example a breed, while heterosis is normally associated with breed (or strain) crosses.

Calculation of inbreeding

The degree (or amount) of inbreeding is expressed by a **coefficient F**, which indicates the proportion of heterozygocity that is lost relative to a given starting point. The inbreeding coefficient is always a measure relative to some assumed or specified starting point, some generations back, for which inbreeding is assumed to be zero (F = 0). The inbreeding coefficient is therefore a measure of *relative*, and not of absolute, *loss of heterozygocity*.

Table 9.1 Some common inbreeding coefficients of individuals

Relationship of parents of individual	Inbreeding coefficient (F)*
Full sibs	0.25
Parent and offspring	0.25
Half-sibs	0.125
Related by 2 grand-parents in common	0.0625
Related by 1 grand-parent in common	0.0313

* Assumes that for common ancestor F = 0.
Note   The figures can be interpreted as showing the proportion of heterozygocity (e.g. 25%, 12.5%, etc.) which has been lost relative to the population at the start.

Inbreeding calculated by tracing back the ancestry of particular animals can only be carried out if the pedigrees of the animals are recorded. Even then, ancestry cannot usually be traced back for many generations. However, as shown in Table 9.1, the contribution to inbreeding of ancestors 3 or 4 generations back is far less than the contribution from ancestors 1 or 2 generations ago.

136

As heterozygocity declines, homozygocity increases. Animals that are unrelated to each other are more likely to carry different alleles, for particular traits, than animals which are more closely related. Inbreeding reduces the likelihood, therefore, that two different alleles for the trait will come together from sperm and egg. Put the other way around: if the individuals mated together in a population are more closely related than average, it increases the proportion of individuals in the offspring generation which carry two identical alleles at any one locus. The inbreeding coefficient can be regarded as the probability of increasing homozygocity occurring.

The inbreeding coefficient (F) of an animal is calculated by the following formula:

$$F = \text{the sum of } \{1/2^n (1 + F_A)\}$$

n = number of individuals in each path linking the parents of the animal to a common ancestor (counting the parents, the common ancestor and every other individual in the path).

F_A = the inbreeding coefficient of a common ancestor (when this is not known it is taken as being zero).

The inbreeding coefficient can vary from 0 (non-inbred) to 1.0 (all of the initial heterozygocity lost, now totally homozygous). Alternately, it can be expressed as a percentage from 0% to 100%. See examples 9B and 9C.

EXAMPLE 9B CALCULATION OF F: COMMON ANCESTOR OF THE ANIMAL (X) IS A GRANDFATHER

The dam and the sire of the animal had the same father (D).

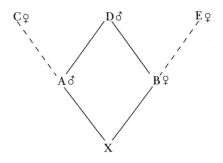

Inbreeding coefficient of animal X = $F_{(X)}$:
    Path ADB,
    n = 3
    $F_{(X)} = 1/2^3 = 0.125$

EXAMPLE 9c CALCULATION OF F: SEVERAL PATHWAYS JOINING ANCESTORS TO
THE ANIMAL (X) THROUGH BOTH ITS PARENTS

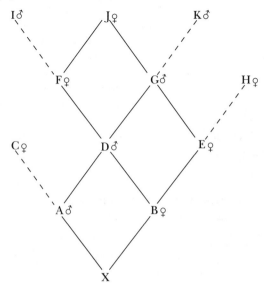

Table 9.2 Data from pathways for calculation of F

Path	n	$1/2^n$	Inbreeding of common ancestor	Contribution to $F_{(X)}$
ADB	3	0.125	0.125	0.1406*
ADGEB	5	0.0313	0	0.0313
ADFJGEB	7	0.0078	0	0.0078
			$F_{(X)}$	0.1797

* $0.125 \times (1 + 0.125) = 0.1406$

Common ancestor D is 'inbred' because his parents F and G are half sibs. (Note also that D and E are half sibs and cause some inbreeding in B, one of the parents of X, but this fact produces no further relationship link between A and B and therefore does not contribute to the inbreeding coefficient of X.)

NOTE   No individual must appear twice in the same path. (A fuller description is given by Falconer 1989.)

9.3 Inbreeding in small populations

When a population of animals is relatively small, inbreeding can occur by chance – when inbreeding is neither deliberately avoided or attempted. Under these circumstances the extent to which inbreeding increases in the population can be roughly estimated from the number of males used as sires and the number of females to which they are mated.

The formula for the rate of inbreeding, provided mating is at random, is:

Rate of inbreeding = 1/8Nm + 1/8Nf
Nm = number of males used as parents.
Nf = number of females used as parents.

When the number of females is large, the rate at which inbreeding increases in the population is almost entirely due to the number of males.

EXAMPLE 9D CALCULATION OF RATE OF INBREEDING

If 5 bulls are used with 400 cows, then:

$1/8Nm = 1/(8 \times 5) = 1/40 = 0.025$ (or 2.5%)
$1/8Nf = 1/(8 \times 400) = 1/3200 = 0.0003$ (or 0.03%)

Total rate of inbreeding (per generation)
$= 1/8Nm + 1/8Nf$
$= 0.0253$ or (2.53%)

Most of the inbreeding in the example 9D is due to the small number of sires used. Even if a very much larger number of females had been used, the rate of inbreeding would not fall below 0.025 (2.5%) per generation – the amount determined by the number of males alone. This demonstrates the point that:

• the number of males used in a population should be kept large if the harmful effects of inbreeding are to be avoided.

This is especially important if a new breed is imported which might ultimately be wanted in large numbers in its own right or, following crossbreeding, to be included in synthetic breed formation. (It should be noted that the above formula will underestimate the probable rate of inbreeding if mating is not at random.)

EXAMPLE 9E EFFECT OF INBREEDING ON 4 TRAITS IN SHEEP

1 *Survival of the ewe over a period of 3 years (from the time she was first mated) (Figure 9.1.)*
2 *The number of lambs born per ewe giving birth to lambs (Figure 9.2.)*
3 *Lamb survival from birth to weaning (Figure 9.3.)*
4 *The total weight of lamb weaned (at 15 weeks old) per ewe mated (Figure 9.4).*

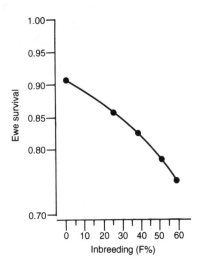

Fig 9.1 *Effect of rapid inbreeding on ewe survival from first mating (at 1.5 years-old) to 4th lambing (5 years-old)* (after Wiener, Lee and Woolliams, 1992)

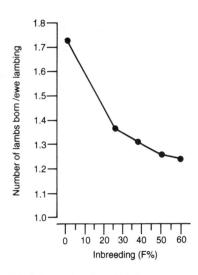

Fig 9.2 *Effect of rapid inbreeding on number of lambs born per ewe lambing* (after Wiener, Lee and Woolliams, 1992)

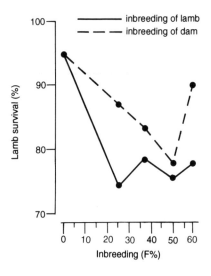

Fig 9.3 *Effect of rapid inbreeding on lamb survival from birth to weaning (15 weeks-old) by inbreeding of lamb and that of its dam* (estimated from data of Wiener, Woolliams and Macleod, 1983)

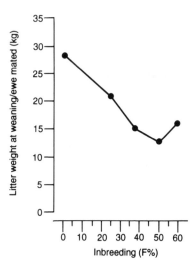

Fig 9.4 *Effect of rapid inbreeding on litter weight at weaning per ewe mated* (update of data of Wiener and Woolliams, 1982)

Traits 1, 2, and 3 are components of the reproductive process. Trait 4 is a composite trait which incorporates the success of mating, the number of eggs shed by the ewe and fertilised, survival of the embryo(s) to birth and of the lamb(s) to weaning, and growth of each lamb to weaning.

Inbreeding in this particular trial with hill breeds of sheep in Scotland, was carried out by mating parents to their offspring for successive generations. This produces a very rapid rate of inbreeding. The trial was undertaken to study the consequences of such inbreeding and not as a means of sheep improvement. At each of the five stages of inbreeding involved (coefficients of 0, 0.25, 0.375, 0.50 and 0.59) the levels of performance of the different traits were recorded (Figures 9.1–4).

It can be seen that inbreeding had a large effect on performance:

1 *Ewe survival declined from about 92% to 74%.*
2 *Number of lambs born per ewe (which had a lamb) declined from 1.73 to 1.26.*
3 *Lamb survival (when related to the inbreeding of the lamb) was reduced from about 95% to about 74% after one generation of inbreeding and then did not change very much.*

In consequence of these harmful effects and similar effects on other characteristics including growth,

4 *the total weight of lamb weaned for each ewe originally mated decreased from 28 kg to about 13 kg – a dramatic reduction due to inbreeding.*

The visible sign of inbreeding depression is also illustrated in Figure 9.5 which shows two animals from example 9E. They are of the same age and breed and they have the same father, but different mothers. The larger lamb is non-inbred because the sire and dam were not related, but the smaller one is highly inbred (inbreeding coefficient F = 50%).

It was possible in the study which produced these results (example 9E) to look at the effects of the inbreeding of the individual separately from the effects of the inbreeding of its dam (because each dam gave birth to offspring of various level of inbreeding – depending of the dam's relationship to the ram to which she was mated).

In general, for traits which are normally under maternal influence, such as lamb survival or growth of the lamb, inbreeding of the dam also had a large effect. This is shown for lamb survival by the broken line in Figure 9.3: survival declined continuously over 3 generations of inbreeding (F = 50%) of the dam and after that apparently improved (but the last point on the graph is based on fewer animals and is less reliable than the others). This effect of inbreeding of the dam is additional to the effect of inbreeding of the individual, the lamb itself.

There are many examples of the effects of inbreeding in the published literature, much of it based on relatively small amounts of inbreeding which often occurred incidentally to selection or some other restriction on the number of ancestors (such as a relatively small population which

Fig 9.5 *Effect of inbreeding on sheep (left) F = 50%, (right) non-inbred* (from Wiener and Hayter, 1974, photograph by courtesy of the AFRC Roslin Research Institute, Edinburgh)

The photograph is of 2 female sheep of 15 months-old. Both had the same father but different mothers. One mating produced a lamb which had an inbreeding coefficient F = 50% (left). The other mating produced a lamb which was non-inbred (right).

is closed to outside blood). The effects of inbreeding are then often reported as a change in performance per 1% increase in the inbreeding coefficient. Almost without exception, the results of such studies show a deterioration in the performance of the animals as a result of the inbreeding. This deterioration has the consequence of slowing the rate of genetic progress which might otherwise be expected from selection.

It may also be of interest to speculate that with very slow rates of inbreeding – the inevitable consequence of having populations of finite size – other processes may counteract these otherwise harmful effects. Thus, mutations, even though they occur rarely, will help to maintain variability in the genetic make-up of whole populations and counteract the effects of very slow inbreeding. Also, the genetic phenomenon of crossing-over and recombination (page 31) may counteract deleterious effects of inbreeding, if the inbreeding occurs slowly enough.

9.4 Past and present uses of inbreeding

Although inbreeding has harmful effects and should be avoided by livestock breeders, it is still of interest to note situations where inbreed-

142

ing has been used in the past and where it may still have a role to play. These examples are not strictly relevant to the livestock breeding practices of individual farmers in the tropics – but the crop plants and animals which have resulted from procedures that include inbreeding do have importance.

Genetic theory – application to inbreeding

As seen in chapter 4, segregation of alleles occurs when gametes are formed. For heterozygous loci, each gamete carries only one of the two possible alleles. When male and female gametes join at fertilisation, different combinations arise. For example, individuals which are Aa at a particular locus produce gametes which contain either A or a in equal proportion. When eggs and sperm of these types combine at random, individuals arise which are genotypically AA, Aa, or aa (in the ratio of 1:2:1).

One genotype in the parental generation has been replaced by three in the offspring generation – two of these being homozygous. Provided the three genotypes survive equally well, nothing new has been added to or taken away from the population in terms of alleles – but the alleles have recombined in new ways.

If, in the next generation, mating is no longer at random but takes place within each of the three genotypes (AA, Aa, aa) the two homozygous types are reproduced as such, and the heterozygous type is again dispersed into three genotypes. In total, the proportion of homozygous types increases, relative to the population at the start. Also, whilst the three genotypes are associated with different performance, the animals within each of the types are similar to each other.

This illustration, because it is restricted to a single locus with two alleles, is a great over-simplification of what happens in practice. This situation can, however, be imagined as repeated over a multitude of pairs of alleles that make up the genotypes of individual animals.

- Mating *heterozygotes* to each other leads to a dispersal of genotypes and an associated increase in *variability*.
- Mating of like *homozygotes* to each other leads to *genetic uniformity*.

Inbreeding can be considered as analogous to that simplified situation. When closely related animals are mated to each other they will tend to have alleles in common and the proportion of homozygotes will increase. If there are many such closely related groups in a population of animals, the effect of inbreeding is to create genetic uniformity within the groups but genetic differences between the groups. The distinct groups are usually referred to as **lines**. As inbreeding proceeds, variability in performance *within* lines therefore declines and that *between* lines increases.

The hope of those who practise inbreeding, other than those engaged in producing hybrids (page 145), is that a proportion of lines will carry all the 'best' alleles for performance in the homozygous state. If this were the case the superior performance should be retained by the offspring because these lines, being homozygous for the good effects, will breed true. The fallacy in this argument is that there are too many genes associated with performance for all the 'good' alleles to be present at the same time in a single line.

The second difficulty confronting the creation of superior pure-breeding, homozygous, lines is that, in some circumstances, the fact of being heterozygous can be an advantage in its own right (overdominance, chapter 3) and not only because some 'good' alleles are dominant to some 'poor' ones. A number of experiments have shown that:

• heterozygous animals tend to be better buffered against environmental stress of various types,
• conversely, homozygotes appear to be less well buffered.

Early breed development

Some of the master breeders of the past two centuries, from whom originated some of the famous breeds of today, decided that it was possible to fix the good points of particularly desirable animals by mating them to close relatives (inbreeding) or by increasing the proportion of blood from a particular sire (line-breeding). Many of the traits to which these breeders paid attention were readily visible to the eye and highly heritable – traits such as coat colour, size and shape of the animal, presence and shape of horns, the setting of the udder and size of teats on a cow and fleece type. These are traits for which heterozygocity itself provides little advantage, but which gave the breeds, developed in this way, their distinctive looks.

Perhaps the breeders did not consider the opposite outcome: that inbreeding might also concentrate the 'bad' points of animals. The breeders did not have the benefit of the rules of heredity to help them predict the outcome of their breeding practices (Mendel's Laws of Inheritance used after 1901). However, the depression caused by in-breeding relates to performance traits. A depression in performance would have been noticed only if the performance of the animals had been carefully measured and recorded.

It is also possible that the success of early breeders, and the high reputation which the best of them enjoyed in their day, was reinforced by good performance of their bulls and rams when used in other herds and flocks. If these sires were indeed inbred they would, when mated to unrelated animals have offspring that were not only non-inbred but might also show some hybrid vigour.

Many of the early attempts at creating new breeds failed and the breeds became extinct. The successes, on the other hand, became some of the well-known breeds of today. Most of these breeds, though true breeding (homozygous) and distinct for a number of their external characteristics, are heterozygous for many of their production-related traits.

It is the external characteristics which normally make breeds easily identifiable and distinct. However, many of the breeds which look quite distinct are not nearly as distinct in their performance characters such as fertility, litter size, milk yield and growth rate.

Producing inbred lines for crossing

When it was discovered that heterozygocity could bring benefits in terms of plant or animal performance, some breeders decided to make practical use of that. Apart from devising crossbreeding systems to make use of existing breeds, plant breeders and some breeding companies also started to develop highly inbred lines with the intention of crossing the lines (production of hybrids). Provided the lines themselves were sufficiently homozygous – easy to achieve with plants but difficult with animals – the crosses of the lines would be highly heterozygous and display hybrid vigour for important characteristics.

This process led to **hybrid corn** production and has led to similar developments in the **poultry** industry. These successes were made possible because the species concerned are very fertile to begin with. When reproduction (seed number or number of eggs) is reduced by inbreeding there is still enough fertility and prolificacy left to maintain many of the inbred lines. (In any case, when done on a large commercial scale, by large international companies, the loss of inbred lines and the poor performance of many of the lines simply becomes one of the costs involved in the hybrid production – which is a very profitable business.) In this commercial procedure, only a few of the many inbred lines created go into the final production of hybrids. The lines are selected for their own performance and, most importantly, for their ability to combine successfully with other lines in order to maximise hybrid vigour.

For species having few offspring to start with, such as cattle, sheep, goats and pigs (relative to poultry or plant crops), the inbreeding process leads to too great a loss of lines and too great a loss of performance to be sustainable (as shown in example 9E). The idea of creating large numbers of inbred lines and then testing selected lines for their combining ability is not practicable with low-reproducing livestock – at least with the technology available up to the present.

Changes may take place if advances in reproductive physiology allow a harvest of hundreds of eggs from each animal, with fertilisation of these eggs *in vitro* (outside the body, such as in a test tube). At present, this is not possible outside a laboratory situation. For the foreseeable future, for the large livestock species, any benefits from crossing inbred lines, in terms of hybrid vigour, are too small relative to the costs of producing the inbred lines.

Testing for recessive defects

It is sometimes advisable to test a male for the possibility that he is carrying a harmful genetic defect before he is widely used on large numbers of females. This situation might arise for bulls which are intended to be used widely through artificial insemination. The testing is worthwhile only if the harmful defect is already known to occur fairly often in the population. In such a case it could be important to start to eliminate the defect from the population – or at least reduce the frequency of its occurrence. The first step is to prevent the defect from being spread further through the use of a bull carrying the allele for the defect.

The problem arises particularly with defects which are controlled by a pair of alleles at a single locus and where the allele responsible for the defect is recessive to its normal allele.

EXAMPLE 9F SOME RECESSIVE GENETIC DEFECTS

1 *Congenital dropsy (an accumulation of fluid in tissues).*
2 *Some forms of dwarfism.*
3 *Bulldog calves (so called because of the shape of their heads).*
4 *Atresia ani (closed colon).*
   Many hereditary defects are lethal at birth or lead to the death of the animal soon thereafter.

There are a number of possible tests for detecting whether a bull is a carrier of a particular defect or not. Such a bull is heterozygous at the locus concerned: carries one copy of the recessive allele as well as the normal, dominant allele which suppresses the action of the recessive. Such a bull, a carrier bull, will pass this recessive allele to half his offspring. If, by chance this creates a homozygous offspring that individual will display the defect. (This will happen if the recessive allele from the bull is paired up with the corresponding recessive from a female to which the bull was mated.)

Tests generally depend on mating the bull to females whose genotype, in respect of the defect, is known. This is not easy to arrange – hence a test which does not depend on knowing the genotype of the females is described in example 9G.

*Mate the bull to a number of his daughters. If the bull carries the defect but does
not show it, he is expected to pass the allele responsible to 50% of his daughters.*

*If he is then mated to his own daughters, the expectation is that, on average,
12.5% of them will have offspring which are homozygotes for the recessive and
show the defect.*

*23 normal offspring from such matings (and no defectives) would provide
reasonable confidence that the bull was not a carrier, but it would not prove it.
There is still 1 chance in 20 that this number of normal offspring, without the
occurrence of a defective, fails to detect the bull as a carrier.*

*By contrast, the occurrence of even a single calf with the defect would prove that
the bull was a carrier of the defect.*

9.5 Avoiding inbreeding

Strictly speaking, to avoid inbreeding implies minimising inbreeding by
taking appropriate measures:
- Avoid mating closely related animals.
- Keep the number in the parental generation (the number of sires and
  dams) as large as possible.

In a selection programme, which restricts the parents to the best of
those available, there has to be a compromise between the increased
progress that can be achieved by selecting more intensely – restricting
the parents, especially the sires, to ever smaller numbers – and the harm
this can do through inbreeding depression.
- When importing males (or females) for purposes of crossbreeding, it
  is important to ensure that the animals imported are not themselves
  closely related to each other and that the numbers imported are large
  enough to avoid matings of relatives later in the breeding programme.
- Do not use sires in a herd or flock after their own daughters have
  reached mating age.
  Co-operative schemes, such as sire circles (chapter 6), will help to
  avoid inbreeding by restricting the use of any one sire in a herd or
  flock to only a short period of time.
- Do not replace a sire in a single-sire herd or flock by a son or other
  close relative (and in herds using more than one sire, take care that
  sons, if kept, are not mated to their relatives).
- If substantial inbreeding has arisen in a herd or flock (or larger
  population) it can be counteracted by using, as sires, males from
  another, unrelated population.
- Animals which are substantially inbred, because their parents were
  closely related, should themselves be mated to unrelated animals.

10 Special considerations for species and traits

The preceding chapters were concerned mainly with the principles of genetic improvement which apply to all species and all characteristics of livestock. Practical breeding plans, however, have to be adapted to particular circumstances. These depend on where the animals are kept, how they are kept and in what numbers, on the attributes and functions of each class of livestock and on the needs of the farmer. It is not possible in a book such as this to provide specific breeding plans for the many combinations of these different circumstances. It is, however, possible to review the main factors associated with these circumstances and to show how they affect thinking about genetic improvement.

Other books in this series *The Tropical Agriculturalist* provide important background for different livestock species and types. Some of the factors associated with livestock production in the tropics are discussed below to show their importance to decisions about breeding programmes.

10.1 *The environment*

Climate

The vast area generally referred to as the tropics, including the subtropics, is not a uniform whole. It comprises several ecological zones from the extremes of hot, humid, tsetse fly-infested areas to hot and very arid areas. The principal livestock areas are those varying from the semi-arid to the humid (but free of tsetse fly) and the relatively temperate highlands. Each of these environments needs a different emphasis for livestock improvement. Local adaptation, including an ability to cope with disease and heat stress, will be of prime importance in some areas. Crossbreeding with exotic stock may not be successful in all environments. When selection within a local breed is the best option, the environment will influence the priorities to give to different traits.

Culture

Cultural and religious differences affect animal production and determine what are acceptable animal products. This, in turn influences what is required from animal breeding. Keeping animals as a financial reserve, for social or religious reasons, or as a form of food insurance against crop failure, is not uncommon. These uses of livestock will not be considered here as far as breeding plans are concerned.

It is important to realise that keeping animals for the sake of their numbers alone is a barrier to improvement. It prevents the culling of unproductive animals and reduces the amount of feed available to each animal and is not likely to be sustainable in the long term.

Exchanging cattle between families, for example as part of marriage settlements, will encourage the mating together of unrelated (or less related) stock and thus counteract inbreeding.

Type of herd or flock

Pastoralists
The herds and flocks of pastoralists (involved to varying degrees in migration) usually have reasonably large numbers of animals. Pastoralists nearly always have to rely entirely on the available natural herbage as feed for their livestock and it is difficult to improve on those conditions. Cattle are usually kept for milk with meat as a secondary product. Sheep and goats are usually kept for meat, although milk can be an important secondary product. Selection within such populations would be a sensible policy as it is less likely than a crossbreeding programme to produce much larger animals which would need more food and better conditions than can be provided.

Co-operation of several flock owners would be a big advantage for progress from selection and should also reduce the risks of inbreeding.

Milk yield would be an obvious selection criterion where milk is the main product. For sheep and goats larger body size, which is positively related to total meat output, would be a relatively simple trait for selection – but it has the disadvantage that larger animals may not be wanted because they need more feed. The other traits of likely importance, such as regularity of breeding and good mothering ability of the females, as well as good survival of the young, are hard to change genetically – especially without good records and perseverance over many years. The motivation for selection over a long period of time may also not be present if the herders are not in fact the owners of the animals.

If crossbreeding is really wanted by the herders, first consideration should be given to the possibility of crossing among different local breeds and not to crossing with exotics.

In some areas, migration of flocks and herds is restricted to certain times of the year, for example to exploit summer pastures at higher elevations or to follow the aftermath of crop harvests. This might alternate with more static periods for the animals in the neighbourhood of the villages. Such periodic migration can increase the overall feed supply to the animals. The extent to which it makes supplementary feed available, widens the opportunities for crossbreeding.

Small-holder
The herds and flocks of farmers and small-holders in settled areas with crop production are most often small. The availability of crop by-products and other feed makes it reasonable to think of crossbreeding to produce more productive animals, even though they need more feed. Milk, meat and work are all requirements from cattle and water buffalo in the cropping areas while goats and sheep are also kept for both meat and milk – though the emphasis given to each product will differ from place to place.

Deciding on the objectives for genetic improvement is, therefore, more difficult in this type of herd or flock than in those where a single animal product provides the principal source of income. Males used for crossbreeding can often be shared between several herds or flocks or made available in the village. Such co-operative crossbreeding could very sensibly lead to the formation of a new breed suited to the area. Whilst sharing of males is good genetic advice, it can, however, lead to the spread of sexually transmitted diseases through the male.

When individual flocks and herds are small, selection by the individual farmer would be ineffective except to eliminate unproductive animals. Co-operation among farmers and keeping some records would be essential. An option for genetically improving the existing local breed would be to have central breeding studs to supply sires or semen.

Specialist units
Individual herds or flocks specialise in the production of milk, meat or eggs for large urban populations and, sometimes, for export. The total number of such units may be small relative to the vast livestock population of the tropics but the opportunities for genetic improvement are considerable. Most of these units have relatively large numbers of animals. Management is often better and feed supply less erratic than in some other situations.

Both selection and crossbreeding can be appropriate options. In these herds and flocks, one aspect of production, milk or meat, is usually much more important than the other. This simplifies the breeding objectives.

10.2 *Species*

Cattle

Three attributes of cattle in the tropics are of particular concern to the animal breeder:

* The large majority of cattle are used for both meat and milk; many are used for transport and, in areas of cropping, also for field work.
* Cattle have a low reproductive rate.
* The unit cost of each animal is high relative to the smaller species.
  See also *Dairying* by Richard W. Matthewman in *The Tropical Agriculturalist* series.

Multi-purpose use

The multi-purpose use of cattle makes it particularly important to pay most attention to the trait which will give the greatest improvement in economic terms. This applies to improvement schemes both by selection and by crossbreeding. In many situations economic priority will be to increase milk production, but this can differ greatly between herds and areas. Even in the relatively large herds supplying milk to urban populations, meat cannot be ignored because the males go for slaughter and the cows are eaten at the end of their milk-producing life. In ranch-type cattle production, which is mostly concerned with meat output, milk often provides a useful source of food for the owners, workers and families.

A small-holder with one or two cows, for whom milk, work and meat are all likely to be important, has, perhaps, the greatest problem deciding which criteria to use for culling cows and which type of bull to use for breeding.

Reproductive rate

The low reproductive rate of cattle arises because, in the tropics, cows are often 4 years-old (sometimes older) before they have their first calf. Thereafter, the interval between calves is long (1–2 years). They have normally only one calf at a time and calf mortality is often high. A low reproductive rate makes genetic improvement of cattle slow – yet the financial and social rewards of such improvements can be high in the long term.

It would be useful to increase reproductive rate in some way. Genetic means are not likely to succeed because of the low heritability of reproductive rate and several of its components and low variability (for example twins are very rare). Management and feeding can be used to improve reproduction and reduce calf losses and such improvements can then aid the process of selection by increasing the number of animals among which it is possible to select. An increased reproductive rate will also reduce the interval between generations and thus speed up genetic change. But it is important that better management does not make the environment in which any selection is done atypical of the conditions of the farms in which the improved animals have to live (chapter 6).

Artificially induced multiple ovulation followed by embryo transfer (MOET) is a way of increasing reproductive rate. It has led to new, efficient, selection schemes when used with nucleus herds (chapter 6). It has particular advantages in countries where the infrastructure does not exist for other national schemes of genetic improvement – but MOET needs a high level of technical efficiency to make it successful.

The benefits from improved female reproductive rate also apply to the multiplication stage of an improvement programme – the stage at which bulls are produced for distribution to farmers. A breeding station supplying bulls to farmers will be more effective and profitable if reproductive rate is good and mortality low. There can also be problems of reproduction at the 'receiving end' – the farmer's herd – such as arise from poor detection of oestrus which, in turn, leads to failure in conception and consequent delays in calving.

Male reproductive rate also affects genetic improvement. Semen collection and its subsequent use in AI greatly increases selection intensity because fewer bulls are needed. However, AI in not easy to implement in many countries. The age at which bulls in the tropics are first used is often quite high – this increases the generation interval, to the detriment of breeding progress. Improvements in the methods of rearing of bulls reduce the age at which sexual maturity is reached.

Successful use of AI also needs a good system of distribution for the semen at the right time for the needs of the cows and successful heat detection of the females.

Poor reproductive rate affects not only the progress that can be made in a selection programme but also slows down the speed at which crossbreeding can proceed. It also reduces the farmer's income through lost milk output and lost calf production.

Unit costs

The high unit costs of cattle compared with most other farm species makes investment in breeding programmes more suitable for a national or co-operative enterprise than for individual herds. This applies to:

- Selection schemes aimed at improving indigenous breeds.
- Crossbreeding which requires provision of bulls or semen, or actual crossbred animals, to farmers.

Sometimes, such bulls or crossbreds come from large units which sustain their breeding programmes either alone or in co-operation with each other. At other times, it will involve setting up special breeding

Fig 10.1 *Buffalypso, a strain of buffalo developed for meat production in Trinidad* (photograph by A. J. Smith)

stations for the purpose. Ranching-type operations for meat production are large enough in some countries to have their own, self-contained breeding programmes.

Domestic buffalo

The Swamp buffalo of many countries of SE Asia is used primarily for work. Milk yield is generally low, but milk is taken from these animals. Meat is obtained when the animals are slaughtered after several years as draught animals (a minimum age at which slaughter is permitted is laid down in many countries).

The River buffalo of India, Pakistan and elsewhere is also a draught animal, but its higher milk yield makes it important for milk production too. A few herds exist mainly for milk production. In Trinidad, the buffalypso meat strain has also been developed especially for meat production – with a quality of meat similar to that of beef cattle (Figure 10.1).

The two types of buffalo, swamp and river, differ in the number of their chromosomes. However, they interbreed, but there is conflicting evidence whether chromosome number adversely affects the fertility of the crossbreds.

The reproductive rate of buffalo is no better than that of cattle in the tropics even though, on average, buffaloes live longer. Genetic improvement is made difficult by the fact that most farmers own only one or two animals for crop cultivation, particularly rice, and for transport. However, in some places the buffalo has been recorded as giving more milk and surviving better than cattle under similar conditions. A few genetic improvement schemes for buffalo are on record, especially in relation to milk yield, but perhaps there is a greater potential for genetic improvement than so far attempted. The possibility of improving indigenous buffalo by importing an improved strain, for example a good milking strain, from another country is not readily available to breeders. Veterinary regulations (chapter 1) would be likely to prevent such importation, because most of the countries with buffalo have the disease problems which these regulations are meant to keep out.

Most of the points considered in relation to genetic improvement of cattle apply also to domestic buffalo. An additional consideration is the inherently poor heat tolerance of the buffalo. This is important because it affects the buffalo's capacity for work (draught page 165). To an extent, the buffalo meets its needs for cooling by wallowing in water. Where the opportunities for this, or other means of cooling, are not readily available, the suitability of the buffalo for work is more limited.

Yak

The yak is not an animal of the tropics; quite the reverse – it is remarkable for its tolerance of cold and high altitudes. Yak, however, deserve a mention here because the yak represents precisely the circumstances primarily considered in this book – animals which are used for a number of different purposes and which are kept for prolonged periods of the year (long winters in this case) in conditions of severe shortage of feed and other environmental hardship – and in situations where much of the infrastructure for modern animal breeding is absent.

Milk (mostly for making cheese and butter) provides the most important source of income, followed by income from meat from the slaughter of surplus animals (mostly mature castrate males). However, the use of yak as pack animals, especially in migrant herds, is still important as is the use of the hides and the hair, and the dung for fuel.

The yak (*Bos grunniens*) is a long-haired bovine which is important in the high mountainous regions of central Asia, particularly SW China including the Tibetan plateau, Nepal, Bhutan and parts of Mongolia and northern India. There are several types or breeds of yak differing in size, productivity and coat colour. It is difficult to be certain, because of a shortage of information, just how much of the difference in performance between the types is inherent and how much is due to different conditions in the different areas in which these types are largely found. However, differences between the types of yak have also been recorded

154

Fig 10.2   *Yak, in terraced farmland, Nepal*

when they are kept together, suggesting that at least some of the differences are genetic.

Yak have a different number of chromosomes from other domestic cattle, but will interbreed with them. The crossbred females are fertile, but the crossbred males are sterile. This immediately rules out any yak-cattle crossbreeding system involving the use of crossbred males as sires – as in grading-up to a crossbred level (chapter 8) or to produce a new (synthetic) breed.

Crosses of yak with other cattle give substantially more milk than pure yak and they also grow faster, leading to better meat output – but the extent of such superiority and the success of this policy depends on the breed of cattle used for crossing and on the availability of feed to meet the extra production. It is not proven whether such crosses are as tolerant as yak of the harsh environmental conditions and feed deprivation. Neither is it certain what proportion of the apparent superiority of yak-cattle crosses can be strictly attributed to heterosis – because the strict conditions for the necessary comparisons (chapter 7) have not generally been met.

The normal reproductive rate of yak is also low, with females not generally calving before 3–4 years-old and because perhaps a majority of yak produce a calf only every second year. This can be attributed to the severe nutritional deprivation during the long winters which leads to severe loss of body condition, particularly of pregnant females. These are then thought to require an extra year to recover before conceiving again. The low reproductive rate further limits the opportunities for crossbreeding with cattle, based on producing F1 calves in a sustainable way.

For these various reasons, this author does not share the enthusiasm of some others for yak-cattle crossbreeding, except in restricted circumstances where the benefits can be considerable.

Crossing among the existing different yak breeds may, however, offer opportunities for improvement which do not seem to have been sufficiently widely explored as yet.

Selection of the yak for improved performance is clearly an option worth considering. Some of the conditions for it are favourable. Individual owners of yak may have only small- or medium-sized herds, but many such herds are often found together or in close proximity. This creates effectively large herds which should provide the ideal circumstances for genetic selection, provided the different families owning the yak can agree on objectives.

The best opportunities would exist for choosing superior milking females as the dams of males, and for the selection of males on their own growth performance. Difficulties arise from:
• an absence of record keeping
• from the problem of defining objectives (although milk provides most income)
• knowing what part of the superiority of any animal is due to a better genotype and how much is due to better nutrition.

Also, yak herd owners, as in the tropics, tend to retain animals for the sake of owning larger numbers: this is detrimental to the availability of adequate grazing and especially to the possibility of conserving forage for use in winter – and it is done at the cost of keeping unproductive animals. However, given that some of these problems can be overcome, at least in part, and particularly in the more settled communities, selection may well offer the best option for genetic improvement of the yak in the long term.

Sheep

Hair sheep, which predominate in the tropics, are kept primarily for meat production. None-the-less, milk from sheep has considerable importance in some areas, for example the Middle East, and there are some specialised milk breeds. It is also likely that milk from sheep, in general, has some importance for consumption by the herders and their families. Wool (and hair) production from sheep is seldom the primary aim in African and Asian countries (apart from South Africa) but it is a useful by-product and the basis of some village industry. For more detail on the attributes of sheep and on sheep production in the tropics, see the book *Sheep* in this series by Ruth M. Gatenby.

Most commonly, genetic improvement of sheep is intended to increase meat output. This provides the main economic return, except in breeds specialised for milk or fibre production. The main limitations on meat output from sheep are often low litter size, high lamb mortality and infrequent reproduction and not the growth rate – at least in the first instance. Selection can change body size and growth more easily than reproduction and survival. Crossbreeding can be used to change body size rapidly. Also, some highly prolific breeds exist which pass higher prolificacy to the cross. However, management and feeding need to be improved to meet any extra performance so obtained.

A significant trade exists in live sheep for slaughter on festive occasions. Size, and perhaps fatness, are the main criteria for profit from selling these sheep. Crossbreeding is an easy solution to obtaining larger-framed animals than found in some of the local breeds. Crossing with sheep breeds from temperate regions is not recommended unless feeding and management and climate are not limiting. Nearly all temperate breeds are wool breeds and these do not do well in humid tropics, although they can be considered at higher altitudes and in semi-arid areas. Sheep readily lay down fat when nutrition is adequate. This is regarded as a disadvantage in many western countries but not in most others. Selection against fat, so much part of the improvement programmes with sheep in, for example, Europe and New Zealand, is not a usual requirement in the tropics or the Near and Middle East.

Selection will generally be more appropriate to the larger pastoralist flocks and crossbreeding to the smaller farm flocks associated with crop production. However, co-operative breeding schemes will assist both selection and crossbreeding in all situations. Because the cost of individual sheep is relatively small, it should be easier to persuade flock owners to co-operate either in forming a group-breeding scheme or in exchanging rams to avoid inbreeding.

Goats

There are many similarities with sheep in terms of the attributes of goats in so far as they relate to breeding practices. In many countries of Africa and Asia goats are kept mainly for meat, but milk, surplus to that taken by the kid, is used by the family. In other countries goats are kept first for milk, but with meat an important second product. In general, the reproductive rate of goats is less limiting on breed improvement than it is for sheep. Twins are more common, and very common in some breeds and some areas.

Specialist fibre production from goats is increasingly important in some countries – but normally at higher altitudes. Mohair comes from the Angora goat and involves the whole fleece. Angora bucks can be used to grade-up local breeds for mohair production (see Table 8.9). Cashmere only comes from the undercoat or down of the fleece. The down protects the goat from very severe cold during winter, as in those parts of the world where these goats originated. The down is often harvested by combing it out from below the hairy outer fleece of the animal, but it is also separated from the hair by machine when the fleeces are shorn. Cashmere fibres occur in very small quantities in the fleeces of most goats. The largest quantities come from the cashmere goats of China, Mongolia and Siberia. Crossbreeding and grading-up of local breeds can be used to increase the output of cashmere.

A very large proportion of all goats in the tropics are kept by small-holders and in some countries the landless. Especially where milk production is the main aim, the numbers kept by each farmer is small, perhaps only a single female to provide milk for family use and cash from the sale of surplus milk and kids. In a number of improvement programmes bucks are shared or made available on a village basis. This affects the type of improvement programme which it is sensible to consider. With goats for meat production, numbers kept are often larger and farmers tend to retain their own bucks.

If selection is the sensible option, because the local breed seems capable of worthwhile improvement, it is best done centrally. The improved bucks can then be distributed to villages. As in all schemes where breeding stock is shared, it is important to make sure that it is not also a way of spreading disease.

Crossbreeding offers a simple opportunity for the genetic improvement of goats. For milk production, several of the European and middle-eastern breeds (strains of Nubian) have been surprisingly successful in crosses with local breeds in tropical conditions, provided feeding and management are appropriate – including shelter where necessary. Supply of crossbred (F1) bucks of this type on a village basis can be the best first step.

Goats are also kept by pastoralists, often alongside sheep. The same considerations apply as for sheep.

Hides from goats can have a special value but are not usually the main object of genetic improvement.

Pigs

Pigs are kept for meat. Pig production is very important in Asia but of only minor importance in most parts of Africa. Some pigs kept in villages are allowed to forage. Most pigs, however, are kept under more controlled conditions and fed cereal and other concentrates as a part or the whole of their diet. Pigs and pig production in the tropics are the subjects of another book in this series, *Pigs* by David H. Holness.

It is of particular relevance to the animal breeder that pig production in different parts of the world has much in common, because of intensive production methods – often with housing and in large, specialised units. This, in turn, has led to exotic breeds being incorporated into the pig production of tropical and sub-tropical regions. The aims of faster and more feed-efficient growth, with leaner carcasses, have also been widely adopted because of the relatively large proportion of the total production costs which are due to the feed costs.

Pigs, relative to the species discussed earlier, have a larger litter size and farrow at more frequent intervals. This increases the potential rate of genetic improvement above that expected from the other species. It has also encouraged the supply of improved breeding stock from international breeding companies. An undesirable side-effect of large litter size is that it can lead to accidental inbreeding in future generations. This would happen if too many piglets are kept from each of a small number of sows. To reduce inbreeding, it is better to keep a smaller number of piglets from each of a larger number of sows, but a compromise is needed between progress from selection and inbreeding depression (chapters 6 and 9).

Some Chinese breeds of pig produce numbers of piglets far greater than those of other breeds. This has created widespread interest among animal breeders and has led to breeding programmes which attempt to transfer the high litter size to other breeds without the associated fatness of these Chinese breeds.

Rabbits

Rabbits are kept primarily for meat – apart from Angora rabbits for fibre. Because of the small amount of money needed to start rabbit production it is increasingly recommended as an additional source of food and income for families in many parts of the world. Production systems and different breeds of rabbit are described by D. Fielding in another book of *The Tropical Agriculturalist* series.

The relatively high litter size of rabbits (6–10 offspring) and the frequency with which they can reproduce, provides an ideal opportunity for selecting superior does and bucks even from among the small numbers which most rabbit owners keep. The criteria for selection should usually be larger body size consistent with an adequate litter size. Care is needed to avoid inbreeding if rabbit keepers retain their own male and female breeding replacements.

Several meat breeds are available for crossbreeding. The Californian White and the New Zealand White breeds are widely used.

Poultry

The relatively large number of eggs produced by hens (compared to the number of offspring in other species) should, in theory, allow successful selection for the commercial attributes of hens because selection pressure can be high. The commercial attributes include egg number and egg size, but also body size, because the birds are also important for meat. In practice, long-term breeding plans are often difficult to organise because the large majority of poultry in the tropics are kept as scavengers and ownership is often by the landless. Shared use of cockerels of imported dual-purpose (egg and meat) breeds, many of which are successful in the tropics, offers the most direct opportunity for genetic improvement. The book on poultry in the tropics by Anthony J. Smith, provides details of breeds and management systems, see *Poultry* in *The Tropical Agriculturalist* series.

Large units for either egg production or for meat (broilers) generally use specialised, single purpose, breeds or, increasingly, strains marketed by a few large international breeding companies. Selection based on the individual flocks of farmers is rare. However, genetic selection and crossbreeding, on a large scale, have led to phenomenal increases in productivity – both egg and broiler production – from the levels which were normal as recently as the middle of the twentieth century.

Total egg number per bird depends on:

- the age at first lay
- the number of eggs laid in each clutch (perhaps 10, one after the other)
- the interval (the number of days) between clutches
- for how long the laying process will continue in a season.

(The clutch, after it is laid, represents the eggs a hen would want to incubate and hatch if she was left with the eggs and allowed to go broody.)

From the point of view of the geneticist, total egg number is thus a compound trait (chapter 4). Some of the components may be more limiting for total egg number than others. Rather than selecting on the compound trait it may be more effective to combine the components into **an index**, according to their genetic and economic importance and genetic inter-relationships.

A good practical and economic measure combining all the factors has been found to be the total egg production from time of hatching over, say, the next 500 days. In large-scale operations, the total output from the hens per hen-house is often considered the main criterion of merit.

Egg size and certain defects of eggs are also under genetic influence.

For meat production, size, growth rate and efficiency of converting feed into meat are the most important criteria.

Selection and crossbreeding and combinations of the two are effective methods of improvement. There is, however, a small negative genetic correlation (-0.1 to -0.2) between egg number and body size: increasing the size and growth rate of chickens would reduce egg production if no action is taken to counteract this effect. There is also a negative genetic correlation (around -0.3) between egg number and egg size – the more eggs the smaller each egg. Since these several traits are important for the success of commercial egg production, a selection programme has to take these various inter-related effects into account, for example in constructing a selection index.

10.3 *Traits*

In addition to the main products from each type of livestock there are always by-products – skins, horn, dung and so on. Some of these have great importance in a few situations, but attention will be focussed on the main characteristics which are common to more than one species and are the most frequent concern of the animal breeder.

Reproductive traits

Irrespective of species, reproductive traits generally have a low heritability but high variability (bovines excepted). It is this high variability which allows successful changes to be made by selection, but only if a long-term commitment can be made to selection.

To improve reproductive rate is particularly appropriate where meat is the main product, such as in sheep, because it is usually the number of offspring which determine profitability. When animals are kept mainly for milk, or wool, or work, the performance of the animal itself matters most. In these cases, producing offspring can often be regarded mainly as the means of renewing the capacity to produce milk and to provide replacements.

As for other traits, if selection is considered a possible route for improvement, thought must be given to the components of reproductive performance, which include:
- the age at first breeding
- the interval between the successive occasions at which offspring are born (parturitions)
- the number born on each occasion
- survival and longevity in the wider sense.

Records on all of these are helpful to identify whether any one component is the major limitation. In cattle especially, it can be useful to record the number of matings needed to obtain a pregnancy in order to identify whether that is the cause of long intervals between successive calvings.

Reproduction is greatly affected by climate, feeding and management, and to a greater or lesser degree, depending on species, by season. Heat stress reduces fertility. These various factors need to be recorded for the animals concerned and taken into account in comparisons among animals or groups. It will often be necessary to correct (adjust) the data for these environmental causes of variation (chapter 2).

The various components of reproductive rate can be combined, at each age, into a single measure by noting the total number of young surviving from birth to a particular age (for example weaning) for every female mated. However, neither that composite trait, nor most of the separate components, apart from litter size, provide a ready basis for successful selection – although the records will identify unproductive animals and show where management might make improvements.

Litter size (the number of young born) is the most usual of the reproductive traits considered for selection. In sheep and goats, a single record of parturition provides very little information about the genotype of the animal (chapter 5).

Selection accuracy is improved if **ovulation rate** is added to the information. In practice, this is possible only in large breeding units or nucleus flocks because of the need to use a **laparoscope** – an instrument which can be inserted through the body wall of the female animal to examine the ovaries for ovulations. Ovulation rate is positively correlated with litter size. When ovulation rate is included along with litter size in the selection criterion, the accuracy and efficiency of selection for increased numbers at birth is improved.

Other indirect methods of assessing female reproductive capacity have been tried. One of these is the testis size (or testicle growth) of rams which is related to the breeding characteristics of females because the same hormones control both. Until now, success with these other indirect methods has been very variable and unreliable for a number of different reasons.

In sheep, goats and pigs, crossbreeding with more prolific breeds will increase reproductive rate. This is useful if the crosses are what is wanted in other respects and if nutrition and management can sustain the larger numbers.

Meat production

On an individual animal basis, **body weight** is the major component of meat production. Weight at a given age has a reasonably high heritability (and generally greater in older than in very young animals – see chapter 4).

There is considerable variation within breeds and there are large differences in body weight between breeds. Selection has been shown to be successful and crossbreeding has brought big changes. However, the growth of animals is also influenced by feeding and environment. Appetite, the desire of an animal to eat, is reduced by heat stress.

Since the size of an animal at a given age is perhaps more readily measured or judged than most of the other economically important traits, farmers can make some genetic improvement in the production of their flocks or herds simply by *not* using poor, small individuals for breeding. It is particularly useful to castrate poor males so that they do not leave offspring. Great care must be taken to avoid inbreeding – which might occur if only one male is used by himself in a herd or flock and is then followed his son (chapter 9).

Differences in the proportions of bone, muscle and fat, and in dressing-out percentage (the proportion of the live animal which ends up as saleable meat) all have lesser importance than body size, especially in the tropics. For most meat production in the tropics the main factors are:
• total weight
• age of the animal.

Younger animals have more tender meat than older animals and are generally less fat. Weight at a given age is the most obvious criterion for a selection or crossbreeding scheme.

Before using selection or crossbreeding to increase body size it should be remembered that larger animals also eat more food and need more – although their maintenance requirements are lower per kg live-weight. It will depend on the production system whether increased weight is an advantage or a disadvantage.

In the tropics, the effects of body size on heat absorption and dissipation can also be important. Large animals have a smaller surface area in relation to their body weight. Big animals should, therefore, absorb less heat from the sun – relative to their weight: small animals should be better at dissipating heat because of their larger surface area relative to weight.

The importance of reproductive rate to the total output of meat from a herd or flock has been mentioned earlier (page 161).

On most farms in the tropics there are no **weigh scales** for cattle or for adult sheep and goats. For animals which go for slaughter at special abattoirs there is an opportunity to record their weight at that time. Weight at the time of slaughter, even if age is known, is an inefficient way of improving growth rate because that information can be used only in choosing *surviving* relatives.

Linear body dimensions can be used as a way of estimating weight. **Heart girth** alone and several combinations of animal length, height and depth have been used. The correlation of these measurements with weight depends on species, breed and other circumstances. Age of ruminants, when date of birth is not recorded (as it should be in a breeding programme!) can be estimated approximately from the number of teeth that have erupted. The species-related books in this series provide guidance on these points.

Carcass quality

Carcass quality is sometimes of economic importance in the tropics if animals are produced for export to places which pay extra money for superior carcasses or are sold in some other markets catering for a luxury trade. In such circumstances it is useful to pay attention to carcass quality in an improvement scheme. The quality traits are also heritable, but difficult to measure. Three factors are usually involved in carcass quality: shape of animal, fatness and tenderness of meat.

1 Shape of animal is important because in these specialist markets hind-quarters are prized above fore-quarters.

2 Fatness involves the proportion of muscle to fat but mainly because excessive fat is not wanted in animals for these specialist markets. Fatness can be estimated by scoring the condition of an animal from 0 for

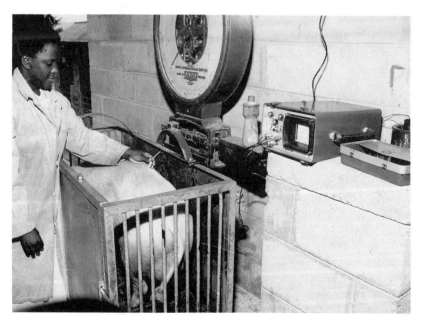

Fig 10.3 *Ultrasonic measurement of backfat thickness in the pig* (photograph by D. H. Holness, reproduced from *Pigs, The Tropical Agriculturalist*)

164

emaciated, to 5 (or some other number) for very fat. Especially for pigs, various ways of mechanically probing backfat thickness in the live animal have been used for a long time; now superseded by the use of **ultrasonic equipment** (Figure 10.3). For other species, the most 'accurate' way, in the past, was to determine composition after slaughter.

Measurements after slaughter are too late for choosing the animal itself for breeding, but not too late to use the information in order to select a son or daughter, or other close relative, as the breeding animal. Such carcass evaluation, however, is too expensive for commercial application. In the past, it has provided a large amount of useful information on variability in fatness, muscle and bone within and between breeds for use in breeding trials. Ultrasonic equipment of various levels of sophistication is now available for use on the live animal and it provides information which is quite well correlated with actual fatness and lean tissue area.

3 *Tenderness of meat* in practice is related to the age of the animal and its rate of growth. Well-finished cattle of 2 years-old will have more tender meat than an old cow after a life of milking or work.

The difficulty in measuring carcass quality traits means that these traits are more easily built into crossbreeding than into selection. The breed or type of sire used to produce the slaughter generation of progeny (often called the **terminal sire** or terminal sire breed) can be chosen to have particular merit for quality meat production.

Milk production

The main criterion of performance in a milk production unit is the amount of milk produced. Milk composition (fat and protein percentage) is of secondary importance unless the percentages are very low in situations where cheese or butter are the main product. **Lactation length** and the **daily amount** given determine the total output of milk. The daily amount given by a female usually increases for some weeks after parturition, then often remains relatively constant for a period before it declines as the end of lactation approaches. Season of year also affects yield. The daily yield can vary for many other reasons if animals have contracted mastitis, or have become bloated, or have, perhaps, been disturbed during milking.

A single measurement of milk yield is, therefore, never enough for an accurate estimate of lactation yield. For this purpose, morning and evening milk yields need to be recorded on a number of occasions throughout lactation. In addition, when using the records in a selection programme, it is nearly always necessary to correct the records of individual animals for some of the environmental factors which affect yield.

Milk yield for a lactation has a moderately high heritability (around 0.25 – Table 4.1) and milk composition a higher heritability. Most of the components of milk production are heritable too. There is much variation in yield within breeds and there are big differences between breeds. Both selection and crossbreeding are effective ways of changing milk yield and milk composition.

The first requirement for improving milk production is to measure it. Some of the problems are discussed below.

Recording Cattle milk yield.   In many western countries, the most effective frequency of recording milk yield, taking into account the costs of recording, has been found to be every three weeks. In large institutional herds in the tropics there is usually no problem in adopting this system.

In many other herds recording will be regarded as a problem, especially in herds with indigenous breeds which do not let down their milk without the presence of the calf. Where this occurs, it is important not to allow the calf to suckle longer than the minimum time for the cow to let down her milk. The calf should also be removed between successive milkings, or the amounts collected will be deficient by the amount the calf has taken – even that may not always be practical. If so, the only advice that can be given is that all cows should be compared on the same basis, whatever system is adopted, in order to choose among cows. That implies comparing cows of the same age and stage of lactation at the same time.

Even the production on a single day measured in a graduated bucket is better than nothing, and better than a simple guess – it would not be an accurate measure of total milk production but might help to cull some poor producers and perhaps pick out some of the best. It might also be the way of verifying the yield, on the owner's farm, of any cows notified as being exceptionally good in a population screening exercise (chapter 6).

Milk composition usually has to be determined in a laboratory and is relevant only to large-scale schemes and where butter or cheese production is the main object of milk production.

Recording milk yield of goats.   The same applies to milk goats as to dairy cows, except that the shorter lactation length makes it necessary to sample more frequently in order to cover the yield over a whole lactation.

Recording milk yield of sheep.   Assessment of milk yield can be important when the milk is used for human consumption and because of its effect on lamb growth. Generally, ewes that give more milk produce better and heavier lambs than those which produce less. Except in flocks specialis-

166

ing in milk production where the ewes are always milked, one method of estimating milk yield is to weigh lambs before and after sucking the ewe. On the day in question, lambs have to be kept apart from the ewes for several hours at a time so that when the lambs are allowed to suck they receive a measurable amount of milk. This should be done 3 or 4 times over a 24-hour period. Another way of estimating milk production of ewes is to weigh lambs at birth and again at 3 and 6 weeks. Over these periods the milk from the ewes is almost the only source of food for the lambs. Their growth depends on it. Conversion factors are available which allow a given increase in weight to be related to a given amount of milk. If lambs manage to steal milk from ewes which are not their own mother, this makes the relationship between lamb growth and its mother's milk production less reliable.

Hair and wool

Quantity of fleece is usually more important than quality, except in the specialised production of fibre. **Fineness** (measured as diameter) and **length** are the main components of fibre quality. Objective measures of quality, usually fibre diameter and fibre length from a representative number of fibres, are more difficult to obtain than subjective judgements, but lead to greater improvement. Merino sheep breeders in Australia adopted the objective approach many years ago. The weight of fleeces, though correlated with body size within a breed, has a moderately high heritability and shows much variation between breeds. Fibre diameter and fibre length have even higher heritabilities and also differ greatly between breeds. Both selection and crossbreeding can therefore change both quantity and quality quite readily and can reduce fleece defects.

Mohair, from Angora goats and rabbits, depends for its value on lustrous, white locks which curl or wave. Individual fibres are fine and long. **Cashmere**, the downy undercoat from the coats of goats, has even finer fibres, but they are short. Quantity and quality are influenced by both heredity and environment and crossbreeding with specialist fibre breeds is very effective in introducing these traits to local breeds.

Draught

Cattle and buffalo are widely used in the tropics for work, both in the cultivation of land and for transport.

There are differences in the capacity for work between breeds and strains and also among animals within breeds. The capacity for work is not, however, a function of only the power output of the animal. **Heat tolerance** is of major importance and affects the work output. Work itself generates heat and puts an additional stress on the animal when working in already, hot climatic conditions. Work output is regarded as a combination of **tractive (pulling) power**, **speed** and **persistence** at work. Several of these factors, including heat tolerance, may be capable of genetic improvement – although perhaps not worthwhile in practice (see below).

Tractive power itself is positively correlated with liveweight, which is readily changed by selection or crossbreeding. Larger and hence more powerful animals, however, also need more food, which is generally in short supply. Increased body size is of benefit only where the feed supply is plentiful. Since draught animals are used for work in fields and rice paddies for only a relatively small part of the year, the maintenance feed costs of the animal are a major consideration. Small animals can, therefore, have an advantage over large animals, even though they take longer to plough a given area.

Body size is also related to heat absorption from the sun and to heat dissipation, (as noted for meat production, page 162). This factor is perhaps of even greater importance for draught animals which generate extra heat through work.

The appropriate conditions for genetic improvement are particularly difficult to meet in the case of draught animals for a number of different reasons:

- Individual farmers usually own only a very small number of draught animals, often only one or two – this provides few opportunities for choice.
- By the time draught animals are trained for work and able to show their value, they are perhaps more than 5 years-old. This would lead to a long generation interval if selection were considered.
- Reproductive rate is particularly poor, perhaps because of the harsh conditions under which the animals are kept. This greatly limits the rate of genetic improvement which can be made (chapter 5).
- A large proportion of draught animals are castrated males and thus not capable of breeding.

Most breeds of draught animal are also used for meat or for milk. The breeding goals, if any, should therefore combine these characteristics with the draught properties.

Some of the above considerations would also prevent successful crossbreeding to improve performance. There is the added problem that larger, heavier breeds that might be used for crossing may also not be sufficiently well adapted to the conditions under which the crossbreds would have to live and work.

It seems inevitable, therefore, if any genetic improvement were to be brought about, that it should be done in large, national breeding herds. As far as tractive power itself is concerned there is a good case for finding and then selecting for a genetically correlated trait with heritability of the right order (chapter 5) and measurable at a *young* age – so as to obtain the benefit of a shorter generation interval.

Two such traits which deserve further investigation of their suitability are:

1 Some measure of pulling power in the young animal before it is properly trained for work.
2 A measure of heat tolerance.

In any centralised breeding scheme it is of great importance to make sure that the conditions under which the animals are selected are relevant to the conditions under which animals have to work in the villages. Otherwise, the results may not apply to village conditions.

EXAMPLE 10A   SELECTION CONDITIONS RELATED TO LOCAL CONDITIONS

It has been found that a single well-fed animal can often do the work of two poorly-fed animals. But this finding will not allow the efficient use of single-yoked animals in villages if the feed is not available to put that animal into good condition.

In the same way, an animal selected as a good worker under good conditions of feeding and management could be useless under village conditions.

The genetic considerations are well discussed by Vercoe et al. (1985).

Non-genetic changes have large effects on the work done by animals. These changes include improvements in feeding, disease control, changes in management practices and the design of implements.

The work output of many, perhaps most, draught animals suffers because they are ill-fed and because disease and parasite burdens are high. Management practices, such as restricting ploughing to cooler parts of the day and the provision of shade and cooling improve work output. The design of equipment, for example for ploughing, is very important. Improvements in design can make it possible to use smaller animals for work, with the advantages of lower maintenance costs for the animals and better heat dissipation in relation to body weight.

It is probably these areas of non-genetic improvement which should have priority over attempts at genetic improvement of the work output of draught animals – at least in the first instance.

Disease resistance

Individual farmers can do almost nothing to change the disease resistance of their animals by genetic means, apart from the small opportun-

169

ities offered in the choice of breeds and from crossbreeding which can improve general survival. The subject of genetic disease resistance has received much interest over many years and many research projects are devoted to it because:

- Ill health and disease cause great losses to farmers through loss of production and premature death of animals.
- Prevention and treatment of disease are costly and not sufficiently available in most countries of the tropics.

Diseases are grouped broadly as:

- Diseases associated with bacteria, viruses and fungi.
- Those connected with internal and external parasites.
- Diseases related to metabolic disturbances and deficiency, or excess, of specific nutrients.
- Hereditary defects.
- Losses from environmental stress, heat in particular.

Hereditary defects, the least significant, are usually inherited in a simple way, with just one or two pairs of genes responsible. Such defects are rare in occurrence and not important in the overall losses which occur among livestock. It is usually enough to cull the defective animals and their immediate parents and possibly brothers and sisters which might be carriers. The culls should not be passed on to other farmers who might breed from them. Strictly speaking the defective animals and relatives should be slaughtered. The strategy for coping with the unusual situation of a known and widespread defect was described in the context of testing for recessive defects (page 146). This applied to bulls (or other males) which are intended to be used widely through artificial insemination.

Occurrence of any of the other types of ill-health or of full-blown disease is never a simple matter. The symptoms of ill-health or disease arise from an interaction of the causative agent and other factors of the animal's environment and its own innate abilities to resist harm. Thus:

1 **Bacterial or viral infections** are more effectively resisted if the animal has had a previous mild exposure (which is often provided by vaccination) than if it has not.
2 **Internal parasites** will cause much more harm and may kill if the animal is poorly fed but pass unnoticed in a well-fed beast.
3 Ill-health associated with **mineral or trace element deficiencies** are often the result of some nutrient imbalance, or due to the excess of some other constituent, and not due to an absolute deficiency of the element associated with the disease symptoms.

In all cases, management, feeding and direct preventive treatments make a major impact in reducing the incidence of disease and the losses it causes. These facts alone indicate that variation in the incidence of disease due to heredity is likely to be small.

Genetical disease resistance

There are some general indications that heredity plays a role in disease resistance and especially in the overall ability to survive adverse conditions.

- **Local adaptation** – in the tropics, the most important indication is that tropical breeds of livestock are better able to cope than European or North American breeds with the diseases, the variable feed supply and the climatic stresses of the tropics. This is what is generally meant by local adaptation.
- Crossbreds have a better survival rate than the exotic breed contributing to the cross.
- A crossbred of two local breeds may occasionally have a better survival rate than that of either parent breed.

There is also evidence for a degree of genetic resistance to some specific diseases. The following are some examples:

1 Zebu breeds are susceptible to trypanosomiasis whilst some humpless African breeds, e.g. the N' Dama, are relatively resistant in tsetse fly infested areas.
2 Australian evidence has shown a genetic component in the resistance to parasites of the gut and to ticks.
3 Genetic resistance to bloat in cattle has been demonstrated.
4 Deficiency of a trace element (e.g. copper) has been shown to affect some breeds of sheep more than others (because of genetic differences in the efficiency with which the element is absorbed).
5 Selection against mastitis in dairy cattle has started in Norway, in spite of the very low heritability of mastitis incidence. This has been made possible by a national disease recording scheme which has identified that the daughters of some bulls have a higher incidence of mastitis than the daughters of other bulls.
6 In pigs, the occurrence of sudden death from stress, e.g. during transport on the way to slaughter, is known to be inherited. It is now part of the breeding programme of large breeding companies to eliminate this defect which is present to a different extent in different pig breeds. (This stress factor is also associated with some carcass traits.)

For a few major diseases for which there is already good evidence for a genetic component to resistance (e.g. trypanosomiasis), research is proceeding to discover whether specific genes controlling resistance can be located. Such genes might be identified directly or indirectly through their linkage to some other recognisable gene, a marker gene (chapter 12), for which selection could occur.

In the past, blood groups, and the types of albumin, haemoglobin and transferrin have been examined in relation to trypano-tolerance in, for example, N'dama and Baoulé cattle (Queval 1991; Toure 1987). Current work is aimed at extending the range of marker genes. Whilst still including the earlier genetic factors as markers, the latest work is increasingly directed at studying the DNA strands (chapter 12).

For a wide range of diseases, research interest is now focussed on discovering the manner in which animals protect themselves against disease and whether the defence mechanisms can be genetically manipulated. Protection against specific disease organisms, whether by vaccination or by some possible genetic means, has the disadvantage that micro-organisms can change their genetic structure relatively rapidly, because of the rapid turn-over of their successive generations. This has the consequence that any specific protection provided for animals at one point in time may not be effective subsequently.

More hope is now attached to the idea of discovering general defence mechanisms which might be present in the animal, or might be created by a process of genetic engineering (chapter 12). That is, however, a long way from providing genetic solutions to disease problems which individual farmers can apply for themselves now.

11 Breed conservation

Many breeds of livestock, including many from the tropics, have become extinct or have declined to numbers which put them in danger of extinction. A publication by the Food and Agriculture Organisation of the United Nations (Wiener 1990) provides some of the evidence and lists the names of endangered breeds of all species of livestock and in every continent. It is certain that many more breeds will be added to such lists as more attention is paid to the subject of conservation and more information becomes available on the decline in numbers of animals of particular local breeds. Included in such lists are, for instance:

1   Many of the criollo types of Latin and South America.
2   Several of the local breeds in Africa, such as the Kuri cattle of the Lake Chad area and the Barotse of Cameroon.

Cattle feature prominently in these lists because, in general, more attention is paid to this species than to others. Many of the native pig breeds of China and all indigenous poultry breeds of India are on the endangered list. Worldwide the lists include breeds of buffalo, camelids, donkey, goat, horse, pigs, poultry and sheep.

While many of the named breeds are down to numbers which make the future of these breeds very insecure without action to conserve them, others are in imminent danger of extinction if nothing is done: for example the Tokara breed of goat in Japan, was said to number only 30 individuals.

11.1 *Causes*

One of the most frequent causes of decline stems from the crossing of such breeds with other, more popular, breeds. Typically, individual flocks and herds of numerically endangered breeds are small. This in turn makes their maintenance difficult. It becomes difficult in such breeds to avoid inbreeding and the problems which derive from that (chapter 9).

A second genetic problem facing populations with small numbers of animals is that of **genetic drift**, whereby the genetic constitution of the breed may change by chance – with a resultant change in gene frequencies and the possible loss of some alleles and the fixation of others. This can lead to marked changes often to the detriment of the breed. The owners of animals of a numerically small or declining breed may also not obtain a sufficiently good return (financial or in terms of productivity) from animals of such breeds compared with that from more popular breeds. The owners, therefore, have little commercial incentive to keep animals of such breeds.

11.2 Breed names

In the absence of Breed Societies and records on the animals, it can be difficult to know whether a particular breed type is in fact genetically distinct from others. A local name for a particular type of animal is not proof that it differs from a possibly similar type by another name elsewhere. This creates confusion for those who want to conserve numerically endangered breeds and provides an opportunity for those who oppose conservation to claim that a particular breed is not unique after all.

11.3 Reasons for conservation

The topic of conservation is the subject of great interest across the world because the breeds concerned are regarded by many as a genetic resource which could not be replaced if lost. Much genetic improvement in plant breeding has been obtained by introducing genes from wild, otherwise unproductive, species into the cultivated crop plants of today. So the argument goes that if this is beneficial for plant breeding why not also in the world of animal breeding?

Maintaining genetic diversity

The principal scientific justification for conservation or preservation is the maintenance of genetic diversity. It is always possible that a breed in danger of extinction may possess characteristics which could be useful in the future – especially in relation to resistance to disease and adaptation to stressful environments. The difficulty is to identify what these particular attributes might be, to discover how, once identified, they are inherited and how to incorporate them genetically into perhaps another breed at a future time. The other major difficulty is to decide who pays for the costs of conservation and for the evaluation of the breeds, on which their future use depends. This may involve record keeping and other measures which would not normally be carried out.

Safeguarding the future

The matter of the costs and potential benefits have been considered in some detail by Smith (1985). He has suggested that the objectives for genetic selection which are favoured now may be less appropriate in the future. This possibility represents an element of risk for current breeding practice. This risk can be reduced by maintaining or creating lines with different attributes, not all of which are commercially favoured at the present time but which could be important in the future in some specified way. Smith has calculated that the national costs of creating 'specified' diversity of lines are very small relative to the potential financial returns – even if only a small proportion of these additional lines ever become of commercial value.

Special attributes

Some of the numerically small breeds of livestock may represent such diversity. It is, however, difficult to specify what might be important in the future. One might assume that anything to do with disease or stress resistance would qualify as well as anything which might prepare future animals to eat novel types of feed and crop or industrial by-products. Here lies yet another difficulty: breeds in general in the tropics have not been adequately evaluated. Their particular attributes are often not known and especially not the attributes which are largely unspecified at present but might be of use in the future.

A contrary view is that, in the absence of inbreeding, there is little evidence that genetic variability has been reduced to undesirable levels in commercially useful breeds, or that these could not be made to generate 'new' types if required. This view is based largely on analysis of genetic variation in the performance of the breeds which are recognised as useful at the present time – although there is also some evidence of variability at the gene level obtained by new techniques. This, however, is a view based on past breeding practices and may not be a good guide to the future. There are several indications that current livestock breeding practices, particularly in the more highly developed countries, may create ever greater genetic uniformity. There may be, therefore, a need to counteract this trend by maintaining diversity through breed conservation.

175

Social and cultural considerations

Apart from the scientific reasons for conservation, other reasons include social and cultural considerations and the provision of pleasure and recreation. These should not be judged lightly. Many people derive pleasure from seeing and observing wild species of animal. These animals are widely regarded as part of the world's heritage which it is the duty of the present generation of people to keep for future generations. Why, the argument goes, should farm species of livestock not be equally regarded as a part of the world's heritage and provide interest and pleasure to future generations – especially those of the large urban populations who are not familiar with farm animals?

11.4 *Definitions*

Conservation is the term normally applied to maintaining breeds for which numbers have greatly declined and may continue to do so to the point of extinction if no rescue measures are adopted. The term **preservation** is usually applied to breeds where the numbers surviving are so small that normal reproduction is unlikely to save the breed and special measures are needed to assist the process.

11.5 *Questions on conservation and preservation*

The questions to be answered concerning conservation and preservation are:
* What breeds should be conserved (or preserved)?
* In what number should they be kept?
* What techniques should be used?
* Who should be responsible?
* Who should pay?
* How should the 'rescued' breed be maintained?
    An answer to the first of these questions may come from considering the points discussed earlier in this chapter.

11.6 *Numbers required*

On the question of numbers, experts differ in their recommendations of what constitutes the minimum numbers required for conservation. Some suggest 150 females and 20 (unrelated) males as a 'working' number. Others have proposed much larger numbers, for example 1500 breeding females for sheep. Avoidance of inbreeding is always a critical element and, where possible, representative samples of animals should be chosen from many herds or flocks in preference to the conservation of a single herd or flock – even if relatively large.

Linked to the question of numbers is the **conservation strategy**. Not all sectors of the animal industry in a country lend themselves equally to conservation of a particular breed. Thus, farmers with highly intensive systems of production and with high capital inputs will certainly want to rely on highly productive, probably exotic, breeds or crosses. At the other extreme, nomadic systems may not lend themselves to the disciplines of a conservation programme. The sector of farming suitable for and capable of breed conservation, perhaps alongside breed development, thus needs careful consideration.

In the case of a breed which is virtually extinct, and which it has been agreed to preserve, the question of numbers is academic, since every available animal or cross of that type may be needed, for possibly a prolonged period of time.

11.7   *Techniques*

The techniques for conservation (and preservation) involve
• either the maintenance of live animals
• or cryogenic storage (usually through the storage of frozen embryos or semen).

Often conservation will involve a combination of both methods. Recent developments in biotechnology also provide the prospect of conserving chromosomes, or sections of DNA, but these methods raise additional problems of identification and of testing after the pieces are incorporated into new genomes. These most recent developments are some way off practical application in the context of conservation of the livestock breeds of the tropics and will not be discussed further here.

Use of live animals

In the case of breed conservation or preservation through the use of live animals, a decision is needed whether the animals are to be maintained without selection or whether they are to be 'improved' to make them more commercially viable. Some of the people concerned with countries of the tropics and developing parts of the world insist that concurrent 'improvement' is necessary to reduce the costs of maintaining the population. It is then a matter of hope that the improvement process does not eliminate the special properties which could make a breed valuable in the future. If crossbreeding with other breeds is avoided the dangers of

177

that happening will be greatly reduced. Selection within the breed should be the only method of 'improvement'. However, if that is done, the number of animals (both male and female) which need to be kept is larger than required for conservation with mating at random. This is because inbreeding would occur to a greater extent if selection is also practised (chapter 9).

When only a very few animals of a breed survive it might be necessary to cross these with other breeds in the first instance as the only way to preserve its genes and spread them more widely. Provided a male or males of the near-extinct breed are available, a process of backcrossing to the rare breed might then restore it, in time, to something like its former type. Multiple ovulation and embryo transfer (MOET) can also help to increase numbers – although the technical problems are greater when little is known about the breed and how it will respond to the hormonal and other treatments involved.

Cryogenic storage

With cryogenic storage either embryos or semen can be kept. Embryos have the advantage that a breed can be quickly restored to life by simply transferring the embryos to recipient females when required. The animals that are born are then the required breed or strain. With frozen semen, only half the genes of a breed are passed on to the progeny when the semen is used, as it usually will be, on females of another breed. A process of grading-up is then required over several generations to restore the former breed. If the number of bulls from which semen was kept is small, it will be difficult or impossible to avoid inbreeding during the grading-up process.

Choice of technique

Cryogenic storage is only a method of preserving the genotypes (or part of the genotypes) of a breed. Keeping live animals has the advantage that the characteristics of the breed might still be evaluated while the breed numbers are being maintained or increased. Also the live animals can fulfil some of the other criteria for conservation – that people might see and derive pleasure from a rare, unusual breed of livestock.

11.8   *Responsibilities*

'Who should be responsible for conservation and preservation?' is to some extent linked to 'Who benefits and who should pay?'. These are questions to which there are many different answers and which are the subject of international debate. The problem is that many of the endangered breeds of different species are kept by owners and in countries least able to spend money on non-commercial livestock.

The beneficiaries, social and cultural considerations apart, may well be much more widely distributed and should perhaps be regarded as the livestock breeders of the world. On that argument, the money to pay for conservation and preservation should be international. The responsibilities might then be more widely shared. A start with international cooperation in this field is seen in the establishment of a Global Animal Genetic Data Bank supported by the Food and Agriculture Organisation of the United Nations, other United Nations bodies and the European Association of Animal Production.

Where specific needs are already recognised, for example in relation to disease resistance in poultry, there is little doubt that the breeding companies, which would be the immediate beneficiaries, should also bear costs and responsibilities for conservation. The problem is that breeding companies may legitimately regard the results of their efforts as accessible only to themselves and not for wider use. However, if arrangements are made for the costs to be shared between several parties there is then every reason to expect the benefits also to be shared.

11.9 *Location*

Some livestock breeds which are near to extinction are found in small numbers in zoological and national parks. This can be of great benefit if the joint emphasis is on conservation. Exchange of breeding stock between the small groups of animals at different locations will help to maintain the population and its diversity. In a few countries, charitable or private organisations have been created to promote rare breeds and many of the animals are kept by enthusiastic breeders.

For a majority of the endangered breeds, and particularly those of the tropics, it seems inescapable that the breeds should be maintained in their native locality. This will require whatever assistance national or international bodies can give to encourage the process and to subsidise the costs.

12 Postscript: The advance of biotechnology

A book on animal breeding requires at least a reference to:
- The possible impact which advances in biotechnology are having on livestock production in general.
- The possibility of creating entirely new genotypes which can be multiplied in new ways.

12.1 *Earlier advances*

Over recent decades advances in the rate of change in genetic improvement have been aided by:
- Better understanding and better application of the genetic principles underlying animal breeding.
- Improved statistical and computational methods for assessing genetic merit.
- Great increases in the power of computers to undertake the necessary calculations.
- Methods of increasing reproductive rate both to speed up and spread genetic change.

Genetic principles

Better understanding of the principles has led to a faster rates of change because it has focussed attention on economically important traits. It has also encouraged better methods for coping with the problems of multiple-trait selection. It has provided a systematic approach to the exploitation of crossbreeding. It has also shown how to maximise progress in the animal population as a whole as distinct from individuals. This involves understanding the way to reach the best compromise between the different factors which affect an animal breeding programme.

Better understanding has also led to more effective systems of testing genetic merit and to refining the techniques of performance and progeny testing. Some help has been given to this process by technical advances such as those for assessing carcass traits in the live animal and by the discovery of some physiological traits which might be used to assist selection because they are correlated with the trait that is being improved (for example hormone levels related to milk yield or ovulation rate related to litter size).

Statistics and computing

The improved statistical techniques now available have increased greatly the ability to make proper allowance for all recorded factors which affect performance of an animal and to build these into the assessment of breeding value. The new techniques also allow information from all recorded relatives of an individual to be used in assessing breeding value (and to estimate heritability). Models have been devised to deal in a more comprehensive way with the interactions which arise among different factors. Two widely used, complementary procedures are **Best Linear Unbiassed Prediction** (BLUP) and **Restricted Maximum Likelihood** (REML). Both are increasingly replacing older, but still powerful, multiple regression forms of analysis.

None of this would, however, have been possible without the enormous increase in the power of computers to do the necessary calculations – and to have them done in a timely fashion. The usefulness of having comprehensive calculations ready before decisions on breeding are made cannot be over-stressed. In the past, breeding decisions were usually made on very inadequate assessments of genetic merit. The computer-aided technology also makes it possible to obtain better rates of genetic improvement by culling breeding stock on the basis of continually updated estimates of genetic merit, instead of at fixed ages.

In the context of animal breeding in the tropics, however, worthwhile progress can be made even without the sophisticated computational aids – provided the breeding principles are applied in the best way possible. It is just that the speed of improvement will be less than the maximum possible.

Reproduction

Advances in reproduction came most notably with the introduction of **artificial insemination** (AI) and the consequent widespread use of superior sires – particularly in dairy cattle. This in itself led to new methods of selection particularly:

• The use of progeny testing to identify genetically superior sires.

- To spread the improvement more rapidly through the cattle populations than possible before (chapter 6, Nucleus centralised breeding schemes).

More recently the increase in the number of offspring that females can produce, with, among others, the help of **multiple-ovulation and embryo transfer** (MOET), is having a similar effect on the development of breeding programmes and on the rate of genetic change (chapter 6).

The use of frozen embryos and embryo transfer is also making it easier to transfer breeds or genetically selected material from one country to another where, previously, animal disease considerations might have prevented such shipment.

The use of both AI and of MOET in tropical countries, however, also raises problems which can arise from variation in the reproductive physiology of different breeds and from variable responses in different environments. Moreover, the widespread use of progeny testing, allied to the use of bulls by AI, usually requires a network of performance recording on farms and the presence of relatively large herds – conditions which are not widely met in the tropics.

Nucleus Breeding Scheme

The most important outcome of all these changes for breeding programmes in the tropics has been the development of the concept of the **nucleus breeding scheme**, the **open nucleus** in particular, and the methods for exploiting it (chapter 6). This, combined with improvements in reproductive capacity, through MOET in particular, opens new doors for breed improvement.

Population screening to accumulate an elite group of stock for use as a nucleus deserves particular consideration in developing regions where recording of animal performance is not widespread.

12.2 *Recent advances and prospects*

Genetic engineering

Research in genetic engineering is very active and worldwide. Technological progress, as well as advances in the recognition of genes and understanding of their construction, is so rapid, that techniques which appeared to be in the realms of science fiction only recently seem possible now, and those things which seemed just possible a short while ago are now probable or actually achieved. It is unlikely that anything written here will not be superseded, perhaps within a short period of time, by new solutions to existing problems. The intention is to provide some background and indicate where, especially in relation to animal breeding in the tropics, some problems in the potential application of genetic engineering arise.

DNA manipulation

The new technology involves direct interference with the DNA (chapter 3) which is the stuff of the genes. There are genes which control the multitude of structures of the animal and genes which control the multitude of functions of the animal (and also the way in which the structural genes themselves act; for example, they may be turned on or off by function genes).

Individual genes are not single points strung out along the strands of DNA, but are segments of DNA of varying lengths sending out a variety of chemical messages to create a particular protein or to do a particular job. It has now been found possible to extract genes, or parts of genes, from the DNA strand, to multiply (clone) these extracted genes, to combine them in various ways into what are called constructs, and to introduce them into the DNA of other organisms, including larger animals and farm animals.

It has also been discovered, in principle, how to turn off genes with unwanted effects, but this has proved to be even more difficult to achieve as yet.

The source of a 'new' gene may be from the same or from another species, or could be artificially created. The main application to date has been in the creation of new vaccines and in altering the composition or digestibility of feed products. One of the early demonstrations of gene transfer in mammals was the introduction into mice of many copies of gene constructs with the growth hormone gene from the rat. Mice carrying these rat growth hormone genes grew much larger than control (normal) mice, but they were also infertile and unhealthy.

Application to livestock

As yet the technology and the understanding is insufficiently advanced for much direct impact on animal breeding. Some of the reasons for this and for caution about future application will be referred to later. To obtain livestock with new characteristics not present before, four steps are involved:

* The detection or the creation of useful genes.
* Transferring the desired gene (DNA) into a genome where it did not occur before.
* Testing the expression of the new genome in the whole animal and groups of animals in different conditions.
* Spreading the new genotype to a wider population.

Finding and using genes

The basis of the whole approach is to find and use genes with a useful and major effect on some characteristic of the animal. A few such genes are known to exist in livestock populations, but whether they are useful or not (or even harmful) depends on the farming conditions to which they are applied. Examples of genes with major effects include:

1 A gene conferring a greatly increased litter size on sheep: known as the Boroola gene because it was first discovered in the strain of Merino of that name in Australia.

2 The gene (or genes) causing an extra development of muscling (called double muscling) particularly in some European breeds of cattle.

3 The halothane gene in pigs, with both harmful effects on stress susceptibility and beneficial effects on lean meat output.

4 A gene creating a particularly good carpet type of fleece in sheep, the N-type fleece in New Zealand Romney sheep, now developed into the Drysdale breed.

All of these genes (1–4 above), and any similarly simply inherited traits, can already be introduced to other breeds by conventional cross-breeding. That of course also introduces half of all the other characteristics of the breed carrying the special gene. If those other characteristics are not wanted they can be largely eliminated by several generations of backcrossing to the breed into which the 'new' gene is being introduced – making sure that the desired gene remains in the new population. This needs a large breeding programme and, in many cases, test matings to make sure the new gene is still present in either single (heterozygous) or double (homozygous) dose.

The new technology offers, at least in theory, the opportunity to find, isolate, extract and multiply the fragment of DNA carrying the particular gene and transfer it to its new setting. This could be another breed or another species or could be done across former taxonomic barriers, for example a transfer of genes from bacteria to higher animals or vice versa. The animal into which the new gene has been introduced should then have the new characteristic controlled by that gene without any of the other traits of the animals from which the gene came.

The major problem facing researchers in this area of genetics is that in order to find and isolate a gene, that gene has first to be recognised by some immediate product, a protein. With the possible exception of the *halothane* gene, no such product is as yet identified for most naturally occurring genes with potentially useful effects.

There are, however, a number of other genes which can be recognised. Some affect physiological function of the animal, such as the growth hormone gene, which has effects on growth, on lean content and on milk production. Other genes which are being discussed as of potential use are those affecting the nature of certain proteins (for example caseins, important in cheese making), or to supply more of some amino acids which are in short supply in the diet.

Novel uses for farm animals are being investigated. There is the prospect of making sheep, goats or even cattle secrete products in their milk which are of use in human medicine. Bacteria are already being used to produce insulin and factors which assist blood clotting in individuals who lack that ability (haemophiliacs). Farm animals, however, have advantages over bacteria in making such products because animals make these products in a form more nearly suitable for humans. So far, the methodology is working, and the amounts produced in milk are approaching being enough for commercial use.

It is the battle against animal disease which provides possibly the most important immediate challenge for genetic engineering of livestock for the tropics. The prize, so far not attained, is the prospect of finding genes which confer extra resistance to disease in general or to specific diseases, and the ability to transfer these to livestock which are useful in the tropics. (Some of the considerations applying to disease resistance were considered in chapter 10.)

Transferring genes
The general principle underlying the techniques of transferring genes is DNA manipulation (page 183). At the present time the several possible techniques for achieving incorporation of a new gene in the genetic make-up of an animal have a rather low rate of success. Mostly, an attempt is made to introduce the new DNA material directly into a fertilised egg (Figure 12.1) or something which will develop into one.

At present only about 1% of eggs injected in such a way develop into individuals carrying the new gene. These are called **transgenic animals**. Each egg which is thought to carry the new gene has to be given the chance to develop into an animal. Many recipient mothers are needed to raise the developing embryos, even though many will be found not to carry the new gene. Many other embryos fail to develop normally to full term. Much research effort is currently going into identifying those of the injected eggs which have actually incorporated the newly introduced DNA into their own genetic make-up. When that work succeeds many fewer embryo transfers to recipients will be needed from any one batch of eggs which were treated in the first place.

Testing for the expression of the gene
At present the process of DNA transfer is a little 'hit and miss'. There is not much control over the position on the DNA strand in which the new material will become incorporated – although research is directed at making this more precise. Also, there may be one or many more than

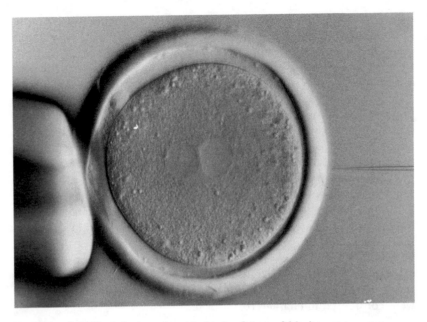

Fig 12.1 *A fertilised sheep egg (zygote) showing 2 pronuclei in its centre – one containing the chromosomes from the female and the other those from the male* (photograph by Dr J. P. Simons, courtesy of the AFRC Roslin Research Institute, Edinburgh)
The blunt pipette for holding the egg cell is on the left of the picture and the pointed pipette on the right is for injecting DNA into one of the pronuclei. The next step in the process would be for the injection pipette to penetrate the cell's wall and enter the pronucleus. Confirmation that DNA has been injected is then provided by looking for swelling of the pronucleus.

one copy of the new gene incorporated in its new home. These factors influence the way in which the newly introduced gene will act and what size of an effect it will have. When a new gene is introduced into a new genotype, which differs in many respects from the genotype from which the gene was taken, it may behave in ways which were not expected or wanted. Thus, the mice which received growth hormone genes from rats certainly grew more (or some of them did), but they were also infertile and less healthy. This has, so far, been the experience with many experimentally-produced transgenic animals. They display the new characteristic to a greater or lesser extent, but they are also worse in other ways – less fit in an evolutionary sense.

Transgenic animals will have to undergo a strenuous testing programme before they can be judged advantageous to animal production.

Spreading the new genotype

If and when it is established that a newly created transgenic genotype is of value, it still has to be spread through the population. Artificial insemination can help to speed up the spread of the new type if it is found in males and induced multiple ovulation and embryo transfer if found in females.

It can be assumed that the testing and spread of a new genotype would take at least three generations. If the generation interval is on average 3 years it would be 9 or 10 years before the new type is available to farmers. During that time no other 'improvements' would take place in the animals concerned. Over such a period of time genetic improvement could be made by 'conventional' means (for example a nucleus breeding scheme using MOET). The rate of such improvement can be expected to be at least 1% per year or, say, 10% over the period. Therefore, any extra value to the farmer of the newly-introduced gene would need to be of at least that 10% magnitude if it is to be economically worthwhile.

Marker genes
It has been possible since the 1920s, but in a very limited way, to identify where some genes with major effects were located on chromosomes. This was achieved by complicated mating patterns and studies of how often different characteristics were inherited together (linkage and crossing-over, chapter 3).

One of the advances from the new biotechnology has been the ability to identify genes which produce characteristic protein bands on gels, when subjected to certain laboratory techniques. For an increasing number of these genes their position on the DNA strand has now been identified. Most of these genes do not themselves have effects on the performance of the animal – at least not effects which are easily recognisable. But their occurrence can sometimes be associated with particular aspects of the performance of animals.

In this way the technique could provide **markers** to the regions of the DNA which control important traits and functions of the animal. This, in turn, may make it easier in future to isolate identified regions and to transfer desirable characteristics or eliminate harmful ones.

More important for the present, such marker genes might also become useful in conventional selection for the associated performance traits or diseases, such as trypanosomiasis (chapter 10).

12.3   Other developments

A few other developments are taking place which might have substantial effects on livestock production and on the speed with which improvements can be made.

Increasing the reproductive rate

Multiple ovulation and embryo transfer is widely promoted in, for example, Europe and North America. Successful application in the tropics requires technical skills and facilities which are often unavailable. The techniques also need further trials to find out whether the procedures which are successful with temperate breeds will succeed with the breeds of the tropics. New methods or treatments may have to be devised.

Research is in progress to harvest larger numbers of cells (oocytes) from ovaries and to mature these *in vitro*. Such techniques, if successful, would greatly increase the number of offspring that can be obtained from a female. Even if the animals concerned are genetically desirable there will be risk of additional inbreeding because of the small number of females used as parents (chapter 9).

Cloning

The creation of possibly large numbers of *identical* individuals from a single cell or from genetically identical cells is implied by cloning. In nature, identical twins, derived from the splitting of a single fertilised egg, are not uncommon. The new techniques aim to do this on a large scale. A possible advantage of clones of animals would be that they have the same requirements for feed and management. They also share, however, the same susceptibilities to disease and stress.

Clones hardly seem a good idea in situations, such as the tropics, where variability among livestock is one of the insurances against disease and stress – so that not all animals are equally susceptible to harm. Clones also create populations with reduced or even zero genetic variability so that future opportunities for making genetic changes are compromised.

Sex determination

The techniques exist for determining the sex of embryos and even of pre-determining the sex. Although not really sex determination, there is also now the prospect, by genetic engineering, of enhancing the male sex characteristics of ordinary males. Sexing of embryos is already totally effective, but costly. Semen sexing in cattle has now (1993) also been claimed with a high probability of success.

The practical benefit of any of these procedures arises only if one sex is much more valuable than the other. Where this is the female (for example for milk production) there is no problem in maintaining the population or even increasing its numbers. Where the male is the preferred sex (for example for draught or for growth rate) there could be unfavourable effects on the ability to reproduce the population, because of too few females. For the design of breeding programmes, the possibility of determining the sex of embryos has both advantages and disadvantages, which may neutralise each other.

Products which help animal production

Biotechnology is helping to provide:
- New aids for diagnosing animal disease.
- New vaccines to prevent disease.
- Improved feeds and aids for reproduction, growth and milk production, for example through genetically engineered hormones.

12.4   Uniformity and diversity

Many of the changes in the animal production of the already highly developed parts of the world are aimed at creating uniformity:
- of product
- of the animals to provide the products
- of production, feeding and management system in sheltered, relatively disease-free and highly controlled environments.

Many of the biotechnological aids assist the process of attaining uniformity.

Animal production in the tropics, on the other hand, is largely an exercise of responding to diversity. It still has to be shown whether biotechnology can be successful in serving the needs of diversity – except in providing better feeds and better disease prevention or cure.

12.5   Investment in livestock breeding

The livestock breeders of the tropics, and developing parts of the world in general, have one great advantage over their counterparts in most of the more 'developed' countries.

In the industrialised countries, further investment in animal production can increasingly be justified only by profit from small improvements in the desirability of the products (for example by changing the flavour or tenderness of meat) or from reducing the costs of production. Some of the investment in animal production which does still take place simply replaces one product by another (for example more poultry meat and less beef). Some investment has also been directed at developing more 'animal-welfare conscious' or 'environment-friendly' systems of production.

In the developing world, by contrast, there is still an immense scope for increasing livestock production to keep pace with human population growth and to meet the rightful demand for more and higher quality food for each person. Investment in livestock production in general, and animal breeding in particular, can be justified, therefore, on both economic and social grounds. The animal breeder in the developing world can look forward to a continuing, useful application of the science and technology of breeding for a long time to come. Genetic engineering of farm livestock in the tropics, through DNA manipulation, is at the present time still no more than a possible aid to genetic improvement of the future – and even then its application will be expensive.

The current methods, based on the application of quantitative genetics and aided by other techniques and technology, have been shown to be successful. These methods are already powerful and appropriate tools for changes and improvements in livestock production.

Glossary

Additive (of gene action)   Joint effect of genes is the sum of the effects of the separate genes (applied to genes from different loci or to alleles at a single locus).

Additive genetic variation   Variation of breeding values (the main cause of resemblance between relatives) in the offspring will, on average, be half-way between the values of their parents.

Adjustment factor   *see* correction factor.

Allele   One or more alternative forms of a gene occupying the same site (locus) on a chromosome.

Allele frequency   *see* frequency.

Amino acid   Structural unit of all proteins (there are 20 different amino acids).

Artificial insemination (AI)   Technique of inserting semen, and the associated sperm, into the female reproductive tract. The term, AI, is often used to describe the whole process including dilution and storage of semen.

Artificial selection   Selection carried out by humans and not by nature.

Backcross   Offspring from mating F1 animals to one or other of the parents or parent breeds.

Breed   Population of animals which is distinguished from another population of the same species by some recognisable genetic characteristics.

Breed structure (also breed hierarchy)   The way in which herds or flocks of a breed are organised into different levels of importance in terms of their genetic contribution to the breed.

Breeding value   Genetic worth of an animal in respect of a particular trait or combination of traits.

Cell   Basic unit of living tissue.

Chromosome   Structure (seen under the microscope as rod-like during cell division) which occurs in the nucleus of cells and on which are located the genes.

Clone (in genetic engineering)   Copy of a specific DNA sequence (for example, from sheep) maintained usually in a viral or bacterial host.

Cloning (in reproduction)   Production of many identical individuals from one.

Closed nucleus (of breeding schemes)   Nucleus (*see* below) group of animals into which no other animals are allowed from outside.

Compound trait   *see* trait.

Confounding (in animal breeding)   Describes the situation where different factors contributing to performance cannot be separated because they always occur together. (For example, if breed A is measured only under intensive feeding and breed B only on grazing, it is not possible to determine how much of any difference between A and B is due to heredity and how much due to feeding.)

Conservation   Maintenance of (breeds of) livestock to retain adequate numbers for further breeding and to prevent a decline in numbers or extinction.

Contemporaries   Animals born at the same time and treated in the same way.

Controls (of populations)   Unselected population or group of animals with which other groups are compared.

Correction factor   Numerical amount calculated to adjust performance records for environmental factors which differ between animals, for example, the difference between twin- and single-born animals.

Correlation   Statistical measure of the degree to which traits change together or are associated with each other (hence, correlated traits). Two traits are said to be **positively** correlated if they go up or down together, and **negatively** correlated if as one trait goes up the other goes down.

Crossbreeding   The mating together of animals of different breeds or strains. The offspring of such matings are called **crossbred**.

Crossing-over   Mutual exchange of segments of homologous chromosomes which occurs during meiosis and has the effect of breaking linkages between different loci on each chromosome.

Cryogenic storage   Storage by deep freezing (usually of early embryos and sperm).

Culling   The discarding of animals, usually for poor performance. The discarded animal is called a **cull**.

Dam   Female parent of an animal.

Deviation   Difference in performance between an individual (or group) and some fixed point, often the average of a larger group or population from which the individual (or group) was drawn.

Diploid   The normal state in the nuclei of cells (except gametes) where all chromosomes are doubled up into pairs. (Homologous chromosomes are paired.)

DNA (deoxyribonucleic acid)   Complex chemical compound which makes up the structure of genes.

Dominance (of alleles)   Condition whereby the action of one allele masks the effect (partially or totally) of the other (recessive) allele – hence, dominant allele.

Donor (in embryo transfer)   Female from which early embryos (or germ cells) are taken.

Dressing-out percentage (or killing-out %)   Weight of carcass expressed as a percentage of liveweight of the animal at slaughter.

Egg   *see* ovum.

Embryo   Animal organism in an early stage of development (from a few cells to many) in the uterus of the female.

Embryo transfer   Mechanical transfer of embryos at a very early stage of development from one individual (donor) to another (recipient).

Environment (in relation to animal breeding)   All the factors affecting performance or expression of a trait which are due to the treatment and surroundings of the animal and not due to its genes.

Environmental correlation   A correlation among observations due to shared effects from factors of the environment.

Environmental variation   *see* variation.

Enzymes   Substances (proteins) in the cells of animals which cause various and specific biochemical reactions to take place.

Epistasis   Interaction of genes which are at different loci and the interaction of the effects which such genes have.

Exotic (in relation to breeds)   Describes a breed brought in from another area, such as breeds from temperate regions taken to the tropics.

F1   Offspring (or offspring generation) from the first cross between two breeds or strains.

F2   Offspring (or offspring generation) from matings of F1 × F1; followed by F3, F4 and so on.

Frequency (in relation to genes)   Statistical term used to describe the number of times that a particular allele of a gene occurs in a population expressed as a percentage, or as a proportion out of 1. (The frequencies of all the different alleles of any particular gene add up to 100%, or to 1.)

Gamete   Reproductive cell: sperm in the male; egg or ovum in the female.

Gene   Basic unit of hereditary transmission: a segment of DNA.

Gene interaction (non-allelic interaction)   *see* epistasis.

Gene transfer (in genetic engineering)   Transfer into the DNA of an animal of a segment of DNA from elsewhere and representing a new gene or additional copies of an existing gene.

Generation interval   Average age of parents when their offspring are born.

Genetic correlation   A correlation among observations on different traits due to the effects of genes.

Genetic engineering   Science and technology of manipulating and modifying genes in the DNA directly.

Genetic variation   *see* variation.

Genome   All the genes carried by an animal.

Genotype   Genetic composition of an animal in terms of all the alleles it carries; the total effect of all the genes (apart from the environment). Can be applied to specific traits.

Genotype-environment interaction $(G \times E)$ Situation where the effects of particular genes in one environment differ from their effects in another environment, for example the *difference* in milk yield between two breeds may be different in two separate environments.

Germ cells   Cells from the ovaries of females and the testicles of males from which the gametes are derived.

Grading-up   When two breeds are involved, the successive backcrossing to one of the original parent breeds. Males of one of the parent breeds are mated each time to the previous generation of crossbred offspring. Similarly, grading-up can be to a crossbred type (for example an F1) instead of to a pure breed.

Group-breeding scheme   An association of several breeders into a joint, co-operative breeding programme.

Half-sib   *see* sib.

Haploid   Half the normal (diploid) number of chromosomes as produced at meiosis in the formation of gametes. (In the haploid state, the chromosomes are not present in pairs.)

Heat (of breeding females)   *see* oestrus.

Heritability (h^2) Proportion of phenotypic variation which is due to genetic variation. Relative importance of heredity in determining phenotypic value of a trait in a population. (The usual form of heritability – based on the additive genetic variation – can also be defined as the proportion of the observed superiority of selected parents, above the population mean, which reappears in the progeny. This is also called the heritability in the **narrow sense**. Heritability in the **broad sense** is the ratio of the whole of the genetic variation in a trait to the whole of the phenotypic variation for that trait in the population.)

Heterosis   Condition and extent to which crossbred progeny differ in their performance from the average of their parents. **Positive** heterosis (when the cross is better than the average of the parents or better than the better of the parents) is also called **hybrid vigour**. The term, heterosis, is normally applied to groups of animals and not to individuals (for example the average performance of reciprocal crosses compared with the average of the two parental breeds).

Heterozygote   Individual which has two different alleles of a gene on the two homologous chromosomes. Such an individual is said to be

heterozygous for that gene.

Hierarchy (in a breed) *see* breed structure.

Histogram Diagram in which columns represent the number of observations at each of a range in performance levels.

Homologous chromosome Each of the two members of any particular chromosome pair. Homologous chromosomes carry the same array of genes in the same order and hence affect the same traits, but they do not necessarily carry the same allele of each gene.

Homozygote Individual which has the same allele of a gene on the two homologous chromosomes. Such an individual is said to be **homozygous** for that gene.

Hormones Biochemical substances secreted by glands of the animal which affect various and specific functions.

Hybrid vigour *see* heterosis.

Inbreeding Any mating together of related animals – but usually having an ancestor in common in the last 2–3 generations.

Inbreeding coefficient (F) Numerical value which describes the degree of inbreeding which is the proportional amount by which heterozygosity has been reduced, relative to some arbitrary starting point. F values are between 0 and 1 (or 0–100%). Zero signifies an absence of inbreeding (no common ancestor in the pedigree of the animal) while 1 (or 100%) signifies that no heterozygocity remains – all loci are homozygous. (Total homozygocity is unlikely in animal populations, but occurs in plants, especially those that are self-fertilising.)

Inbreeding depression Reduction in the level of performance associated with inbreeding (due mostly to the loss of favourable dominance at heterozygous loci).

Independent assortment Two alleles of a gene pair on one chromosome segregate independently from two alleles of a gene pair on another chromosome.

Independent culling levels When more than one trait is to be improved at the same time, it is the performance level, set separately for each trait, below which the animal is culled irrespective of merit in the other traits.

Index Computed estimate of the genetic value of an animal based on a number of different traits and considerations.

Index selection When more than one trait is to be improved at the same time, selection is on an index which combines performance in the different traits into an overall criterion (economic or biological value). With index selection, good performance in one trait can compensate for poor performance in other traits.

Interaction When two or more traits, or two or more factors, act on each other.

In vitro   In a test tube or culture dish (outside the animal body).

In vivo   In the animal body.

Linkage (of genes)   When different alleles affecting different traits are situated on the same chromosome and are, therefore, passed on together. Closeness of their positions on the chromosome determines how tightly linked they are (*see* crossing-over). Different traits can be said to be linked (or correlated) due to their inheritance being associated.

Locus (plural: loci)   Position on a chromosome where a particular gene is located.

Marker gene   A gene, with a distinctly recognisable effect, for which the location on the chromosome (or on the strand of DNA) is known and which is linked to other genetic characteristics not controlled by that gene.

Maternal effect   Non-genetic influences of the dam on her offspring. Difference in performance between reciprocal crosses due to the mothering properties of the dam.

Mean (or average)   Total (for example milk yield) divided by the number of observations.

Medullation (of fibres)   Cavity or hollow space inside fibres.

Meiosis   Cell division in the germ cell when gametes are produced in which the diploid number of chromosomes is halved to the haploid number.

Mitosis   Division of (body) cells where each daughter cell receives the same full, diploid, set of chromosomes.

Mutation   Change which occurs in a gene resulting in an allele which has a different effect from the original.

Multiple ovulation   Shedding by the ovary of many eggs at a time (often in the context of artificially induced ovulation).

Natural selection   Selection effected by the influences of nature and not of humans. *See* artificial selection.

Non-additive variation   Variation attributable to deviations from additive action of different factors (for example, if offspring are better or worse than expected from the average of their parents). Dominance, epistasis and genotype-environment interaction cause non-additive variation.

Normal distribution (normal curve)   Bell-shaped distribution which describes the variation of most continuously variable performance traits in a population of animals.

Nucleus (of breeding schemes)   Herd, flock or group in a breeding scheme containing the best (elite) animals in which genetic improvement is practiced and from which breed improvement flows.

Nucleus (of cells)   The part in the cell containing the sets of chromosomes.

196

Oestrus Period of time when a female will stand to be mated (also called being on heat).

Oocyte One of the cells in the pathway producing the egg in the female. (Primary oocytes contain the diploid number of chromosomes, secondary oocytes the haploid number.)

Open nucleus (of breeding scheme) Nucleus group of breeding animals which remains open to the introduction of animals from other herds or flocks.

Ovary Organ of the female that produces the ova (eggs).

Over-dominance Where the heterozygote is superior in performance to both the homozygotes.

Ovulation Shedding of an ovum or ova from the ovary.

Ovum (plural: ova) Female gamete (also called egg).

Parasite Small animals which live on or in others. (For example: ticks externally; nematodes internally.)

Pathogen Organism causing disease.

Performance-test Evaluation of an animal by its own performance (production).

Phenotype Outward appearance or performance of an animal resulting from the joint expression of all genes and all environmental (non-genetic) factors affecting the animal.

Phenotypic correlation A correlation due to an association between the phenotypic values of one trait with the phenotypic values of another trait for the animals in a population (usually the overall correlation).

Phenotypic variation *see* variation.

Pleiotropy Where one gene affects more than one trait at the same time.

Polar body Cell cast off from the oocyte in the cell divisions leading to the development of a mature ovum.

Polled Without horns.

Polygenic (of traits) Affected by several genes.

Polypeptide Compound formed by the chemical linkage of ten or more amino acids.

Population Group of potentially inter-breeding animals. (For example, a breed; sometimes used to describe a group such as a herd or several herds together for purposes of breeding.)

Preservation (of breeds) Maintenance, by any means, of the genotypes of breeds faced with extinction.

Probability Likelihood of an event occurring (usually in a statistical sense).

Progeny Immediate offspring (descendant) of a father or a mother or both.

Progeny test Evaluation of an animal by the performance of its progeny.

Protein   Complex molecule made up of amino acids linked into polypeptide chains. An essential organic constituent of all animal cells; the major constituent of muscle and other tissues (apart from fat), wool, enzymes and so on.

Quantitative genetics   Concerned with the inheritance of continuously variable traits and with differences among animals in degree (greater or smaller) rather than with differences in kind (such as having horns or not).

Random mating   Where each male has an equal chance of mating with each female.

Recessive (of alleles)   The allele which has its action or its effect masked by the action of another (dominant) allele at the same locus. For example, in Hereford cattle the white face is dominant over the coloured face.

Recipient (in embryo transfer)   Female into which early embryos are placed to complete their development.

Reciprocal cross (in crossbreeding)   Reversal of the male and female parent breeds or strains. (For example, male of breed B mated to female of breed A is the reciprocal cross of male A × female B.)

Recombination   Re-association of segments of homologous chromosomes which have been exchanged during crossing-over. (The association of the different alleles which have come together in this way.)

Regression   Statistical term to describe by how much one trait changes as another changes.

Repeatability   Statistical term to describe the probability that the measurement of a trait will be repeated when the trait is measured again. (The correlation between repeated measurements of a trait).

Rotational crossing   When two or more breeds are involved in crossbreeding, the males of each breed are mated to progeny of the previous generation in strict rotation in each successive generation. (For example with 3 breeds: generation 1 – breed A; 2 – B; 3 – C; 4 – A; 5 – B; and so on.)

Screening (of populations)   Search for and identification of exceptionally good individuals.

Segregation   Separation of two alleles of a gene pair into different gametes (at meiosis).

Selection   Choice of some animals in a population in preference to others. Usually the choice of animals as parents of the next generation.

Selection differential (S)   Difference in performance between the average of the animals selected as parents and the average of the population from which they came.

Selection intensity (i)   Deviation of the selected group from the mean of the population, expressed in units of standard deviations. (Can be directly derived from the proportion of the population selected.)

Sex chromosome   A chromosome specifically associated with the determination of sex.

Sex limited (of a trait)   Trait expressed phenotypically in one or other of the sexes only. (For example milk yield in the female.)

Sex linkage   Traits controlled by alleles located on a sex chromosome are said to be sex linked (hence X-linked – alleles on X chromosome; or Y-linked – alleles on Y chromosome).

Sib (sibling)   The relationship of one animal to another which shares a parent or both parents. Full sibs share both father and mother; half-sibs share either the father or the mother, not both.

Sire   Father of the offspring.

Sire circle   Breeding scheme where sires are used in rotation in different herds or flocks.

Sperm (spermatozoan)   The male gamete.

Spermatocyte   One of the cells in the pathway to producing sperm in the male. (Primary spermatocytes have the diploid number of chromosomes, secondary spermatocytes the haploid number.)

Standard deviation   Measure of variability of a trait in the population. Statistical term to describe, in standardised units, the amount of variation around a mean, related to the normal distribution. (Square root of variance.)

Strain   Genetically distinct population within a breed.

Stratification (of animal production)   Where different breeds or strains are kept for separate purposes usually in different areas.

Stratification (of a breed)   Division of herds or flocks into different levels of genetic importance in the breed (*see also* breed structure).

Synthetic breed   A breed created by interbreeding of two or more established breeds.

Tandem selection   Selecting for one trait until it is changed to a predetermined level before starting selection for another trait (in situations where it is intended to improve more than one trait in a population).

Teaser   Male acting as a normal male, usually to detect oestrus in females, but unable to pass sperm because he is vasectomised or because the penis is prevented from penetrating the female.

Testicle (or testis, plural: testes)   Organ of the male that produces the sperm.

Trait   Characteristic or attribute of an animal.

Transgenic   Animal carrying in its genome, a new gene or an altered gene, introduced by genetic engineering.

Truncation   Point in a distribution of values on one side of which animals are retained and on the other side of which they are culled.

Variation   Measure of the differences among the animals of a group or population, often prefixed by some attributive term. For example: genetic variation – that due to the action of genes; phenotypic variation – that pertaining to the phenotypic values of a trait in a population; and environmental variation – that due to factors of the environment.

Zygote Cell formed from the fusion of two gametes – following fertilisation of an egg by a sperm.

Bibliography

Recommended further general reading indicated by ★

Ahmad, M. and Kahn, B. B., 1984, Improvement in quality of mohair from Angora crossbred goats, *Pakistan Journal of Agricultural Research*, **5**: pp. 255–258.

Barlow, R., Hearnshaw, H. and Hennessy, D. W., 1985, Breed evaluation research in the sub-tropics of New South Wales. In *Evaluation of Large Ruminants for the Tropics*, ACIAR Proceedings Series No. 5 (ed. J. W. Copland) pp. 120–125.

Bonnes, G. et al., 1991, *Amélioration génétique des animaux d'élevage*, Les edition Foucher, Collection INRAP, Paris. ★

Bradford, G. E. and Berger, Y. M., 1988, Breeding strategies for small ruminants in arid and semi-arid areas. In *Increasing Small Ruminant Productivity in Semi-arid Areas*, ed. E. F. Thomson and F. S. Thomson, ICARDA, pp. 95–109.

British Society of Animal Production, 1988, *Animal breeding opportunities*, Occasional Publication No. 12, British Society of Animal Production, Edinburgh. ★

Copland, J. W. (ed), 1985, *Evaluation of large ruminants for the tropics*, ACIAR Proceedings Series No. 5, Canberra, ACT, Australia. ★

Cunningham, E. P. and Syrstad, O., 1987, *Crossbreeding* Bos indicus *and* Bos taurus *for milk production in the tropics*, FAO Animal Production and Health Paper 68, FAO, Rome. ★

Falconer, D.S., 1989, *Introduction to quantitative genetics*, Longman Scientific & Technical, Harlow, Essex. 3rd edn. ★

FAO, 1990, *Production Yearbook*, **44**, FAO, Rome.

Faugere, O. and Faugere, B., 1986, *Suivi de troupeaux et contrôle des performances individuelles des petits ruminants en milieu traditionnel africain. Aspects methodologiques*, Revue d'Élevage et de Médecine Vétérinaire des Pays Tropicaux, **39**: 29–40.

Faugere, O. and Landais, E. P. N., 1989, *Fascicule 1: Le suivi sur le terrain et la tenue des fichiers manuels; Fascicule 2: Le fichier informatique. Saisie et organisation des données. Interrogation de la base de données; Fascicule 3: Annexes: fiches de terrain, cartes individuelles, fishiers informatiques, écrans de saisie, guide d'autopsie.* ISRA-IEMVT, Paris, 134: pp. 200 and 260.

Hunter, A.G. (ed), 1991, Biotechnology in livestock in developing countries, *Proceedings of Biotechnology 1989*, University of Edinburgh, Centre for Tropical Veterinary Medicine, Edinburgh. ★

Mason, I. L., 1988, *A dictionary of livestock breeds*, 3rd edn, CAB International, Wallingford, Oxon.   ★

Mason, I. L. and Buvanendran, V., 1982, *Breeding plans for ruminant livestock in the tropics*, FAO Animal Production and Health Paper 34, FAO, Rome.   ★

Matheron, G. and Planchenault, D., 1992, La caractérisation des races: expérience de l'IEMVT/CIRAD. In *African animal genetic resources: their characterisation, conservation and utilisation*, ed. J. E. O. Rege and M. E. Lipner, Addis Ababa, ILCA, 19–21 December 1992, pp. 31–34.

Maule, J. P., 1990, *The cattle of the tropics*, University of Edinburgh, Centre for Tropical Veterinary Medicine, Edinburgh.   ★

Nicholas, F. W., 1987, *Veterinary genetics*, Clarendon Press, Oxford.   ★

Nicholas, F. W. and Smith, C., 1983, Increased rates of genetic change in dairy cattle by embryo transfer and splitting, *Animal Production*, **36**: pp. 341–353.

Park, Y. I. and Kim, J. B., 1982, Evaluation of litter size of purebreds and specific two-breed crosses produced from five breeds of swine. *Proceedings of the 2nd World Congress on Genetics applied to Livestock Production, Madrid, 1982*, **VIII**, pp. 519–522.

Planchenault, D. and Salut, C., 1990. *Mise en place d'un suivi de troupeaux bovins, ovins et caprins. Utilisation du logiciel Pikbeu.* Rapport technique 1. IEVMT, Maison-Alfort, France.

Queval R., 1991, *Unité d'immunogénétique. Rapport succinct d'activités 1991*, CRTA, Burkina Faso, pp. 11–16.

Shaw, A. P. M. and Hoste, C. H., 1987, *Trypanotolerant cattle and livestock development in West and Central Africa. Vol. 1: The international supply and demand for breeding stock*, FAO Animal Production and Health Paper 67/1, FAO, Rome.   ★

Shaw, A. P. M. and Hoste, C. H., 1987, *Trypanotolerant cattle and livestock development in West and Central Africa. Vol. 2: Trypanotolerant cattle in the national livestock economies*, FAO Animal Production and Health Paper 67/2, FAO, Rome.   ★

Smith, A. J. (ed), 1984, *Milk production in developing countries, Proceeding* of the conference held in Edinburgh 2–6 April 1984, University of Edinburgh, Centre for Tropical Veterinary Medicine, Edinburgh.   ★

Smith, C., 1984, Rates of genetic change in farm livestock, *Research and Development in Agriculture*, **1**: pp. 79–85.

Smith, C., 1985, Scope for selecting many breeding stocks of possible economic value in the future, *Animal Production*, **41**: pp. 403–412.

Syrstad, O., 1990, A genetic interpretation of results obtained in *Bos indicus* × *Bos taurus* crossbreeding for milk production, *Proceedings of the 4th World Congress on Genetics applied to Livestock Production, Edinburgh, 1990*, **XIV**: pp. 195–198.

Taneja, V. K. and Chawla, D. S., 1978, Heterosis for economic traits in Brown Swiss-Sahiwal crosses, *Indian Journal of Dairy Science*, **31**: pp. 208–213. (As quoted by Cunningham and Syrstad, 1987.)

Thorpe, W., Cruickshank, D. K. R. and Thompson, R., 1980, Genetic and environmental influences on beef cattle production in Zambia. (2) Live weights for age of purebred and reciprocally crossbred progeny. *Animal Production*, **30**: pp. 235–243.

Thorpe, W., Cruikshank, D. K. R. and Thomson, R., 1981, Genetic and environmental influences on beef cattle production in Zambia. (4) Weaner production from purebred and reciprocally crossbred dams, *Animal Production*, **33**: pp. 185–177.

Timon, V. M., 1987, Genetic selection for improvement of native highly adaptive breeds, *Proceedings 4th International Goat Conference*, FAO, Rome. ★

Toure, S. M., 1977, La trypanotolérance; Revue des connaissances. *Rev. Elev. Méd. Vét. Pays Trop.* **30**: pp. 157–174. ★

Vaccaro, L. P. de, 1990, Survival of European dairy breeds and their crosses with zebus in the tropics, *Animal Breeding Abstracts*, **58**: pp. 475–494.

Vercoe, J. E., Frisch, J. E., Young, B. A. and Bennett, I. L., 1985, Genetic improvement of buffalo for draught purposes. In *Draught Animal Power for Production, ICIAR Proceedings Series No. 10*, ed. J. W. Copland, pp. 115–120.

Wiener, G. (ed), 1990, *Animal genetic resources. A global programme for sustainable development.* FAO Animal Production and Health Paper No. 80, FAO, Rome.

Wiener, G. and Hayter, S., 1974, *Crossbreeding and inbreeding in sheep*, Agricultural Research Council, Animal Breeding Research Organisation Report 1974, HMSO.

Wiener, G., Lee, G. J. and Woolliams, J. A., 1992, Effects of rapid inbreeding and the crossing of inbred lines on conception rate, prolificacy and ewe survival in sheep, *Animal Production*, **55**: pp. 115–121.

Wiener, G., Woolliams, C. and Macleod, N. S. M., 1983, The effects of breed, breeding system and other factors on lamb mortality. 1: Causes of death and effects on the incidence of losses. *Journal of Agricultural Science* (Cambridge), **100**: pp. 539–551.

Wiener, G., and Woolliams, J. A., 1982, The effect of crossbreeding and inbreeding on the performance of three breeds of hill sheep in Scotland, *Proceedings of the World Congress on Sheep and Beef Cattle Breeding*, ed. R. A. Barton and W. C. Smith, Dunmore Press, New Zealand, **1**: pp. 175–187.

Woolliams, J. A. and Smith, C., 1988, The value of indicator traits in the genetic improvement of dairy cattle, *Animal Production*, **46**: pp. 333–345. ★

Woolliams, J. A. and Wilmut, I., 1989, Embryo manipulation in cattle breeding and production, *Animal Production*, **48**: pp. 3–30. ★

Index

additive genetic effect 27, 43, 105, 127–9
age, and generation interval 56
AI 89, 93, 181, 182
  cattle 152
  for conservation 178
  for genotype spreading 187
allele 25, 25–7, 103–4
  frequency 32–6, 52
  in segregation 27–9
  see also gene
Angora 158, 159
animal production 1, 2
annual rate of progress 64

backcross 28–9
  F2 performance
    comparison 112
  heterosis determination 110–11
  nomenclature 106
backcrossing, continuous *see*
  grading-up
backfat thickness 165
beef cattle, crossbreeding 130
body size, and heat tolerance 168
body weight 162–3, 163–4
breed
  comparison 5, 15–16, 104–5, 107
  conservation *see under*
    conservation; decline
  development 144–5
  exotic 7–8
  genetic differences 104
  names, and conservation 174
  reference 99
  synthetic 123–5
  variation within 49–51
  see also genotypes

breed hierarchy *see* breed pyramid
breed pyramid 88, 89
breeding age, and generation
  interval 56
breeding scheme, nucleus 182
breeding value (BV) 65–6, 67–8
buffalo 153–4
  draught 167–9

carcass quality 74, 164–5
cashmere 158, 167
categorical distribution 59
cattle 151–3
  cost 152–3
  draught 167–9
  milk yield 166
  reproductive rate 151–2
cell division 19–22
chance 16–17, 30
chromosomes 18, 19, 24
  in sex determination 22–3
climate 6, 148
cloning 188
comparison, basis for 49
computer
  for records 15, 16
  selection programme 84, 181
  statistical analysis 17, 181
confidence 66–8
confounding 5, 112–13
conservation, 176
  breed 173, 174–6
  live animals 177–8
  numbers required 176–7
  techniques 177–8
contemporary comparison 92
control group 86, 126
correction factors 13–14
correlated traits 51, 73–4

crisscrossing   121–2
crossbreed, population for   113–15
crossbreeding   103
  additive genetic effect   105
  for disease resistance   171–2
  heterosis   105–7, 113–14
  maternal effects   107–8
  for meat production   163
  yak   155–6
  see also heterosis
crossbreeding systems
  F1 production   119–120
  grading-up   117–19
  monitoring   125–6
  rotational crossing   120, 121–3
  synthetic breed   123–5
crossing-over   31
  and inbreeding   142
cryogenic storage   178
culling
  intensity of selection   60, 62
  levels   81–2, 82–4
  records for   12, 14
culture   149

dairy cattle crossbreeding   126–9
dairy cattle survival   129
database   15
decline, breed   173–4
defects, testing   145–6
diploid number   19
disease
  and genetic engineering   185
  improvement constraint   6–7
  resistance   169–72
distribution transforms   59
DNA   19, 24, 183
dominance
  genetic   104
  incomplete   36
dominant alleles   25–6
draught animals   153, 167–9
  management   169

efficiency   1–2, 12
egg production   160–7
embryos, frozen   87
endangered list   173
environment
  heredity interaction   *see* genetic-
    environment
  traits   84–6
  variation   44–5

epistasis   30–1, 104, 125
  heterosis   112–13, 115
  synthetics   125
epistatic deviations   43–4
Europe, selection progress   101–2
exotics   118–19, 129
extreme performance
  screening   96–8

F1   114, 119–20
F2 herd, and heterosis   114–15
family selection   79–80
feed, improvement constraint   6
fertilisation   22
fertility, and hybrid
  production   145
first cross   *see* F1
flock size   7; *see also* herd
frequency distribution   38, 39–40

gametes   19–22
gene   24
  additive effects   43–4
  expression testing   185–6
  frequency   32–6
    alteration   34–6
    constancy   34
  interactions   30–2; *see also*
    Mendelian rules
  marker   187
  and mutation   25
  segregation   37–8
  transfer   183, 185, 186
  variation in performance   40–1
  see also allele
generation interval (l)   56–7
genetic change   3, 180–1
genetic consequences of
  selection   52–4
genetic disease resistance   171–2
genetic diversity   174–5, 175
genetic drift   174
genetic engineering   182–7
  and uniformity   189
genetic improvement
  advantages   2–3
  and computing   181
  inbreeding   142
  MOET   95
  sheep   157
genetic uniformity   75–6, 143, 189
genetic variation apportioning
  43–4

genetic-environment
  interaction   32, 45, 86, 99
  traits   24
  variation   48–51
genotype   24
  conservation   178
  frequency prediction   33–4
  spreading   186–7
goats   157–8
  crossbreeding   132–3
  grading-up   133–4
  milk yield   166
grading-up   117–19, 133–4
group breeding schemes   89–92

hair   167
  goats   157–8
  rabbits   159
  sheep   156
haploid number   20, 21
Hardy-Weinberg law   34
heat tolerance   154, 167–8
herd size   7
herd type   149–50
hereditary defects   145–6, 170–1
heredity/environment   see genetic-
    environment
heritability (h^2)   45–8, 56
  estimates   46–8, 50
  and indirect selection   75
  low, and selection   79
heterosis   105–7
  cattle herd survival   129
  crossbreeding criterion   113–14
  dairy cattle crossbreeding   127–9
  determination   108–13, 112–13
  epistasis   115, 112–13
  physiology   115
  reference group   111
  rotational crossing   122
  synthetics   124–5
heterozygocity
  heterosis   105
  loss   136, 137
heterozygote   25, 103; see also
    overdominance
high-yielding animals   1–2
homologous chromosomes   19
homozygotes   25, 103
  inbreeding   143, 144
hybrid production   145
hybrid vigour   see heterosis

improvement   1, 6–8
inbred lines   145–6
inbreeding   75
  avoidance   147
  closed nucleus   90
  conservation   177
  effect   135–8
  effects   139–42
  family selection   79
  genetics 143–4
  MOET   95
  occurrence   134–5
  rate   139
  sire circles   99–100
  small population   138–9
  uses   142–6
inbreeding coefficient (F)   136–8
inbreeding depression   75, 135–6,
    141, 142
incentives, extreme
    performance   97
independent assortment   29–30
independent culling levels   81–2,
    82–4
index selection   82–4
indirect selection   74–5; see also
    correlated traits
individual selection   77–8
infrastucture, and improvement   7
inheritance   27–30; see also gene
intensity of selection   60–2

lactation yield   see milk yield
lines   143–4, 175
linkage   31
litter size   162
local breed, as reference   111

males
  and annual rate of response
    64–5
  MOET selection   94–6
  restricted, and inbreeding   135
  sterile   155
management
  disease prevention   170–1
  grading-up   119–20
  herd improvement   125
  production improvement   102
maternal effect
  crossbreeding   107–8
  heterosis determination   112

meat production   41–2, 162–5
meiosis   20–1
Mendelian rules   27–30
milk production   74, 165–7
milk records   11–12
milk yield
   estimation   111–12, 165–6
   and pastoralists   149
   recording   166–7
mitosis   19, 20
MOET   94–6, 182
   cattle   152
   in conservation   178
   for genotype spreading   187
mohair   167
multiple ovulation and embryo
      transfer   see MOET
multiple traits selection   80–4
multiplier group   88, 89
mutation   25, 142

national herds   124
normal distribution   39, 55, 58–9
nucleus breeding scheme   182
nucleus flock   89–90
nucleus-centralised breeding
      schemes   92–3
nucleus-group breeding
      schemes   89–92

observations, repeated   67, 69
offspring, and selection   70–1;   see
      also progeny testing
offspring/parent comparison
      49–50
open nucleus breeding
      scheme   90–1
overdominance   26–7, 106, 144
ovulation rate   162

parents, and selection   70
parks, for conservation   179
pastoralists   149–50
pedigree   70
performance, and
      inbreeding   139–41
performance depression   135–6
performance records   9–14
   using   14–16
performance test   77
phenotype   24
pigs   158–9

backfat thickness   165
   crossbreeding   133
population screening   96–8
poultry   160–1
preservation   see conservation
progeny   see offspring
progeny testing   70–1, 79, 92, 93
progress rate   64, 100–2

rabbits   159
recessive alleles   25–6
recessive genetic defects,
      testing   145–6
reciprocal crosses   107
recombination   31, 142
records
   choice of animals   10
   and confidence   66–7
   content   10–14
   correcting   13–14
   efficiency   12
   keeping   8
   performance   9–16
   using   14–16
reference breeds   99
reference sires   92
relatives
   and inbreeding   134
   and selection   69–71
   variation within   49–51
repeat observations   67, 69
reproduction   181–2
   sex determination   188–9
reproductive capacity
      assessment   162
reproductive rate, increase   188
reproductive traits   161–2
response to selection (R)   62,
      64–5
rotational crossing   121–3

sample size   105
segregation of genes   27–9, 37–8
selection   52
   environment   84–6
   family   79–80
   genetic consequences   52–4
   individual   77–8
   methods   77–87
   objectives   52
   relatives   69–71

selection — *continued*
  response   50
  tandem   81
  see also performance records
selection differential (S)   53–4,
    55–6
  components   60–2
  and variability   62–3
selection intensity (*i*)   60–2
  multiple traits   73
  response   64
selection programme
  computers in   84
  correlated traits   74
selection progress monitoring
    86–7
selection schemes   87–100
  breed structure   87–9
  efficiency loss   102
  MOET   94–6
  nucleus-centralised   92–3
  nucleus-group   89–92
  population screening   96–8
  and progress rates   100–2
  reference breeds   99
  sire circles   99–100
  sire referencing   98–9
sex determination   22–3, 188–9
sex linkage   31–2
sheep   131, 156–7
  milk yield   166–7
sib testing   79
sibs
  and selection   71
  variation comparison   50
sire circles   99–100
sire referencing   98–9
skewed distribution   40
small-holder   150, 151
standard deviation   17, 58, 59–60
standard error   17
statistical analysis   17
statistical confidence   16–17
statistical efficiency   113

stratification   116
synthetic breeds   123–5, 144–5

tandem selection   81
terminal sire   165
testing station   93
tractive power   168, 169
traits   3–4
  compound   41–2
  correlated   51, 73–4
  disease resistance   169–72
  genetic/environmental
    factors   24
  hair/wool   167
  meat production   162–5
  milk production   165–7
  multiple   72–3, 80–4
  qualitative   37–9
  quantitative   39–41
  reproductive   161–2
  see also genetic-environment
transgenic animals   185, 186
transmitting ability   66
trypanosomiasis   171, 172
twins   49

ultrasonic equipment   164, 165
uniformity   189

variability, and selection 62–3
variation   59–60
  apportioning   42–4
variation in performance   41, 42–5
  component estimation   48–51

weight   *see* body weight
wool   156, 167

yak   154–6
yield fluctuation   121

zebu cross   129
zoological parks   179
zygote   22